Victim Vulnerability: An Existential-Humanistic Interpretation of a Single Case Study

VICTIM VULNERABILITY: AN EXISTENTIAL-HUMANISTIC INTERPRETATION OF A SINGLE CASE STUDY

ERIC ANTON KREUTER

WITH A FOREWORD BY EUGENE I. TAYLOR

Nova Science Publishers, Inc.
New York

For permission to use material from this book please contact us:
Telephone 631-231-7269; Fax 631-231-8175
Web Site: http://www.novapublishers.com

Library of Congress Cataloging-in-Publication Data

Kreuter, Eric Anton.

Victim vulnerability : an existential-humanistic interpretation of a single case study / Eric Anton Kreuter.

p. cm.

Includes bibliographical references and index.

ISBN 1-60021-282-4

1. Victims of crimes--Case studies. 2. Victims of crimes--Psychology. I. Title.

HV6250.25.K74 2006

362.88--dc22 2006018051

Published by Nova Science Publishers, Inc. ✢ New York

Dedication

This book is dedicated to Robert's brother, Joseph, who will always be remembered. Robert's willingness to contribute his case history for researchers, psychologists, and law enforcement is a testament to the resiliency of the human spirit where we have both the capacity to move forward and also to remember those whom we have lost.

CONTENTS

ACKNOWLEDGMENTS

I wish to acknowledge Robert as it is a distinct privilege to be entrusted to investigate your life story, which is deserving of the utmost respect. Your candor, insight, and eloquence have made this work possible. I also wish to acknowledge with gratitude the efforts of my learned doctoral committee: Eugene I. Taylor, Ph.D., Ruth Richards, M.D., Ph.D., and Robert Flax, Ph.D. Your guidance and support has made a significant difference in my life and in my research. As well, my family and friends deserve recognition for their steadfast support, especially my beautiful wife Meryle F. Kreuter, LCSW and my amazing and talented children: Christopher, Cathleen, Matthew, and Aaron. I also wish to thank several individuals who have graciously provided editing support and well as commentary over content and philosophical contributions: Robert's mother, Diane K. Kanca, Esq., and Andrew D. Decker, M.D.

FOREWORD

I am particularly grateful for the opportunity to comment on the project launched by my erstwhile and very able student, Dr. Eric Kreuter, especially because this particular case study presents some interesting features.

First and last, while the project should be considered in process and still on-going, it is always about a real person, studied from the standpoint of a person-centered science. We must resist at every turn the urge to categorize, to classify, and to diagnose the person whose story is told here. Instead, we must remain open to the complexity of his experience—to see the person as a total gestalt. Just as this study is also, personality too is an on-going process of evolution over the life span.

Second, we should view the person in terms of the relation between the biological, material environment, in other words, his physical and economic conditions; the world of relationships, which refers to his relation to others and his ability to love and be loved in return; and the interior life world of the individual, which refers to his thought, feelings, preferences, perceptions, attitudes, as well as his imaginal and dream life. Such a view focuses not only on a description of the person's total life circumstances, but also on an awakening to the experience of self-knowledge, the aim of which is the actualization of one's highest potential.

Third, this case study highlights the nature of the transference. That is, the nature of the relationship of the subject to his parents and the ways in which this relationship has shaped subsequent relationships, especially the ability to attract a compatible partner of the opposite sex, sustain a family, and to establish adequate and enduring friendships with others. All relationships are colored by these original bonds, which become especially important in the therapist-patient relationship and in the outcome of therapy. There is also the sibling relationships to consider, especially the impact of the brother's premature and untimely death from illness. But more to the point, the transference helps us to understand in the present study the relationship between the subject and the researcher, who is not a therapist but who plays the role of friend, advisor, and confidant to the subject in an attempt to understand his condition.

Fourth, We tend to emphasize objects rather than the flow of experience. We ask first what the person's job is, where they live, their socioeconomic status, and their level of education, and so on—what is fixed about them. We do not tend to inquire into the subject's ability to experience transcendence into an expanded state of higher consciousness or what he knows about spiritual freedom. And as a result of this emphasis on objects rather then on their relations, we ourselves are not free. Berdeyev's horizontal versus vertical modes of time, and the expansion and contraction of consciousness along those continua, are worth noting. We view a person in terms of a linear progression from birth to death, not knowing how to ask about the expansion and contraction of consciousness along the way or the function of insight in the process of self-realization. We cannot make the alcoholic stop drinking; he has to come to that realization himself. We cannot command the pilot to stop following the perpetrator of his identity theft. There needs to be that spark of self-motivation that comes from within him to cease that behavior. The individual has to want to change and will do so along the lines of our fondest desires if we extend to that person empathy, unconditional positive regard, and a spiritual equanimity that raises perception of one's self to a whole new level of seeing.

Finally, the existential and phenomenological viewpoint reminds us that there is an important difference between description and interpretation. The need, press, vector theory of personality functioning describes the person, but it does not explain the person's unique trajectory through life, the person's goals and aspirations and their potential actualization as a result of this encounter. That is left in the end to the psyche of the investigator, who, as an existential investigator, is now able to see that the nature of the journey he has taken with the pilot is itself a worthy and sufficient goal.

Eugene I. Taylor, Ph.D.
Executive Faculty
Saybrook Graduate School and Research Center
San Francisco, California

PREFACE

An examination of the psychological literature on victimization shows disproportionately that that we know more about the predator than we do the victim. Moreover, almost all the literature on the victim is presented from either a reductionistic or cognitive-behavioral point of view. This book examines the psychology of a victim of repeated criminal acts from the existential-humanistic perspective. The method used is the single case study. The subject, currently age 51, a pilot, was the victim of identity theft, extortion, and duress. These crimes, some of which are treated under federal law as violent by their nature or effect, resulted in a large, unrecoverable financial loss, suspension of the pilot's medical certification required to operate aircraft, abrupt termination of his chosen career, a continuing governmental record of being delusional despite overwhelming proof to the contrary, lasting emotional and physical distress, as well as other consequences. Meanwhile, the predator has harmed dozens of individuals, forming a diverse cohort. A life history of the subject is presented as a context for the specific chronology of events defining his victimization, which is followed by an existential interpretation. Interviews and archival data, including written and audio forms of documentation, have been incorporated into the study. Seven criteria were selected from existential-humanistic psychology that have been applied in the exploration of the behavior and personality of the victim: (1) the interior life-world of the person; (2) self-actualization needs vs. adjustment to social norms; (3) meaning through suffering; (4) being in the face of non-being; (5) attitudes toward death and annihilation; (6) dreams, visions, and mythic experience; and (7) existential use of the void. The study found characteristics of the psyche of a particular victim that may have made him vulnerable. These characteristics include: being overly trusting; being under the influence of a hero-rescuer archetype; and being overly reliant on instruments due to training as a pilot. Mainstream psychology has ignored this dimension, which is needed to understand the total person. The book ends with an epilogue that describes the principal researcher's recent encounter with a woman who perpetrated a scam on him and the similarities between the psychopathic predator Robert encountered and this person.

Chapter 1

INTRODUCTION

In June 1995, a commercial airline pilot (Robert) returned home after several days of flying, set up his new computer system, and registered his first screen name with a popular Internet service provider. Within minutes, he received an Instant Message from a woman (Connie). She was quite provocative in her choice of words, including occasional flirtatious comments. Initially, Robert was intrigued at the novelty of this new form of communication. A relationship developed over a period of weeks through e-mail and telephone contact, but then the messages from Connie became anxious. Initially, Connie engaged in friendly and diverse conversations with Robert. Eventually, she alluded to herself as an informant who was involved in a governmental investigation into organized crime based on her alleged personal friendship with the target. Robert began to have concern for her safety. Messages were sent to Robert from other identities (including actual persons used in false portrayal), all pressuring him to cooperate and help her. Robert received messages from these identities, but never met any of them. On some occasions Robert came home from a multi-day flying sequence and found that his apartment had been searched by someone, though apparently not by Connie. The identities indicated that they knew much about Robert and were initially cordial in their communications with him. Robert was uneasy about their familiarity, but also felt there was nothing he could do about it. These messages became threatening, mainly against him, but some of the messages also threatened Connie. The e-mail first established that the entities behind them had vast knowledge about Robert and was presented as if a police investigation was done. The velocity of the ongoing dialogue led to Robert's reluctant assistance, mainly for Connie's benefit. This acquiescence and events that followed led to Robert's victimization, eventually leading to Robert being coerced into allowing Connie to stay with him temporarily. Over $100,000 was stolen under the duress of extortion over a period of time allegedly by these entities from Robert's bank accounts. Other activities occurred, which caused Robert to be concerned for his safety and that of his family. Only after the damage was done and the threats were made, Robert hired a private investigator in an effort to prove that Connie and co-conspirators were responsible for the harm done to him. Connie used his credit identity to make numerous purchases and cash withdrawals. Robert eventually learned that new credit accounts were established using his identification, but she controlled access to the cards that were issued.

Connie created an elaborate scheme involving a number of characters, some of whom are quite famous.[1] These characters engaged in extensive e-mail dialogue with Robert. Each character maintained a distinct and consistent personality structure. The dialogue was centered on Connie's relationships with these characters and how Robert's involvement with her was either troublesome to some of the characters or helpful to others. Robert became increasingly interwoven into Connie's world as a result of her clever use of these personalities.

Connie explained to Robert that she was forced to be part of a government investigation into organized crime and illegal gambling within professional baseball by ballplayers. Connie was a fan who closely followed a particular team. Connie convinced Robert that she developed a relationship with one of the baseball players after she and Robert met. This fact made her ideal for the supposed investigation, which was being conducted by a State Trooper, who was more than ten years older than both Robert and Connie. Connie and this officer had a serious relationship since she was in high school. The persona of the State Trooper established contact with Robert and convinced him that he was involved with Connie. Connie explained how she was forced to submit to physical, mental, and sexual abuse as part of her role. She presented to be quite distraught as she explained these events to Robert. Robert became concerned for Connie and tried to persuade those involved to leave Connie alone. Eventually, Robert threatened to go to the authorities, but then the characters, who, from Robert's perspective, presented as law enforcement identities, began to directly threaten Robert as well as Connie herself and Robert's family.

Robert was faced with many bizarre events, but could not prove that Connie was behind them. The events included threats by one or more of the cyber identities and they were very direct and very frightening. Connie assumed the role of victim, resulting in Robert trying to cater to Connie's needs instead of dealing with the mysterious nature of the events himself. Robert reported that he did so not simply altruistically, but because Connie distracted him from his attempts to investigate the causes with dramatic displays of what others reportedly did to her. In one instance, Connie told Robert that she was forced into a car and had her vagina burned with a lit cigarette. Robert did not believe her and insisted she show him the burn marks. She lifted her skirt and revealed fresh burn marks. Robert later hired a private investigator to confront Connie. Connie admitted the wounds were self-inflicted solely to convince Robert to believe her story.[2] Connie explained to Robert that her captors instructed Connie to tell Robert that these burns were meant to instill fear in him and that the next time similar harm would come to Robert and his family.

Robert was getting to the point of deciding to report the crimes after the cumulative effects of all the events to date had taken their toll on him. The last story Connie told him was that she was jogging along the Delaware River when she was confronted by two individuals that Connie linked to the façade of the investigatory team. She told Robert that these men tried to force her into a car so they could talk with her about elements of the case. She said she escaped the situation by jumping into the Delaware River at a nearby marina. When Connie described this event to Robert by telephone, she was very dramatic, was crying, and her voice suggested that she was shivering.

---

[1] It is important to note that the names of famous personalities referred to in this book were used by the predator to create various illusions of their involvement, but there was no such involvement.

[2] Connie admitted to being under the influence of Demerol at the time of the self-injury.

Eventually, Robert reported the criminal activity to the Federal Bureau of Investigation (FBI), which began an investigation. The investigation that was done was very sparse and apparently did not include running a criminal background check on her. Had they done so, they would have learned of her history of arrests and incarceration for crimes related to credit card fraud, narcotics addiction, property theft, false use of identity, insurance fraud, and even fraudulent use of a credit card in the name of her older daughter. The FBI agents contacted Connie by telephone. She spoke to them a few days following the announcement of the guilty verdict in the case of the bombing of the Oklahoma City Federal Building. She used this current event to her advantage and told the agents that Robert was a sympathizer of Timothy McVeigh. Connie explained that Robert liked to stretch the truth.

Despite the fact that Robert's father accompanied him to the FBI office in New York City and corroborated Robert's report of crime, Robert's story was deemed not credible by the FBI. Robert's father provided first-hand information about the crime as he had become exposed to Connie and he had knowledge that others might have been involved. Even Roberts parents had become frustrated and frightened at the bizarre nature of what they have seen occur in Roberts life. The FBI agents felt they did a complete and comprehensive investigation and believed they had enough information to act as they did. The agents gave Robert and his father assurances to believe they would investigate the reported crimes and help Robert. Ultimately, their actions harmed him. It was during this era that the FBI was developing a reputation for lack of accountability and their investigation into Roberts claims is a blatant example of their monolithic arrogance and unchecked power. Because of their misguided conclusions and faulty reasoning and the lack of a thorough investigation, the agents notified the Federal Aviation Administration (FAA). The FAA concluded that reporting of non-existent crimes indicated there may be psychosis.[3] On the strength of this highly unusual letter from the FBI, the FAA, in a case of blind reliance, suspended Robert's license. They did so because of allegations by the FBI of Robert's reporting of crimes that they believed had not occurred.

Though this scenario may seem very unusual, many of us become victims at some point in our lives. Meanwhile, certain people find themselves in the role of victim over and over again. (Spence-Diehl, 1999; Gross, 2000; Winkel, Blaauw, Sheridan, and Baldry, 2003). In this study, this will be called victim vulnerability.[4] Mainstream psychology might view this as a pathological condition. However, this investigation will show how an existential-humanistic interpretation of events might differ from one based on mainstream psychology. While mainstream psychology might view the situation through a diagnostic lens, an alternative and less obvious interpretation is presented through an existential analysis of the individual's response as part of his personal journey towards self-actualization. This means that the manner of response by the pilot is part of his working towards a resolution of his personal identity and purpose in life. Further, the risks taken by the subject to help Connie may have contributed to his vulnerability.

---

[3] The FAA issued a rare Immediate Order of Suspension of Robert's First Class Medical Certificate on the basis of suspected psychosis. The FAA required Robert to undergo psychological and psychiatric evaluations to determine his mental status. Robert has not piloted aircraft again since that date.

[4] Henry A. Murray stated: Almost every theorist has to be a neologizer – a coiner of words – or, at the least if he does not create new words for his theory, he needs to use ordinary dictionary words in new ways or with unusual frequencies or emphasis" (Schneidman, 1981, p. 97).

Robert extended help to Connie because she presented herself as a helpless victim. Robert did not realize at the time that Connie actually was a predator. When the threats started to become heightened, Robert felt trapped and forced by the cyber-stalking activities of the identities, who Robert had not met, to continue helping her even though he would have preferred to remove himself from the situation. These identities were orchestrating criminal activity through a pattern of power and control over Robert.

This book uses the phrase 'power/control crime' to refer to any behavior involving an attempt to exert power or control over another person by any means, violent or otherwise (Bojij, 2005). This term should also be taken to encompass behaviours that may or may not be illegal. For example, Bocij (2004) (see also Bocij et al, 2003) notes that some of the behaviors associated with cyberstalking are perfectly legal when viewed in isolation. Robert felt that the only way to protect himself was by helping Connie. Robert chose not to divulge any of this to his family in order to protect them from harm.

The subject's behavior may have also contributed to his vulnerability. By not discussing his problems with his peers, family, or friends until it was too late, he denied himself outlets that may have led to a different manner of handling the situation. The subject was unsure of the true source of the problems he was encountering because of the elaborate setup and execution of a complex and dangerous scam. In retrospect, because he always left open even the smallest of possibilities that she was being truthful about her victimization, he had decided not to shun her, but the situation eventually became intolerable. Connie's truthfulness or deceitfulness was at issue. Robert would not decide to see Connie as fully culpable until he had convincing evidence in the matter. Connie's scam endured because she was able to keep open the possibility that she was being victimized.

The victim in this case could also be considered to have been bullied because people who use bullying typically prey upon vulnerable individuals. As part of the scam, Connie, herself, created the image of being the victim of bullies. "Bullying is when a person is picked on over and over again by an individual or group with more power, either in terms of physical strength or social standing" (Nemours Foundation, 2005, p. 1). Some bullies use psychological control or verbal insults to put themselves in charge. "One of the most painful aspects of bullying is its relentlessness" (p. 2).

Because of the type of elaborate scam described in this book, it becomes important to inquire about the personality issues that are involved in the phenomena of victimization (see, for example, Turvey, 1999a; 2001a; Winkel, et al., 2003). The subject's personality profile, presented through a life chart, reveals a series of vulnerabilities, which will be described later in detail. These vulnerabilities likely have resulted in his selection by the predator, the harm first caused by her, the fictitious identities she created to fool him, and by the inappropriate actions of the FBI. Her initial contact of the pilot was through an Instant Message, which led to their subsequent dialogue.

Robert was age 41 at the time Connie first made contact with him. Though he has moved several times since 1995, Robert has lived mostly on the East Coast, currently in New York.

Robert involved himself in several previous criminal situations, involving others, where he aided the victims. These situations (to be elaborated later) resulted in personal danger to himself. As his life was greatly disturbed subsequent to the crimes committed against him, he became more passive, taking on the role of victim. Because Connie was an offensive stalker, Robert later protected himself, becoming a defensive stalker and used various methods, at a distance, of monitoring and subterfuge to lure Connie into certain scenarios so that he could obtain vindication. Though Robert acknowledges that his actions could be viewed as wrong, it is important that these actions not be taken out of context. His actions were meant to protect himself from further harm from her. Connie's actions ultimately led to her arrest and incarceration as well as ostracizing herself from her Alcoholics Anonymous group. Thus, he endured a transition from power to powerlessness through various important existential moments in his life.[5] This notion of powerlessness can be explained less as a result of being targeted by a psychopath, but more as a result of a system of government and components of a system of forensic psychology that are inept and unethical.

The principal investigator's previous research explored the various theories of psychopathy (Kreuter, 2003a), theories of victim vulnerability, and how predators select victims (Kreuter, 2002; 2003b) from cognitive, behavioral, and experimental perspectives. Through a process of interviews and review of documents, it was discovered that the personality of the subject suggested vulnerability. His vulnerability is the subject of this research because of the unusual nature of events that triggered his particular responses. This case study explores a particular victim's vulnerability as well as drawing parallels between his personality characteristics and those of other members of the victim cohort. What has not been done is an interpretation of victim vulnerability from the existential-humanistic perspective.

The focus of the research is on the question: What is the psychology of the victim from the standpoint of a whole person? This perspective includes the entire milieu of an individual's personality and environment, thoughts, feelings, attitudes, behaviors, aspirations, fears, dreams, and capabilities. Rogers (1963) wrote on what a science of the whole person looks like. He categorized psychology into three major ways of knowing. The experimental perspective covers the objective; the psychodynamic perspective covers the subjective, while the existential-humanistic tradition also considers the interpersonal, and reframes the subjective. The third approach in psychology considers a person as a subjectively free, responsible architect of his own personality. From these ways of knowing, Rogers thought of knowledge as consisting of hypotheses, which we attempt to verify in a three-fold manner: subjectively, objectively, and interpersonally.

"One important way of knowing is through the formation of inner hypotheses which are checked by referring to our inward flow of experiencing as we live in our subjective interaction with inner or outer events" (p. 74). In this interpersonal or phenomenological way of knowing, the focus of empathy is toward the other individual. Rogers felt that one of the consequences of this phenomenological-existential trend is that psychology will become a more inclusive science. Thus, psychology will now be capable of including not only behavior, but also the person and perspective of the observer, and the person and perspective of the observed. In terms of understanding the importance of the self, Rogers felt that the interpersonal is the most important: "Instead of measuring all sorts of peripheral behaviors, we can go straight to what is often hypothesized as the dynamic core of the personality and a most significant influence upon behavior" (p. 82).

The present study strives toward that picture by investigating interpretations of the subject's experiences from an existential and humanistically oriented depth psychology. Mainstream psychology looks at certain aspects of a person without integrating the analysis in

[5] Robert's mother, an accomplished artist, painted a young figure, a victim, behind shattered glass. This painting (in grayscale) appears at the end of Chapter 7.

context of the entirety of a person. In doing so, some complexity of understanding is missing. The person as a whole is a gestalt, not the mere sum of the parts.

As a way of looking at the whole person, the principal investigator's contribution towards understanding the psychology of the victim is based on the single case study. There is precedent for this in the history of psychology: Sigmund Freud's development of the field of psychoanalysis involved the introspective study of himself. Psychologist Gordon Allport, a pioneer in the field of personality psychology, advocated a study of the whole person, which he presented in his case analysis: *Letters From Jenny* (1965). Henry A. Murray's work in the area of personology is recapitulated in his single case study of Herman Melville (Eugene Taylor, Ph.D., personal communication, February 14, 2004).

This study explores several constructs: those associated with the perpetrator: psychopathy and constructs associated with the victim: victim vulnerability; victimology; learned helplessness; depth psychology; and existential-humanistic psychology. An understanding of these constructs will help to illuminate the experience of the subject. Psychopathy involves the exploration of a particular pattern of psychological behavior. Victim vulnerability involves analysis of how victims respond to crime as well as other forms of harm. Victimology is the study of a style of personality. Learned helplessness examines a trait approach towards understanding the person. In this study, depth psychology refers to personology, and existential-humanistic psychology.

In the present case study, archived documents as well as interviews provide the material for analysis of the psychological profile of the subject. The data includes seven hours of the subject's tape-recorded monologue, made in 1997, wherein he described with great emotion what happened and how he was harmed by the actions of the predator.[6] The seven hours of tapes were made in one sitting and at the height of the extortion. At this time, it is important to remember that the subject did not know that Connie was the perpetrator. These tapes are in the researcher's possession and have been transcribed.[7] In addition, voluminous correspondence between the subject, the perpetrator, and fictitious personas created by the perpetrator will be used in this research.[8] Kreuter (2003b) identified and interviewed over a dozen known victims of the same predator[9]. Data received from the subject's cohort demonstrate common criminal patterns used by the predator. Court transcriptions and personal interview data have been used to illustrate the crimes and their impact on the subject.

For various reasons resulting from being victimized, the pilot has undergone a number of psychological evaluations of his mental functioning.[10] The results of these evaluations will be elaborated later. One limitation of this dissertation is that consented two-way e-mail access to the predator by the principal investigator was active between March and April 2005, after she was released from prison, and through text-messaging between April and May 2006, but the

[6] The subject made these tapes while he was in a severely depressed mood. He considered the potential that those who were stalking him would physically harm or even kill him. The tapes were hidden in the closet of a friend of the subject's parents and were retrieved a year later.

[7] At the conclusion of this research, the original tapes will be returned to the subject.

[8] These written records exist because the subject maintained much of the printed e-mail he received as he thought that one day these would become important as evidence of the crimes.

[9] In this research, the predator is given a provisional diagnosis of psychopath by the principal investigator on the basis of her conduct and behavior through there is no independently verifiable professional clinical assessment of her that is available. A Parole Officer did confide that Connie's file contained references to a diagnosis of antisocial and statements made by other credible persons did describe Connie in a similar manner.

[10] These reasons included insurance claims, legal proceedings and a required forensic evaluation.

dialogue abruptly ceased each time.[11] Despite this limitation, some data on the predator is available. Certain voice recordings, handwritten documents, and e-mail communications are included in the archive. Thus, the perpetrator's rationale for choosing to victimize the pilot and the cohort is limited to what can be inferred from the archived data and personal interviews with others.

The archive consists mainly of raw data: 529 pages of e-mail communication (including notes made at a later date by the subject) between the pilot and the predator, including the fictitious personas set up by the predator. In addition, interview notes taken by the principal investigator, transcriptions of audio tapes, and court documents comprise the balance of the archive. The archive is a duplicate of original records compiled by the subject and given to the principal investigator to conduct this research. Quotations in this research from specific documents will be referenced to the archive.

Correspondence from the predator to others, including the principal investigator indicates that she received a diagnosis of bipolar disorder at some point in her life. A research sub-question explores how these aspects fit into the existential-humanistic interpretation.

In the mid-90s the Internet arrived and, along with it, its contribution to our society. But it also created the opportunity for criminal exploitation (Douglas, 2003). Thus, someone with criminal intent could transfer his or her predatory skills into the high-tech world. People can be vulnerable in cyberspace because, there, a person in the home environment feels they cannot be reached and, by doing so, lose some of what the principal investigator refers to as their self-protective instincts.

Identity theft (ID) is on the increase. As recently as 1996, identity theft was not designated a crime. Today, it is classified as a felony under the Federal Identity Theft and Assumption Deterrence Act of 1998 and ranks as the nation's top consumer fraud co6 laint, according to the Federal Trade Commission in Washington, D.C. (Wells, 2002). "ID thieves also can hide in the virtual shadow of the Internet" (Carozza, 2005, p. 38). Victims of identity theft and fraud often spend many hours researching and tracking the crime that has occurred against them, correcting credit reports, and incurring expenses to restore their financial standing.

The predator in this research first encountered the subject by the Internet. Her use of the computer to orchestrate her crimes against the subject leads to consideration of computer addiction (Suler, 1999). She is known to have spent long hours on the computer devising many schemes, including the one against the subject. Cyberspace addiction is an addiction to virtual realms of experience created through computer engineering (Suler, 1999). The subject also became engrossed in computer research and defended himself from future attacks following his discovery that the predator was responsible for the harm he suffered. He hoped this effort would help vindicate and exonerate himself from not only the crimes, but from what the FBI and other aspects of the legal system and forensic psychology did to him. Ferris (2002) suggests that Internet addiction disorder is characterized by increasing tolerance of long online hours (repetitive stimulus), withdrawal, and unsuccessful efforts to control one's

[11] It seams clear that the predator attempted to manipulate the principal investigator through direct communication, which included admissions of guilt, statements of self-condemnation, and statements blaming others for harm done to her victims.

own Internet use. Lucks (2001) found that identity-seekers pursue targets that might give them an identity.[12]

The subject in this research chose flying aircraft as a career. Choice of occupation has an impact on a person. As Von Hentig wrote: "To the selective function of an occupation is added the formative virtue. Vocations model human beings. By long observance and practice traits are developed which become characteristic of the vocation" (1948, p. 306). A profession (including airline pilot) belongs to the category of public service and bestows power on the agent. "The splendor of the uniform and the enjoyment of authority draw into the police force individuals who are highly responsive to such allurements" (1948, p. 306).[13] Robert reported that he was allured by the pleasure of flying long before it occurred to him that he could make a living at it.

In summary, this research explores the psyche of a particular victim to discover aspects of his personality that may have contributed to his vulnerability. This, in turn, may contribute to an overall body of knowledge known as victim vulnerability.

The existential-humanistic tradition may provide an alternative way to help transcend the limitations of the approach taken by mainstream science. By examining the science of the whole person, using a selection of criteria, the psychology of the victim can be more fully understood.

Using a case study, the principal investigator explored the phenomenon of victim vulnerability through evaluation of extensive archival data and lengthy interviews. A life chart, summarizing the life of the subject in this study, depicts key events in his life history. It is hoped that analysis of the personality and behavior of the subject will reveal important aspects of his vulnerability, which contributed to his victimization.

The principal investigator hopes to increase our understanding of this phenomenon so that preventive measures could be instituted, improved treatment plans developed, and laws strengthened in the area of psychopathic criminality, particularly those involving identity theft, Internet fraud, stalking, and cyber-stalking.

Definition of Terms

The case study utilizes a variety of terms which require specific definition:

Buffer: An element of support, which could be in the form of a close friend, family member or ally to assist in the event of a crisis or as a preventive force.

Criminal psychopath: Usually an individual of above average intelligence, who perpetrates illegal activity on others, without any sense of remorse or guilt, despite knowing the result of such actions (Hare, 1993).

Dangerousness: The degree of risk of danger posed by someone, typically a person who has already committed a crime and shows no remorse (McCallum, 2001).

---

[12] The unceasing efforts of the subject to learn all he could about the predator led to his devoting very long days and nights to this process. As a result, his lifestyle became quite different than it previously had been because of the actions of the government and others.

[13] The subject in this dissertation often described the positive feelings he had while wearing his pilot's uniform and the respect he felt was garnered.

Identity theft with extortion: Considered violent by its nature or effect, within the context of Federal law, involving the unauthorized use of the personal identifiers of another individual and the forced manipulation of the protective behavior of victims.

Lack of empathy or remorse: Refers to the common thread of the psychopathic disorder where there is a complete lack of feeling of guilt or remorse for having victimized someone.

Latent vulnerability: Underlying character or personality markers, leading to vulnerability. This may be present in individuals who have few or no outward signs of the condition. These processes are causally linked to the appearance of symptoms. They are not readily observable and are, therefore, difficult to assess.

Learned helplessness: Giving up in the face of uncontrollable events as a habitual pattern. Characterizes the generalization that helplessness is a learned state produced by exposure to noxious unpleasant situations, in which there is no possibility of escape or avoidance.

Modus operandi: An offender's method of carrying out the offense.

Offenders: Refers to those who use various methods to perpetrate crimes and cause harm.

Predator: One that victimizes, plunders, or destroys, especially for one's own gain, often leading to illegal activities. Predators seek power and control over their victim. A related term is predatory, which defines behavior. The usage is not from the psychiatric lexicon, but more a modern device, such as sexual predator. The word psychopath magnifies the meaning of the word predator.

Psychopathy: Refers to a disorder wherein the individual, while being fully capable of normal cognitive functioning, is not insane, and cannot be relied upon to self-govern. "Psychopathy is a deviant development disturbance characterized by an inordinate amount of instinctual aggression and the absence of an object relational capacity to bond" (Meloy, 2002, p. 5). In this regard, psychopaths will often destroy their family relationships through their actions, some of which can include criminality. For this research, psychopathy and Antisocial Personality Disorder, DSM-IV-TR, code: 301.7 (American Psychiatric Association, 2000), while related in their symptomatology, are not considered synonymous. Psychopathy is more severe in terms of behavior.

Resiliency: The internal capability of an individual to withstand the pressure of a trauma or threatened physical or psychological attack. The trauma or attack, if survived, can serve as a point of growth for the individual.

Risk of lifestyle: The choice of lifestyle may or may not increase the probability of becoming a victim.

Stalking: The patterned act of watching, monitoring, or otherwise investigating the location, habits, assets, or other personal data of one or more individuals by one or more other individuals for purposes of possible criminal activity. In general, stalking can be viewed as a primitive instinctual skill, more developed in some than others. Robert's efforts were defensive in nature and served to determine Connie's whereabouts. This is important to distinguish from the stalker who often has criminal intentions. For the purposes of this book, the term 'cyberstalking' is used to describe the use of information and communications technology (ICT) to harass one or more victims. Such harassment may include actions that include the transmission of offensive e-mail messages, identity theft and damage to data or equipment. In this book, 'stalking' means off-line stalking and 'cyberstalking' means harassing individuals with ICT. The terms 'stalking' and 'harassment' are used interchangeably, since all forms of stalking involve an element of threat and/or aim to cause the victim distress (Bocij, 2005).

Victimization: The process of succumbing to an act of wrongdoing. The vulnerabilities of the victim are perceived by the predator who then exploits them.

Vulnerability: The relative state of the exposure of one's physical, mental, or psychological systems to attack or harm caused by sources and events. Broadly, these sources and events include diseases, disorders, and crimes. At issue is also the person's resistance to suggestibility in some cases and hyper-suggestibility in other cases.

Research Questions

This research explores two primary questions:

1. What is the psychology of the victim from the existential-humanistic perspective? The research on the subject's life will be explored to determine why it is he became a repeat victim.

2. What are the characteristics of this subject that made him vulnerable to selection as a victim? Analysis of the data will investigate aspects of the subject's personality that led to his vulnerability.

While the original research questions can be answered from the literature review presented in chapter 2 using the mainstream psychological perspective, the questions have been reframed with emphasis on existential analysis, using seven criteria, which appear in chapter 6. Chapter 7 includes interpretations and the existential perspective followed by the painting as a non-verbal representation of the victim. These reframed questions form a collective that comprise a thorough understanding of the personality of the subject. Drawing from the immense pool of data, numerous moments in the subject's life will be applied to the specific criteria.

Chapter 2

THEORETICAL REVIEW OF THE LITERATURE

PSYCHOPATHY

Our exploration of the aspects of antisocial behavior that is known as psychopathy will help to understand the literature relevant to the psychology of the victim. While the theories of psychopathy continue to evolve, this book treats the psychopath as a person who was likely born that way versus a sociopath who is someone more likely affected by negative life experiences, thus socialized into a pattern of behavior that is antisocial, perhaps criminal. Compared to sociopaths, psychopaths are masters of deception while sociopaths do not generally have that level of sophistication. But, both lack the capability of being loyal, feeling shame or guilt and have no consciousness or a sense of responsibility for their actions. The born psychopath has not developed a sense of cultural values. Their actions serve only themselves at the detriment of their victims. Similarly, the sociopath feeds on the good nature of the victim for their required level of attention or needs. This behavior continues to the point of humiliation, abuse, and attack of the host victim, ultimately sabotaging the relationship, which may have formed under what appeared to be normal circumstances. Vaknin (2006) finds that psychopaths are difficult to distinguish from narcissists. Both the psychopath and the narcissist disregard society. "Psychopaths are deliberately and gleefully evil while narcissists are absent-mindedly and incidentally evil" (p. 1). Psychopaths do not need other people while narcissists are addicted to the admiration, attention, and envy of others (Millon and Davis, 2000, p. 299).

A brief look at the predator will be followed by a discussion on stalking behavior and the personality of the predator.[14] In order to understand victim vulnerability, the elements of psychopathology involved in this phenomenon are needed to gain a more complete picture of a whole person, who is being victimized.

Our understanding of the antisocial behavior known as psychopathy has a long history. The evolution of our theories on this phenomenon has impacted how such persons are labeled, what characteristics are considered in the diagnosis, and how they are treated by clinicians and by the legal system. An examination of this construct is warranted because the predator referred to in this research has been diagnosed by the principal investigator to be a

---

[14] The principal investigator presents only a basic overview of psychopathy in this research as there is extensive material on the topic.

psychopathic personality. The legal system considers her to be a criminal.[15] Various members of the legal system, i.e., her former parole officer, considered her to be antisocial, dangerous, and even capable of murder (Parole Officer, personal communication, 2004).

The syndrome of psychopathy is interesting because it represents a severe form of psychopathology that is concealed by an outer façade of normalcy (Patrick, 2006). Psychopathic individuals can be compared to *Amyciaea Lineatipes*, a species of arachnid that mimics the physical appearance of ants on which it preys. Such individuals readily gain the trust of others because they first appear as likable, adjusted, and well meaning. It is only through continued interaction and observation that the true nature of the psychopath is revealed (p. xiii).

Extensive research exists on psychopathy (Cleckley, 1941/1976; Hare, 1970, 1986, 1991, 1993, 1996, 1998; Davis and Millon, 1998; Blackburn, 1998; Guggenbuhl-Craig, 1999). Much of it deals with violent crimes of a physical nature, such as homicide and rape, although there has been little written on the psychological aspects of the emerging subject of identity theft, extortion, and related criminal activity. Meanwhile, the general subject of identity theft has been widely publicized. The published research on the connection between identity theft and psychopathy delves into use of this form of criminal activity by the psychopathic personality (See, for example, Patterson, 1993; Lucks, 2001). These types of crimes often have severe and long-lasting impact on victims (Kreuter, 2002; 2003b; 2004). The Federal Trade Commission reported that in 2002, identity theft affected nearly 10 million people with an estimated cost to individuals of $5 billion and a cost to business of $48 billion (Identity Fraud, Inc., 2002). Even Shakespeare's *Othello* (Act III, Sc. 3) says: "But he that filches me my good name robs me of that which not enriches him and makes me poor indeed" (Black, 1972, p. 1,189).[16]

Early in the twentieth century, the term psychopathy was used to refer to extreme variants of normal personality and included all personality disorders. It was assumed by Guggenbuhl-Craig (1999) that Phillipe Pinel (1745-1826), who released the mentally ill from dungeons in which they had been confined, was among the earliest to describe psychopathy as a psychiatric condition. He used the term "*maniaque sans delire,* which essentially means craziness without raging" (p. 54). Such behavior was marked by criminality, irresponsibility, and immorality. This diagnosis carried with it a certain moral stigma, similar to insanity. In an attempt to remove the moral stigma of the term psychopathy, the American Psychiatric Association adopted the diagnosis Antisocial Personality Disorder in the DSM-IV-TR, limiting its usage to both Antisocial Personality Disorder and Dissocial Personality Disorder (American Psychiatric Association, 2000). The diagnostic criteria for 301.7 Antisocial Personality Disorder is:

A. There is a pervasive pattern of disregard for and violation of the rights of others occurring since age 15 years, as indicted by three (or more) of the following:

    (1) Failure to conform to social norms with respect to lawful behaviors as indicated by repeatedly performing acts that are grounds for arrest.

---

[15] The predator's long criminal history is evidenced in court records that cite numerous felony and misdemeanor charges as well as civil actions proffered against her.

[16] This line is spoken by Iago, a profligate, bold and versatile liar.

(2) Deceitfulness, as indicated by repeated lying, use of aliases, or conning others for personal profit or pleasure.

(3) Impulsivity or failure to plan ahead.

(4) Irritability and aggressiveness, as indicated by repeated physical fights or assaults.

(5) Reckless disregard for safety of self or others.

(6) Consistent irresponsibility, as indicated by repeated failure to sustain consistent work behavior or honor financial obligations.

(7) Lack of remorse, as indicated by being indifferent to or rationalizing having hurt, mistreated, or stolen from another.

B. The individual is at least age 18 years.
C. There is evidence of Conduct Disorder with onset before age 15 years.
D. The occurrence of antisocial behavior is not exclusively during the course of schizophrenia or a Manic Episode. (p. 706)

Characteristically, people who are given the diagnosis of Antisocial Personality Disorder are egocentric, incapable of love, reveal no ability to express guilt, remorse, and shame, have little insight, and do not easily learn from certain types of experiences, such as causing pain in another person or being convicted of a crime. Some are also engaging and charming. Persons charged with crime are sometimes required to undergo a psychiatric evaluation. The psychiatric diagnosis of Antisocial Personality Disorder (DSM-IV-TR) has caused skepticism during court proceedings regarding the accuracy of decisions and adequacy of punishment. Because of the difficulty courts have in dealing with antisocial persons, the establishment of an effective system of imprisonment and rehabilitation is questionable. Outcome studies also question the efficacy of rehabilitative treatment in the prison system (Carlen, 1986).

Psychopathic individuals typically lie and distort facts in an attempt, often unsuccessfully, to fool their therapist or interviewer (Hare, 1998; Meloy, 2002). "Pathological lying is falsification entirely disproportionate to any discernible end in view, engaged in by observation and cannot definitely be declared insane, feebleminded, or epileptic" (Healy and Healy, 1969, p. 1). It usually manifests over a long period of time, thus such lying represents a trait rather than an episode. Often, pathological liars develop the tendency to swindle. The Healys found:

> Swindling itself could hardly be called a pathological phenomenon, since it is readily explicable by the fact that it is entered into for reasons of tangible gain, but when it is the product of the traits shown by a pathological liar it, just as the lying itself, is a part of the pathological picture. (p. 2)

The Healys, early researchers in forensic psychiatry, referred to the "art of professional criminalistic self-protection" (p. 9). This term applies to the psychopath in this case study, given her strenuous efforts to thwart the legal system and remain out of prison. She has been adept at convincing judges to remand her to drug treatment programs instead of prison.[17] "It is obvious that the typical swindler would find lying his best cloak of disguise" (p. 10).

Hare's (1993) view is that "psychopaths are always getting into trouble in large part because their behavior is not motivated by anxiety or guided by cues that warn of danger" (p. 194). "...many psychopaths are astute students of human nature and, unlike most people, are willing to use what they have learned for their own selfish purposes" (Babiak and Hare, 2006, p. 68). Several studies have been done concerning the return of psychopaths to crime following imprisonment. In one study, psychopaths were not motivated to do well, dropped out of treatment early, and derived relatively little benefit from the program. Following release from prison, their rate of return was much higher than that of the other patients (Ogloff, Wong, and Greenwood, 1990). In another study, psychopaths were almost four times more likely to commit a violent offense following release from a therapeutic community program than were other patients (Harris, Rice, and Cormier, 1991).

According to many years of Hare's research into criminality, 2-3% of the general population meets the strict criteria for psychopathy.[18] His estimates, while clearly very roughly determined, are difficult to empirically dispute. Hare estimates the following prevalence for psychopathy in various populations:

Serious spousal assaulters	10%
Pedophiles	10%
North American criminals (males)	15%
North American criminals (females)	10%
Rapists (incarcerated)	35%
Molesters/rapists	65%
Pimps	50%
Hostage takers/unlawful confinement	50%
Police killers	44%
Serial killers	90%

Among the New York sex offenders who went out on parole, 30.1% were classified as psychopaths (Moran, 1940, p. 14).

Psychopathy can be viewed as a specific personality disorder, an adaptive reproductive strategy, and a clinical construct traditionally defined by a cluster of personality traits and behavior. Hare disagrees with the Diagnostic and Statistical Manual of Mental Disorders (American Psychiatric Association, 2000) statement that Antisocial Personality Disorder is also known as psychopathy.

Hare feels that psychopathy is more predictive of Antisocial Personality Disorder than the reverse. Most psychopaths in prison have Antisocial Personality Disorder. He feels the term psychopathy has become pejorative. Hare believes that psychopaths often hone their skills in prison, which can make the effects of their psychopathy worse.

Blair, Mitchell, and Blair (2005) feel that the classification of psychopathy can be considered an extension and refinement of the DSM diagnosis of conduct disorder and

[17] Court records show that the predator has manipulated and fooled judges into ordering her to seek drug rehabilitation instead of sentencing her to prison. Such evasive actions occurred at least three times.

[18] Lecture given July 7-8, 2005, Lancaster, PA.

antisocial personality disorder. "Specifically, psychopathy identifies one form of pathology associated with high levels of antisocial behavior; individuals who present with a particular form of emotional impairment" (p. 15).

This research explores the possibility that victims of crime are vulnerable as a result of various aspects of their personality, their collective experiences, and the risks that they take (Ingram and Fortier, 2001; Ingram and Price, 2001; Turvey, 2001a; Schneider, 2002). Accordingly, psychopaths prey upon vulnerable victims more easily. This is in contrast to individuals with less susceptibility and those who fall to predatory behavior less easily. Some people are victimized because they are in the wrong place at the wrong time. Though not meant to blame victims, their choices and behavior will contribute to their vulnerability. In general, "...every predatory and scavenging creature seeks out the young, weak, and wounded" (McClurkin, 2001, p. 39). The level of intelligence of a predator refers to the ability of a person to acquire relevant knowledge and apply it in an effective manner. In an analysis of a criminal profile, low offender skill level suggests a lack of criminal experience and poor planning, not necessarily a lack of intelligence (Turvey, 2001a). Offenders may seek individuals whom they know do not have many buffers or ways of using their support. When individuals are victimized, they become emotionally affected in some areas of life. Without buffers (support) they will become incapable of withstanding a potentially devastating event.

Stalking

"Stalking is unwanted pursuit, following, or harassment" (Spence-Diehl, 1999, p. 1). Florida statutes, for example, define harassment as the "engagement in a course of conduct directed at a specific person and serves no legitimate purpose" (Public Law 784.048). The frequency and escalation of stalking behaviors runs the gamut from gathering of information, repeated non-threatening mail, e-mail, instant messaging, and telephone calls, to false reports to authorities, spreading rumors, vandalism, and physically attacking the victim, even murder. Stalking can have a serious impact on the victim. Stalkers and other predators are likely to be attracted to the message board-and chat rooms used by victims. A message board, for example, can become a valuable source of intelligence and might even help a cyber-stalker locate new victims (Bocij, 2005).

The literature on victim vulnerability deals mainly with stalking and prevention strategies. "The most effective way to manage stalking cases is to prevent them" (Ugolini and Kelly, 2001). "Victims should first be encouraged to educate themselves on the dynamics of stalking and their responsibilities in managing it as a way of reducing targeted victim vulnerability" (p. 307). Williams, et al., (1996) discussed the need for law enforcement agencies to make clear their limitations with regard to providing protection, whereby reducing their responsibility and preventing a victim's false sense of security.

Stalking by a perpetrator can give rise to Stalking Trauma Syndrome (STS) in his or her victim. STS is a collection of symptoms that can be related to Posttraumatic Stress Disorder (PTSD) (American Psychiatric Association, 2000). According to the DSM-IV-TR:

> The essential feature of Posttraumatic Stress Disorder is the development of characteristic symptoms following exposure to an extreme traumatic stressor involving direct personal

experience of an event that involves actual or threatened death or serious injury, or other threat to one's physical integrity. (p. 463)

Collins and Wilkas (2001) propose that STS is a condition that can be present when a victim is subjected to repeat and persistent stalking behavior. "In STS, a stalking victim experiences: (1) a cycle of crisis; (2) significant psychological effects, including helplessness and hopelessness, anxiety, depression, desperation, and loss of control as well as behavioral changes; and (3) recovery-based effective coping tools for stalking victims and their families" (p. 317). Such tools help the victims increase their awareness of potential danger and adopt ways to modify their behavior to decrease their vulnerability.

It has only been recently that researchers, psychologists, and law enforcement have begun to take a closer look at the traits and tactics of the everyday stalker. Spence-Diehl (1999) found that the perception of rejection is a common denominator among nearly all stalkers. "The rejection may be either real or contrived in the mind of the stalker" (p. 8). The abandonment (rejection) they hate and fear the most becomes a self-fulfilling prophecy resulting from their own erratic and irrational behaviors" (p. 10). As the stalking behavior persists, the stalker becomes obsessed about the victim. They develop themes of fantasy, often revolving around entitlement, anger, and destiny.

Stalkers may be narcissistic in the sense that they are unable to recognize or respect the needs and feelings of others. Because they lack the appropriate coping skills, they are unable to tolerate discomfort, rejection, loss, shame, or embarrassment.

Meloy (1989), Orion, (1997), and Zona, Palarea, and Lane (1998) found some stalkers developed an erotomanic distortion towards the victims. "In this type the stalkers are delusional" (Leitz Spitz, 2003, p. 505). The psychiatric classification known as erotomania is defined as a rare disorder in which a person holds a delusional belief that another person, usually of a higher social status, is in love with them. It is called De Clerambault Syndrome (El-Assra, 1989) after the French psychiatrist Gaetan Gatien de Clerambault (1872-1934). De Clerambault (1942) published a comprehensive review paper on the subject (*Les Psychoses Passionelles*). De Clerambault was the first to systematically classify erotomania. Since then, much emphasis has been placed in the literature on the higher status or social desirability of the objects, as it is through them that erotomanics believe their unhappy lives can be magically transformed (Davis and Chipman, 1997, p. 166; De Clerambault, 1942).

De Clerambault (1942) originally set up the following criteria for defining erotomania:

1. The delusional belief of being loved by another person.
2. The other person (object) has a higher social status.
3. The other person fell in love first.
4. The other person approached the affected individual first.
5. Sudden onset.
6. The love object remains unchanged.
7. The erotomanic person rationalizes the paradoxical behavior of the love object.
8. The disorder takes a chronic course.
9. Absence of hallucinations

Seeman (1978), in contrast, differentiated between a fixed and recurrent type of erotomania characterized by the following:

1. Fixed vs. variable love object.
2. Chronic vs. recurrent.
3. Object perceived as ordinary vs. more powerful.
4. Actual social contact vs. no contact with the love object prior to onset of erotomania.
5. Dependent vs. independent personality.
6. Subject had heterosexual relationship vs. absence of sexual relationship prior to onset.
7. Defense mechanisms against heterosexual drives involved vs. defense of homosexual drives.

Evolutionary psychology proposes that cognitive and emotional capacities and their corresponding behaviors, much like physical traits, have evolved in order to solve problems of adaptive significance (Brune, 2003, p. 197). Evolutionary principles hold that existing structures can be modified. This is crucial to the explanation in evolutionary terms of psychopathology. Therefore, design flaws are possible within the evolution of human psychological mechanisms. In erotomania, being defined as the pathological variant of a long-term mating strategy, fixation on a single love object was the rule in both men and women (p. 202). "Evolutionary psychology emphasizes the ultimate causes of pathological cognition, emotion and behavior, that is, why, they have come into being in the particular way they did during the phylogenic history of our species (p. 204).

Within evolutionary theory, the so-called sexual strategies theory suggests that women are predicted to prefer long-term mates who are capable to provide sufficient resources; men, by contrast, are more likely to prefer partners who exhibit signals indicating high fecundity (the capacity to produce offspring) (p. 185). Erotomania is uncommon even in psychiatric populations, which explains the lack of reliable estimates of incidence and prevalence rates in the psychiatric literature. "Although numerous anecdotal reports of erotomania exist the syndrome is still poorly understood in terms of its etiology, nosological status, pathophysiology and treatment (p. 186). Traditional explanations of the syndrome have been interpreted primarily in psychodynamic terms (see, for example: Segal, 1989).

In the middle Ages, the syndrome was known as *melancholie erotique* or *amor insanus* (Raschka, 1979). Kraepelin distinguished between erotic madness as a form of primary madness and erotic paranoia, the latter form being associated with hallucinations (Kraepelin, 1883).

Orion (1997), a psychiatrist, wrote about her experiences of being stalked by a former patient:

> Erotomania recently had become part of our national dialogue when Americans sat transfixed by the Senate Judiciary Hearings in which Professor Anita Hill was accused of suffering under the delusion that Judge Clarence Thomas loved her. Since then, erotomania has continued to glow in the national, and even the international, spotlight. (p. 60)

This syndrome can be divided into two distinct, but related typologies: those in which the perpetrator knows the victim from a past intimate relationship and those where the perpetrator sees the victim from afar and wants to establish a physical, sexual, or romantic relationship, which starts by trying to get the victim to notice him (Davis and Chipman, 1997; Davis,

1999). "The goal of the stalker can vary: to have a relationship (attach), be right (vindication), or punish (get revenge)" (Spence-Diehl, 1999, p. 12).

Stalking is a typical predatory behavior. Annually, 1.4 million Americans suffer the experience of being stalked (p. v). Using census data, researchers estimate that approximately 10 million Americans have been stalked at least once during their lives (Rowley, 1997). Such actions can unnerve the victim and result in unpredictable and uncharacteristic behavior. Such new behavior can include what this researcher refers to as defensive stalking, whereby the victim begins to investigate the predator in a quest to uncover information about them (Kreuter, 2003c; 2004). This conduct on the part of the victim can consume the victim's time and financial resources. The outcome can range from intervention by the legal system to frustration and disillusionment in the victim (McClurkin, 2001). Another outcome could be violence against the stalker by the victim or someone trying to protect the victim, even someone seeking revenge. In this research, the subject continues to engage in defensive stalking behavior.[19]

Personality of the Stalker

The literature shows that stalkers have certain typical personality traits. Stalkers_may show some or all characteristics, as there may be multiple profiles or personality clusters: Jealous; narcissistic; obsessive and compulsive; falls instantly in love; manipulative; socially awkward or uncomfortable; family, and others; unable to take no for an answer; and deceptive.

In an effort to create a typology of stalking, various researchers have focused on behavioral, relational, and psychiatric components (Zona et al., 1993; Davis and Chipman, 1997; Meloy, 1998). Davis and Chipman (1997) reviewed several studies of obsessive and intrusive following, stalkers, and stalking between 1992 and 1997 and found that no one particular psychological makeup or profile of a stalker existed.

Meloy (1998) reviewed ten studies published between 1978 and 1995. Typologies across studies were based on various characteristics and included patterns of pursuit, psychiatric characteristics, victim characteristics, and patterns of violence and threats. Significant findings across studies included the prominence of Axis I and Axis II psychiatric disorders in offenders, and patterns of pursuit of the victim.

Harmon, et al., (1995) separated 48 stalking participants into two categories or axes: e.g., type of attachment and whether or not a prior relationship existed between the two participants. On the first axis, two attachment types were identified: affectionate, amorous, and persecutory, angry. For the second axis, six subgroups to describe the prior relationship of the victim to the stalker were created. These included personal, professional, employment, acquaintance, and none. No significant differences were found among the six subgroups on any of the variables tested.

Thus, the behavior of psychopaths comprises a variety of activities aimed at potential victims, some of whom are more vulnerable than others. Due to their lack of feelings of guilt

[19] His daily routine includes computer-based research into the past conduct of the predator in addition to vigilance as to her present activities. This is necessary so as to protect himself and to potentially recover monies she stole from him, which are covered by an outstanding civil judgment.

or remorsefulness, they deny responsibility for harm exacted on others. Psychopaths tend to be very clever and are capable of adapting to varied environments, even prison. The vulnerability of victims blends well with the proclivities of psychopaths.

Victim Vulnerability

The subject in this research succumbed to the actions of the psychopathic predator. The predator used stalking as one means to harm the victim. "Stalkers know whom to target and how to gain access to their victims" (Gross, 2000, p. 61). The predator selected the subject, who merely signed on to join a Chat Room discussion; though he did not contribute to the dialogue. Because his screen name was unintentionally similar to a nickname of a professional baseball team, she sent the subject an Instant Message with a reference to a baseball game in progress. She used this simple approach as a clever way to find a victim. The stalker's objective is to force the victim into a state of surrender. Victims typically respond not with a single reaction, but with a progression of emotions. The principal investigator speculates that the stages may be somewhat similar to those of mourners when faced with loss: denial, bargaining, guilt, anger, and then acceptance (Kubler-Ross, 1997). Victims often participate, albeit unwillingly, in the crimes against them as a sort of silent enabler. They do so by going along with falsified situations created by predators. They may also be vulnerable to the experience of depression, anxiety, and fear. Furthermore, victims may feel like they are overreacting or possibly paranoid. This self-doubt contributes to their reluctance to disclose criminal activity targeted against themselves to others. This may be due to the potential embarrassment victims feel about their predicament. As an example: when the pilot's aunt criticized him by asserting that she, herself, would have been more aware and would have done more to repel the efforts of the predator, the victim felt anger that she portrayed herself as being less prone to being defrauded and she did not fully appreciate Robert's victimization. Speculatively, people who themselves have never been the victim of crime may be less sensitive to the concerns of the victim.

The majority of stalking victims are not public figures, but ordinary people. Victim's rights organizations calculate that "about 700,000 cases are reported annually" (p. 3). Stalkers also prey upon their own family members. Obsessed pursuers will frequently harass a third party, to whom the actual target is attached, in order to gain the intense impact and reaction they seek.

Stalkers, like other predatory criminals, secretly observe and test the potential victim. By doing so, the stalker develops an awareness of the likelihood that the victim will strike back or whether the target will go along with the intentions of the stalker. Victims are manipulated through fear and intimidation at first, then through more sinister means such as duress and extortion.[20] When something is eventually done to stop the abuse, the victim may feel remorse, combined with a sense of culpability. This may feed the obsessive interaction. The victim can become so vulnerable that the stalker's delusional or psychopathic thinking can actually start to sound reasonable. This is similar to the reaction cult followers have after they

[20] In the case of the subject of this research, the reverse sequence took place. This may be partially due to the distance between the subject and the predator and also due to the subject's unwitting trust of the predator very early on in the scheme.

are involved with the cult leader. In cult recruitment practice, as well as in extortions, predators seek to isolate the victim from his or her family, thereby reducing the threat of intervention by a member of the victim's support network.

Thus, psychopathic predators, some of whom use stalking as a mechanism, exploit every clever method at their disposal to identify and exact harm on victims. Predatory activities seem to be habitual in nature. Because their behavior is considered by them to be normal, it is not surprising that psychopaths do not normally seek therapeutic treatment (Hare, 1998).

Vulnerability is viewed as different types of phenomena by different theorists. Depending on the viewpoint, it can be presented as a process, a set of traits, a disorder, or a set of behaviors. Victims are most vulnerable when in transition, in the progress of their lives, from one place to another. "Managing victim fear often presents a case manager with his or her greatest challenge" (p. 308). Victims often believe the pursuer to have extraordinary abilities to get information. Victims also experience a variety of psychological repercussions such as insomnia, depression, anxiety, stress, feelings of futility, and helplessness.

The markers of vulnerability, risk, and resilience refer to similar phenomenon and share a number of features (Ingram and Price, 2001). An important distinction must be made between vulnerability, an internal construct, and risk, an external construct. Vulnerable individuals have one or more features of personality that suggests susceptibility to attack (Ingram and Price, 2001). Risk refers to any variables that are associated with an increased likelihood of experiencing a disorder (Rutter, 1987; Luthar and Zigler, 1991). Therefore, the presence of risk suggests an increase in probability of the occurrence of some type of disorder. Researchers attempting to search for vulnerability markers are essentially searching for predictors of the disorder, absent any symptoms.

There is much research that explores vulnerability to disease. The medical model is mainly concerned with physical disorders and pharmacological intervention. Extensive research has been done on the characteristics of disease as well as the predictability in certain persons to contract disease.[21] Some of this research may be extended to vulnerability to previous victimization related to crime. As Zubin and Spring (1977) suggest: "We regard vulnerability as a relatively permanent, enduring trait" (p. 109). Themes focus on vulnerability as a trait, the endogenous and latent nature of vulnerability, and the role of stress in actualizing vulnerability. Though other investigators have not been as specific, the enduring trait nature of vulnerability is implicit in many of their discussions of vulnerability (Ingram and Price, 2001), likely stemming from a genetic level of analysis. The extent to which a factor is seen as enduring depends on whether the factor is seen as a biological process rooted in hereditary processes or the result of environmentally based trauma or injury, or has been acquired through learning.

Price and Lento (2001) cite the possibility that: "Our measurement of vulnerability constructs still lack the precision to detect subtle distinctions between vulnerability factors" (p. 35). "Even though vulnerability is conceptualized as a trait according to some conceptualizations, vulnerability [to disorder] is not necessarily permanent or unalterable" (p.12). Corrective experiences may attenuate vulnerability.

Two types of vulnerability have been suggested: acute and chronic. Acute vulnerability would be seen in persons who are generally highly sensitive and extremely responsive to events (Ingram and Fortier, 2001). This is in contrast to the chronic type, where there is

[21] For example: genetic predisposition to cancer or cardiovascular disease.

generally a long-term, drawn out impact, extending over a long period of time. Dersch, Palatin, and Gotchel (2002) found the following:

> Although no single theoretical model can fully explain the causal relationship between chronic pain and psychopathology, a diathesis-stress model is emerging as the dominant overarching theoretical perspective. In this model, diatheses are conceptualized as pre-existing, semi-dormant characteristics of the individual before the onset of chronic pain that are then activated and exacerbated by the stress of this chronic condition, eventually resulting in diagnosable psychopathology. (p. 779)

Experiments in the area of stress can be applied to the construct of victim vulnerability. The reactions of victims to previous stressors may lead to a greater degree of vulnerability. Peterson, Maier, and Seligman (1993) found that "The stressors in real life are often chronic, persisting for long periods of time or recurring frequently" (p. 92). Biological systems generally undergo compensatory changes when repeatedly challenged.

Hereditary factors include genetically determined neurobiological processes as well as various dimensions of temperament. Environmentally based factors range from central nervous system damage, resulting from obstetrical and birth complications, to vulnerability factors acquired through socialization and learning processes, such as a lack of control due to overprotective parenting.

Ingram and Price (2001) suggest that the trait nature of vulnerability is perhaps most clearly seen in contrast to the state or episodic nature of psychological disorders. Hollon, Evans and DeRubeis (1990) and Hollon and Cobb (1993) have identified two conditions of vulnerability. One condition has traits present, but is sub-clinical; the other has traits present at a clinically significant level. These researchers distinguished between stable traits of vulnerability that predispose individuals to what they refer to as a disorder, but do not constitute the disorder, and state variables, which represent the occurrence of the symptoms that reflect the onset of the disorder. Perpetrators look for weakness in victims. Such weakness often leads to ill-considered behavior patterns.

While symptoms follow an illness, it is the behavior pattern that perpetrators look for. Therefore, disorder is characterized as a state wherein the essential qualities are relatively stable. Episodes present as profound symptoms, vary between occurrence and remission, but the traits themselves remain generally constant. Thus, an individual may let their guard down even though they were previously victimized. However, with mood swings, vulnerability may not have constancy.

Another perspective is that "frequent experiences with the disorder may increase vulnerability for future onsets" (Ingram and Price, 2001, p. 9). While it might seem likely that prior victimization would lead to increased self-protection, it could also, in some individuals, lead to a weakening of spirit and loss of resolve to prevent future occurrences. Alternatively, tolerance to aversive experiences may build up, which can lead to a kind of strained forbearance and increased ability to endure stress, without serious harm. Thus, a form of tolerance may build up in a victim of ongoing crime.

Vulnerability is an endogenous process and remains stable even though observable states of psychopathology arise and then often diminish. Some investigators have suggested that vulnerability is not easily observable and can thus be conceptualized as a latent process (Ingram and Price, 2001). Thus, the vulnerability is inside a person, whether innately, or through the learning process. Environmental factors and other external sources are also potential secondary forces that may activate vulnerability and possibly lead to aversive interactions. Stress, for example, is conceptualized as the occurrence of significant life events, which, in the case of psychopathology, are undesirable or aversive.

Victim vulnerability can be considered a type of psychological disorder due to the personality and behavioral factors involved. Vulnerability to psychological disorders can often be traced to early life experiences (McNally, 2001; Price and Lento, 2001). This includes postnatal problems from obstetrical complications and dysfunctional learning (Ingram and Price, 2001). Because of its much shorter history, the study of the processes of vulnerability associated with psychopathology in children and adolescents lags behind the study of vulnerability of adult psychopathology (Price and Lento, 2001).

Treatment

There are several approaches to treatment applicable to victim vulnerability. One aspect is to prevent future episodes of victimization from recurring. The other is to treat the trauma created by victimization so that the individual can get past the pain and return to normal life.

Because we do not know much about victim vulnerability, methods of treatment designed to help victims return to productive lives are lacking. Treatment plans begin with a complete assessment of the patients' vulnerability and any resulting trauma. Obtaining family and developmental history is a critical step in both diagnosis and in development of treatment plans.

In most respects, treatment of non-violent offenders is no different from that of people diagnosed with mental illness who have not been referred from the criminal justice system (Dvoskin and Patterson, 1998). Research in the area of institutionalization of long-term prisoners (Kiesler and Sibulkin, 1987) found that unnecessarily long periods of maximum security hospitalization could actually reduce a person's ability to return safely to the outside community. Thus, the best treatment may require progressive movement to less structured, more independent settings where a person can learn or relearn the life skills necessary for a safe return to freedom.

Psychotropic drugs may reduce symptoms of certain psychiatric disorders, which may, in turn, reduce the condition of vulnerability. An example is the use of lithium to control severe mood swings for bipolar or cyclothymic persons. Many psychiatric conditions may also lead to increased victim vulnerability, especially those conditions that decrease cognitive functioning (e.g., promote poor judgment) or increase dependency on others.

Even if vulnerability is altered by medication, the vulnerability still persists with increased risk, following discontinuance of the regimen (Hollon, 1999). Kindling is a neuronal process that intensifies vulnerability to affective disorders wherein each episode of an affective disorder leaves a residual neuronal trace that is rekindled with similar episodes in the future (Ingram and Price, 2001, p. 48). Gradual cognitive impairment may, likewise, be responsible for the decreasing level of stress necessary for a triggered response.

Psychotherapy can also result in a shift from maladaptive learning to positive learning. This, in turn, can lead to attenuation of symptoms and decreased vulnerability. It may be possible to transform the prisoner through rehabilitation using poetry to increase their awareness of their inner pain. The principal investigator has developed a technique for this purpose that encourages the prisoner to write a narrative on their life in retrospect (Who I was), about their current state of being (Who I am), and a projection of their ideal self in the future (Who I want to be) (Kreuter, 2005).[22] The stimulus for the individual narratives is a poem: "Then, I was; now I am; I can become" (Kreuter, 2005, p. 99), which is read to inmates and incorporates the theory in the form of prose. Kreuter (2006a) extends his discussion on the use of poetry in existential-humanistic therapy for prisoners.

VICTIMOLOGY

The Psychology of the Victim

What do we know about the psychology of the victim? In particular, the principal investigator explored the main constructs of victim vulnerability; victimology; learned helplessness; and depth psychology interpreted from the standpoint of personology and existential-humanistic psychology (Kreuter, 2006b). Various sub-constructs will also be discussed. These include: treatment, risk factors, protective factors and resiliency, and victim profiling.

Some individuals respond to the overtures of predators to fill a void in their lives (Turvey, 1999a). Thus, feelings for persons with whom they are infatuated can become amplified. This can result in behavior such as calling repeatedly, only to hang up, or driving by someone's house to see if the object of their infatuation can be seen (McClurkin, 2001).

Though not responsible for the acts of the criminal, victims may somehow inadvertently contribute to the problem. Perhaps there is something about whom the stalker selects and where the stalker finds his or her initial momentum (Spence-Diehl, 1999). Individual's who seem to attract this kind of abuse often suffer frequent victimization (McClurkin, 2001). They can also be individuals who, because of lifestyle, make themselves more exposed or vulnerable to crime, such as men who are victimized by prostitutes. The character attributes of naiveté and gullibility will, at least partially, suggest the level of susceptibility for victimization.

Victims sometimes demonstrate an unwillingness to impose limits and set boundaries for fear of hurting or disappointing someone (Gross, 2000). This phenomenon is often seen in women who have been battered by abusive men. This sends out a clear signal to the stalker that the victim is vulnerable (Spence-Diehl, 1999). They may go along with the situation set up by the predator, especially since their first inclination is to accord the benefit of the doubt to the offender. Usually, the victim knows the stalker and makes excuses for the person's behavior. There can be different responses as a result of the variation of gender and the intimacy of knowledge of the stalker. Also, differences in education levels of the victim will have an effect on the reactions of the victim (Turvey, 1999a). When the situation escalates, Gross states: "victims try to appease their pursuers by meeting his demands" (p. 83). This behavior can serve to enable further abusive conduct.

Targeted victims can become confused and consumed by their own inner conflicts. They may feel terrorized and uncertain if they should call the police or just try to escape from the

[22] Many inmates who have written these narratives have expressed the attainment of a new sense of self-awareness and empowerment in their lives, which, in turn, can lead to transformation and optimism.

situation. Threats of retaliation often result in reluctance to contact law enforcement. Essentially, victims feel trapped and helpless, resulting in loss of self-esteem and increased doubt about their judgments and perceptions. Because victims often fail to sever the connection at the soonest possible opportunity, the stalker's confidence increases (McClurkin, 2001). This results in additional motivation to continue to pursue the victim. Therefore, it is important for people to examine their own tendencies. Often, what we subliminally seek, especially in relationships, we get. If an individual has a pattern of involvement with obsessive people, an unconscious desire to experience what is familiar may dictate future selections. Consciously placing limits on one's accessibility is vital to reduce the chances of becoming a victim (Gross, 2000).

Victimology considers how victims respond to crime. The subject in this inquiry has had his career ruined, his aspirations and security were shattered; and he is steadfastly committed to his ongoing investigation into the life and criminal conduct of the predator. He continues to appeal to elected officials to assist him with his efforts to achieve vindication from the government agency that falsely labeled him as a reporter of false crimes (suggestive of psychosis). The principal investigator conducted a thorough investigation into the validity of the claims of the subject.[23] The evidence provided by the victim, together with independent collection of data (Kreuter 2002; 2003a; 2003b; 2003c; 2004; 2006b), comprise a convincing case of maltreatment of the subject by the government following his victimization from the crime committed against him. He continues to seek vindication as a way to advance his life toward a new career as his former career is ended due to Robert's reputation having been tainted by false allegations.

Victimology has changed from emphasizing crime to studying what is involved in being a victim of crime (Wertz, 1985). Mendelson (1974) suggests that the victim suffers, but questions what constitutes the crime victim's suffering. Drapkin and Viano (1975) note that following victimization, a loss of faith in the justice system with correlated alienation and frustration may in some way further the experience of victimization.

The relationship between the criminal and the victim was explained in detail in 1948 by the German-American criminologist Hans Von Hentig. Von Hentig (1948) studied victims of homicide, and said that the most likely type of victim is the depressive type who is an easy target, careless and unsuspecting. The greedy type is easily duped because his or her motivation for easy gain lowers his or her natural tendency to be suspicious. The wanton type is particularly vulnerable to stresses that occur at a given period of time in the life cycle, such as juvenile victims. The tormentor is the victim of attack from the target of his or her abuse, such as with battered women. Von Hentig's work provided the foundation for analysis of victim-precipitation that is still somewhat evident in the literature today.

Legal categories of criminal and victim are straightforward: one is harmed, the other guilty. Von Hentig (1948) described the types of victims psychologically. Some of these definitions are applicable to the subject in this research. "The detrimental result may be brought about partly by the concurrent effort of the victim" (p. 419). The law assumes that the doer of crime is always active and that the sufferer is always inactive. Von Hentig established a scale to measure the attitudes of the victim:

[23] The principal investigator is a Certified Public Accountant, a Certified Fraud Examiner, and a Diplomat of The American College of Forensic Examiners International.

1. apathetic, lethargic
2. sublimating, conniving, passively submitting
3. cooperative, contributory
4. provocative, instigative, soliciting (p. 420)

Von Hentig suggested that human beings are equipped with a biological sense of fear with which they can imagine danger. Thus, any disturbance of the instinct of self-preservation forms the basis of a dangerous malady. Fatigue also reduces the power of resistance. "The extremely exhausted human being has a much-weakened sense of self-preservation" (p. 422).

The acquisitive person can often become a sucker who believes in his own superior intelligence. Such a person may feel quite able to detect fraudulent schemes or be able to deal with them effectively prior to any real damage being done. The wanton victim has a disposition that may include loneliness, which acts as a process-accelerator (p. 427). In the case of a male, it may be possible for a female to seduce the male victim through clever means, sometimes involving fear.

Loneliness, according to Von Hentig, creates the desire for companionship and can lead to the creation of optical illusions as far as the wished for object goes. "Anything is better than the solitude of a lonesome life" (P. 428). "Most crimes are directed against a specific individual, his life or property, his sexual self-determination" (p. 438).

Sometimes the victim is transformed into a perpetrator. "Many victimized individuals and groups appear to be morally shaken and weakened. Suffering does not make better but worse" (p. 445). Certain victims turn to alcohol to dull their painful feelings. "Without giving up hope, drinking is the true relief from the sting of hopelessness" (p. 445). Being preyed upon is a suggestive experience, which leads the pupil to the practice of preying. "Suffering does not deter but calls forth an imitative venture" (p. 446).

Von Hentig explained that the relationship between the two are often complex, thus the area of criminality and victimization requires a deeper look in order to better understand the inherent dynamics. Of particular interest is Von Hentig's theory that an unknown aspect of the personality manifest itself suddenly, and it depends primarily on the relationship between the criminal and the victim, which has been illuminated by a new and unexpected light through modern psychology (Ellenberger, 1955).

Often the victim ultimately transforms himself into a criminal (Ellenberger, 1955). This theory can be applied to the subject in that he eventually engaged in reactive stalking and used some techniques the predator used in order to discover more about her activities. He used information he gathered by monitoring her Internet usage to provide law enforcement with enough facts about a subsequent victim to warrant seizure of her computer by the police.[24] "...even in the case of individuals who have always led a completely lawful life, a series of grave injustices or vicissitudes may result in their committing a crime. It is accepted that victims of other power/control crimes may sometimes take part in reactive stalking (Bocij, 2005). The Cambridge Advanced Learner's Dictionary defines 'reactive' as 'reacting to events or situations rather than acting first to change or prevent something', while the

[24] Both the subject and the principal investigator provided information about the predator to the computer crimes expert, but the predator has not been arrested as of this date for her new crimes against an elderly man because of the inability of that person to provide testimony. That victim had dementia at the time the predator exploited him and he has since died. It is believed that the predator stole over $30,000 from him. She also stole his car on the day of his stroke.

Merriam-Webster Online Dictionary defines it as being 'readily responsive to a stimulus' or 'occurring as a result of stress or emotional upset'. It can be argued that there are two types of reactive stalker, the 'controlling stalker' and the 'paranoid stalker'. The controlling stalker tends to have experienced the powerlessness associated with being a victim of a power/control crime. As a result, she has become desperate to rebuild her self-esteem and regain a sense of control over her life. One way of achieving this is by gaining power over others (Bocij, 2005).

The paranoid stalker reacts to the fear and anxiety associated with the experience of being a stalking victim by becoming distrustful and suspicious of others. In many cases, these suspicions may be so unreasonable as to border on paranoia. However, the paranoid stalker justifies his/her actions by claiming that they are a necessary part of self-protection; suspicion allows them to stay one step ahead of the stalker. Accepting others at face value involves taking unacceptable personal risks, since anyone might be an accomplice of the stalker (Bocij, 2005).

A different view suggests that reactive stalking can be divided into categories perhaps best described as 'offensive stalking' and 'defensive stalking'. Defensive stalking is carried out in self-defense, usually as a way of gathering intelligence about a stalker and his allies. By constantly checking the stalker's activities, it becomes possible to anticipate and counter his behaviors (Bocij, 2005). Unlike defensive stalking, there is often an intent to cause harm behind the actions of an offensive stalker. Even if people are harmed inadvertently, the offensive stalker may not feel any guilt over what might be seen as acceptable 'collateral damage'.

The concept of reactive stalking might be considered controversial. It is, after all, somewhat provocative to suggest that victims of stalking may eventually go on to become stalkers of their predators themselves. Although users raised a number of concerns, a common worry was that a general acceptance of concepts related to reactive stalking might result in less sympathetic treatment of stalking victims. Reactive stalking also has implications for the criminal justice system. As suggested earlier, some people have little confidence in the ability of the police and the courts to protect them from stalkers and may adopt stalking behaviors (Bocij, 2005). Even the police may not fully understand this particular area.

Hypervigilance has been associated with aggressive or hostile behavior and also as a symptom often associated with PTSD. Hypervigilance can be described as 'extreme sensitivity to cues that may signal presence of feared object or situation' (Health Dictionary, www.health-dictionary.com). Hypervigilance, through its association with PTSD, is sometimes associated with inappropriate aggressive behavior and even violence (Byrne, 2003).

However, Bocij (2005) finds such an argument difficÖLt to accept, since there is evidence that not all stalking victims develop PTSD (Abrams and Robinson, 1998a). For instance, in a study of 100 stalking victims, Pathé and Mullen (1997) found that only 37 developed conditions that met the criteria for a diagnosis of PTSD. Similarly, a more recent study of 100 stalking victims who attended a psychiatric clinic found that fewer than half (47) fulfilled the criteria for a diagnosis of PTSD (Haider and Haider, 2002). Nor are all those suffering from PTSD likely to display all the associated symptoms. Bocif (2005) correctly reports that in order to believe that all the behavior associated with paranoid stalking originates from hypervigilance, one would need to accept that all the message board users who objected to the concept had correctly diagnosed themselves (and others), meaning that all were suffering from PTSD and all had symptoms that included hypervigilance. The term hypervigilance reinforces the victim's self-image as a victim. Any mistrust of others is not only understandable, but may also be justified by the victim's experiences and the possibility of repeat victimization.

The theories of Freud, Jung and Szondi consider the sudden transformation of criminal into victim or into the criminal-victim. In Freud's psychoanalysis, a person carries within their unconscious aggressive, incestuous, and criminal desires. Jung thought each individual in endowed with a group of unacceptable tendencies, which is neither wished for nor self-acknowledged, but are nonetheless active. Szondi created the concept of hidden self, which he saw as possibly the hidden or repressed angel beneath the façade of a criminal. This concept was then used to explain those obscure and mysterious instances where a man, who has been honest and normal up to that point, transforms himself abruptly and transiently into a criminal, into a victim, or into the criminal-victim (Ellenberger, 1955).

Quite a few people commit delinquent acts and then become honest people again when the social situation has returned to normal. Their latent criminal tendencies are transiently manifested. Other individuals suddenly conduct themselves in heroic fashion, while still others put their lives in danger in a totally heedless fashion and act as latent victims. The subject in this research certainly can be described in this manner, having placed himself in danger to help others. Ellenberger stated that some individuals conduct themselves as criminals, then as heroes, and then as futile victims, according to circumstances.

When a latent victim is the perfect negative of a certain type of criminal, a polar relationship develops between them; the criminal act is the bond which unites the complementary pair. Where criminologists have long described the passivity of the victim as well as referred to the victim harshly, such as appallingly stupid or incomprehensibly foolish, a deeper study of the victim reveals the basis for the connection.

The concept of victim dates back to ancient cultures and civilizations, such as the ancient Hebrews. Its original meaning was rooted in the idea of sacrifice or scapegoat – –the execution or casting out of a person or animal to satisfy a deity or hierarchy. The term crime victim generally refers to any person, group, or entity who has suffered injury or loss due to illegal activity. The harm can be physical, psychological, or economic.

Various symposia on victimology have been held (Viano, 2000; Schneider, 2002), which emphasized the damage suffered by the victims due to crimes (Schneider, 2002). Victims of a crime have been found to have a different perception of their status as victim at one stage of the event than those at other stages. These stages start with first becoming a victim, to denial; then to anger; to acceptance; then reducing the vulnerable behavior. As victims work through the trauma of being victimized, they can overcome the fear of doing something about the situation. This will affect their behavior and influence or even determine who will make the transition from one stage to the next and who will not (Viano, 2000).

Certain organizations have been formed to assist the victim. As part of the Third American Symposium on Victimology, held April 2005, a mission statement was devised to define the identity of the organization by recognizing victimology as a distinct discipline that has the victim at the center of its core and to address the needs of victims through research, education, and service (American Society of Victimology, 2005). There is also an international victimology website launched in June 1999 as a resource for all those interested in restorative justice for victims.

It is important to understand the personality of victims to determine why predators select them. Often, in criminal investigations, especially in homicides, "it is not difficult to become distracted by the allure of identification of the criminal's potential characteristics and forget the value of understanding their victims" (Turvey, 2001b, p. 109). This is, perhaps, the more emotionally difficult part of the process of criminal profiling, as investigators try to learn about the life of the victim. It is likely due to the training undertaken by the detectives, which includes development of mechanisms for coping emotionally, for personal detachment, and for dissociation from the victim. The victim is seen as an object. By de-humanizing victims, the investigators block any potential connection of similarity to their loved ones. Were investigators to open up to a process of uncovering facts about the victim's emotional state, personality, and behaviors, they would open themselves up to be affected by the pain and suffering of something that is only an impersonal object of analysis. "If we humanize victims, we know that there is the risk of recognizing that they are not unlike our own daughter, son, mother, father, sister, brother, wife, husband, or friend" (Turvey, 1999a, p. 106). Therefore, in order to maintain this detachment, knowledge about the victim as a person is blocked.

Stressful events, such as victimization, can produce enduring, negative psychological states (Ingram and Price, 2001). The subject in this research has been diagnosed with PTSD by several psychologists who treated him subsequent to the suspension of his pilot's license. This disorder may occur in response to criminal activity. The DSM requires the presence of a major stressor before a diagnosis of PTSD can be made. A review of an earlier version of the DSM reveals that DSM – III required that the trauma satisfy the condition that it be of sufficient severity that it would evoke "significant symptoms of distress in most people" (American Psychiatric Association, 1980, p. 236). DSM-IV provides a non-exhaustive list of typical stressors, which includes robbery. The subject's subjective response to the potentially traumatic event is used to determine whether the fear, horror, or helplessness was sufficiently intense to qualify as a characteristic of disorder.

Briere (2002) notes four broad variables that help explain the amount of posttraumatic symptomatology: characteristics of the stressor, variables specific to the victim, subjective response to the stressor, and the response of others to the victim" (p. 13). Traumatic events may occur in conjunction with variables concerning the victim and the victim's social response after the trauma to determine how the individual subjectively interprets the stressor.

Contrasts can be made when evaluating negative mediators such as psychological health versus pre-existing distress or disorder, adaptive coping responses versus use of denial or avoidance, biologic resilience versus a genetic predisposition toward posttraumatic stress, and a positive social support system versus social isolation or stigma (Briere, 2002). Several of the risk factors for PTSD are also risk factors for traumatic (Criterion A) events per se. Breslau, Davis, and Andreski (1995) found that past exposure to traumatic events and extraversion were predictive of exposure to a PTSD-level traumatic event.

Kessler et al., (1995) found that social inequities increase the risk of victimization, especially for women and people of color in North American culture. The victim's subjective response to the potential stressor is an important consideration in the DSM, where the negative event is not deemed a stressor or trauma unless subjective horror, fear, or helplessness is reported. The posttraumatic stress is more likely and more intense when the individual reports greater perceived threat or danger (Green, Grace, and Glaser, 1985), helplessness (Green, Grace, and Glaser, 1982; Mikulciner and Solomon, 1988), terror (Holloway and Fullerton, 1994), and horror or fear (American Psychiatric Association, 1987).

Those who interpret a traumatic experience more negatively are more at risk for posttraumatic difficulties due to the tendency to view life events as outside of one's control.[25]

Zur (2005) found that "the psychology of victims and the dynamics of victimhood have been largely ignored by scholars and clinicians" (p. 45). The historical tendency of blaming the victim has trended towards exploration into the characteristics of victims and their relationship with the perpetrators (Zur, 2005). Western culture has evolved towards a notion of the inalienable rights of each individual to pursue happiness and supposedly, being victimized blocks that right. Fighting for a right may mean that the person is claiming to have the status of victim. "Today it is fashionable to be a victim" (p. 49). The television talk shows are full of stories about victims from all walks of life (Hughes, 1993).

"In claiming the status of victim and assigning all the blame to others, a person can achieve moral superiority while simultaneously disowning any responsibility for his behavior and its outcome" (Zur, 2005, p. 49). Very few writers have warned against the unrealistic and ultimately patronizing portrayal of victims of crime as total innocents (Viano, 2000). Most scholars avoid this field for fear of being accused of blaming the victim, which has the effect of causing little exploration of the role of the victim. The subject in this research seeks justice and fairness. He has devoted much of his time in this quest and refuses to embark on a new career path until he achieves an acceptable resolution to his plight.

Zur's (2005) work on victimhood, in general, and blame and responsibility, in particular, concentrates on "adult victims and on patterns of victimization established early in life, rather than on the effects of a single trauma" (p. 46). Zur's focus is on victims who have had a prior relationship with an abusive person. His research can be extended to the subject of this research, wherein the victim had a very brief relationship with the predator and the distinctive and elaborate ruse created through the use of false personas in order to fool him.

Victims can exploit their situation by constantly garnering sympathy. "The basic mode of operation of an adult victim is a feeling of helplessness and self-pity, an absent sense of accountability, and a tendency to blame" (p. 54). Victims often have feelings of self-inefficacy. Victims often maintain their behavior as long as there is a perceived net benefit, according to social exchange theory (Worchel, 1984) and behavioral psychology. In this research, the subject's quest for vindication is a type of behavior that provides a benefit to him in the form of a sense of purpose to his life, exempting him, at least temporarily, from seeking a new career. It also provides him with a type of pseudo-occupation: that of researching the life of the predator.[26]

Since the assumption is that there is no gene for victimhood, social and familial forces are most influential in our lives (Zur, 2005). Sykes (1992) found that a single event such as robbery or plane crash, does not transform a person into a victim. It takes a certain consistency in the environment to raise a victim.

The subject in this research fits Mendelson's (1974) original formulation to classify victims according to their relative degree of responsibility and power to control or affect situations. These categories range from total innocence and no guilt to total responsibility and complete guilt. For example, in the not guilty/innocent victim category, included are victims who do not share responsibility for the offense with the perpetrators. The subject fits the

[25] The subject in this case study reacted quite severely to his repeated victimization and felt as though he lost control over his life.

[26] In doing so, the subject was able to discover the true nature of the predator's actions as well as uncover crimes that were committed against other victims.

second category of victims with minor guilt, which includes victims who, with some thought, planning, awareness, information, or consciousness might have anticipated danger and avoided or minimized harm to themselves. There are two categories applicable to the pilot. One is the case of adults who were victimized by being in the wrong place at the wrong time in situations where with some awareness, preparation, and caution, they could have prevented the assault. The second is the case of victims who are conscious and aware of the situation and choose to be part of it. A better sense of danger could have anticipated the damage that occurred.

The psychopath is typically good and finding ways to bond with the victim. "The psychopath's psychological game involves analyzing the individual's expectations and desires, and then reflecting them in a psychological mask that is so convincing the person bonds with him or her" (Babiak and Hare, 2006, p. 79).

Risk's Taken by Perpetrators

Before we can understand how victim behavior plays a role in victimization, it is helpful to understand the different types of risks involved in the criminal behavior of perpetrators. While risk is normally the label for the victim, offenders are also exposed to certain risks. "Offender risk is the amount of exposure to a possibility of suffering harm or loss, such as capture, that an offender perceives when attempting to acquire a victim" (Burgess and Hazelwood, 1995, p. 119). The investigator would be interested to discover what obstacles the offender perceived and how the offender planned, if at all, to overcome those obstacles. Also applicable is the amount of risk of not following the captor's instructions.

In a discussion between the principal investigator and an incarcerated female, the inmate cited an example of a past crime where she staked out a vantage point near an ATM machine, waiting for a victim.[27] When she perceived an opportunity, she robbed the unsuspecting individual and hopped into a taxi for her get-away. Her story revealed her mindset at the time as being devoid of consideration for the ramifications of getting caught, but she was extremely sure of herself that she could execute the robbery safely and do so without detection by law enforcement or injury from the victim. While she did escape with a large sum of cash and the man's wallet, the victim, who pursued her, assaulted her and she suffered a severe eye injury. However, despite experiencing the consequences, some criminals may still return to crime. The diagnostic criteria for Antisocial Personality Disorder (American Psychiatric Association, 2000) supports this concept in the sense that: "failure to conform to social norms with respect to lawful behaviors as indicated by repeatedly performing acts that are grounds for arrest" (p. 706).

Risk and vulnerability have an empirical relation in the sense that the risk of remaining in a stressful environment can lead to the onset of a disorder if one is vulnerable. A physical example is an individual genetically susceptible to arteriosclerosis who continues to smoke cigarettes heavily. Such a person will more than likely develop the disease and possibly others. Therefore, risk factors can be evaluated and correlated to predicted onset of psychopathology and vulnerability, though not synonymous in nature.

[27] Personal communication as told to the principal investigator during a group counseling session as a maximum-security prison.

While certain features of vulnerability are common to risk and resiliency, there are differences between these constructs. Risk refers to variables empirically associated with "an increased likelihood of experiencing and predicting disorder" (Ingram and Price, 2001, p. 13). An example is poverty, which is positively associated with greater psychological dysfunction, such as low self-esteem and dysthymia. While risk refers to increased probability, it is not synonymous with causality.

Empirically validated (intra-personal) risk factors comprising such a profile include: perceptions of external control (as opposed to perceptions of internal control as a protective factor), perceptions of unique vulnerability, and high levels of prior (pre-victimization) life stress (Winkel and Vrij, 1998). Repeat victims are likely to be over-represented in specific categories of crime, such as personal contact crimes with a known perpetrator. "In terms of psychological risk factors, repeat victims relative to singular victims are more likely to report (pre-victimization) perceptions of unique vulnerability, or high prior life stress" (p. 89). Repeat victimization is heavily understudied in victimological research.

A recent study (Winkel, Blaauw, Sheridan, and Baldry, 2003) revealed that a majority of reporters which later exhibited persistent psychological symptomatology, e.g., three to five months post-victimization, were not detected by victim support. The outcome of this study underlies the necessity to implement more formal rules, e.g., checklists for trauma risk – – for police to referral victims for support, which are based on empirically validated risk factors. The findings suggest that "the diagnostic value of such rules might be strengthened if features of repeat victimization are included as an additional referral criterion" (p. 93).

Burgess and Hazelwood (1995) identified categories of risk to victims of crime. Low-risk victims refer to individuals whose personal, professional, and social lives do not normally expose them to the possibility of suffering harm or loss. Medium-risk victims refer to individuals who have the potential to be exposed to harm or loss. High-risk victims refer to individuals whose lifestyle continuously exposes them to the danger of suffering harm or loss. For example, a woman who routinely jogs alone, in a remote section of Central Park, NYC each evening, is at high risk of attack by a mugger or rapist. Therefore, there is a further separation of the lifestyle risk of the victim and the incident risk to the victim. There are also highly vulnerable individuals who are not usually at risk, but who may develop into victims, such as firefighters. Therefore, these individuals willingly place themselves in situations of possible danger by reconciling their drive to help others and possibly some extreme internal manifestations of courage and toughness or a buried neurotic complex to seek out danger.

Risk due to lifestyle refers to the overall risk present due to the victim's personality and his or her personal, professional, and social environments. Certain circumstances, habits, or activities can increase the likelihood of victimization. Turvey (2001a) adapted the following list of traits, representing risk of victimization, from Burgess and Hazelwood (1995): aggressiveness and passivity; anger; emotional outbursts; hyperactivity; impulsivity; anxiety; tendency towards addictive behavior; tendency towards self-destructive behavior; phobias or irrational or inexplicable fears; difficulty with authority (such as high reactivity); personal space or privacy issues; passivity; low self-esteem; depression or hopelessness; negativity; emotional withdrawal; listlessness; need for attention or sympathy; history of self injury; and aberrant sexual behavior.

While it is common to blame the victims, they are not responsible for the predatory acts of offenders. From the victim's point of view, risk to the victim is a subjective determination of the "amount of exposure to a possibility of suffering harm or loss that criminal profilers perceive for a given victim" (Turvey, 2001a, p. 114). It is very subjective, depending upon the knowledge and experiences of the profiler examining a given case. "Many criminal profilers are in the habit of approaching a victim with a great deal of prejudice, born out of a-priori investigative bias developed from initial victim information" (p. 115).

A related concept is incident risk. It refers to the risk of victimization present at the moment an offender initially identifies and engages a victim: "by virtue of the victim's state of mind, and the hazards inherent in the immediate environment" (p. 117). The state of mind of the victim is very important, as an agitated state will result in different behavior, compared to behavior expected in a calm, safe state. Fear is a clear emotion. No-fear could mean anything. "Factors that can increase victim incident risk include: victim lifestyle, victim state of mind, time of occurrence, location of occurrence, number of victims, and drug and alcohol us¢a (p. 117). Awareness of risk factors is important in the treatment of psychopathology.

The efficacy of methods is enhanced through treatment of the underlying symptoms, which are part of the process that you experience. However, existentially, the treatment of presenting symptoms is like putting out a fire, whereas correcting the causal mechanism is similar to finding and controlling the matches. However, a behaviorist would view that if the symptoms are gone there is no underlying cause.

Secondary victimization occurs when a crime victim's report is not considered credible or the impact of crime is not considered serious. Research shows that secondary victimization, generated either by institutions or individuals, is often experienced by victims in the aftermath of crime. Secondary victimization involves a lack of understanding of the suffering of victims, which can leave them feeling both isolated and insecure, losing faith in the help available from their communities and the professional agencies. The experience of secondary victimization intensifies the immediate consequences of crime by prolonging or aggravating the victim's trauma; attitudes, behavior, acts or omissions can leave victims feeling alienated from society as a whole (European Forum for Victim Services, 2005).

Protective Factors and Resiliency

Protective factors offer protection from the condition of vulnerability. Resiliency is the ability to cope with and recover from the experience of victimization. The construct of resiliency can explain why some individuals do not develop psychopathology. Speculatively, if one were to draw the slope of the vulnerability continuum, it follows logically that the greater the resiliency, the higher the threshold for disorder and the lower the risk. Assuming that victimhood is not a psychopathic situation, at the high point of the slope, extreme stress would be required for the highly resilient to approach onset of symptomatology of the disorder.

Victim Profiling

Profiling the victim involves compiling of the victim's history and can provide context, connections, and investigative direction to the criminal profiler (Turvey, 1999b). The key initial question should be: What are the offender's needs that victim selection satisfies? Offenders have needs as do all other human beings. They usually choose strategies to meet these needs in ways that harm others. While this seems logical, speculatively, there may be some psychopathic distortion in some offenders, preventing them from meeting their needs in a more socially acceptable manner (Hare, 1993; 1996; Turvey, 1999b; 2001a).

LEARNED HELPLESSNESS

The theory of learned helplessness expresses that helplessness is a learned state produced by exposure to uncomfortable situations in which there is no possibility of escape (Peterson, Maier, and Seligman, 1993). This research explores theories of helplessness and related personality constructs. The theory of learned helplessness is relevant to this research because the subject became increasingly helpless during his victimization. Presently, research into victim vulnerability largely centers on the theory of learned helplessness (Cole and Coyne, 1977; Abramson, Seligman, and Teasdale, 1978; Peterson, Maier, and Seligman, 1993; Bodner and Mikulciner, 1998; and Geiger and Crick, 2001).

The theory of learned helplessness has been used to try to explain a variety of very complex phenomenon. Learned helplessness leads to a feeling of defeatism where the person feels that there is nothing that can be done to correct the situation, so nothing is done. This research incorporates how the subject reached a point of defeat and succumbed to the actions of the predator.

The theory of learned helplessness consists of three essential components: contingency, cognition, and behavior. "Contingency refers to the objective relationship between the person's action and the outcomes that he then experiences" (Peterson, Maier, and Seligman, 1993, p. 9). The most important contingency is uncontrollability: a random relationship between an individual's actions and outcomes. Controllability occurs when the individual's actions reliably produce outcomes. The theory of learned helplessness has been used to refer to the expectation of helplessness and to passive behavior. For example, behavior refers to the subject's responses to the actions of the predator. Cognition is how he understood the meaning and potential impact of those actions. Contingency is the uncontrollable relationship between the subject's responses and the outcome he then experiences.

Cognition involves the person's perception and how he explains and extrapolates the contingency. For example, a failure might be explained as being caused by tough luck or even stupidity. "Behavior refers to the observable consequences of (non) contingency and the person's cognitions about it" (p. 8).

People can learn to be helpless through the observation of another person encountering uncontrollable events (Brown and Inouye, 1978), as a case of vicarious learning or modeling (Bandura, 1986). In the experiment wherein inescapable shock increases the utilization of norepinephrine (NE) in the brain, the result is a net depletion of NE. In the case of the instinct of the dog to hunt for food, through the years of domestication that instinct is suppressed to an extent, but can be awakened in a need for survival. Dogs adjust to their environments, which can alter behavior, but their basic instinct is still there (Amy Kesner, personal communication, October 1, 2005).

Studies on helplessness typically compare someone's passivity versus activity in new situations. The theory of learned helplessness suggests that other consequences may follow from the individual's expectation of future helplessness, including low self-esteem, sadness, immune changes, and physical illness. The pilot in this research exhibited behavior that can be explained using learned helplessness theory. Hall (1998) found that victims experienced extreme fear, helplessness, paranoia, lost confidence, depression, grief reactions, severe anxiety, insomnia, isolation, relationship difficulties, and an inability to perform their normal daily functions.

Learned helplessness is an extension of learning theory. Originally, the theory of learned helplessness was tested in the laboratory during canine experiments, involving the use of inescapable electric shocks on harnessed dogs (Overmier and Seligman, 1967). Following a series of shocks, the dogs appeared passive. Therefore, the experimenters concluded that the dogs learned that the administered shock was independent of their responses and they expected shocks to be similarly uncontrollable (Maier, Seligman, and Solomon, 1969; Seligman, Maier, and Solomon, 1971). The theory of learned helplessness was initially tested with animal research. However, humans respond in far more complex ways, so several aspects of learned helplessness theory may not be helpful in understanding this research.

Seligman (1998) also found that "Animals can learn their actions are futile, and when they do, they no longer initiate action; they become passive" (p. 23). However, "application of findings from animal studies proved inadequate to explain the full reaction of people to uncontrollable events" (p. 11). The results these experiments support the theory of learned helplessness. The core is that "The impact of inescapable shock does not depend on the shock itself, but rather on its controllability" (p. 25). Thus, when the animal learns that it has no control and expects this to be true in the future, it undergoes motivational and cognitive c ânges that are responsible for its failure to learn to escape.

Other studies on learned helplessness explore whether the theory applies to other populations. Hiroto and Seligman (1975) found that induced helplessness was trait-like, the result of experience. However, Peterson, Maier, and Seligman (1993) argued that experiments on human helplessness, as produced in the laboratory, cannot be completely generalized and have limits across time and situation. Cole and Coyne (1977) as well as Douglas and Anisman (1975), found that helplessness induced in one situation did not generalize to all other possible situations. Simkin, Lederer, and Seligman (1983) demonstrated that small groups could be made helpless by asking the group as a whole to work at unsolvable problems. The early studies of Overmier and Leaf (1965) showed that people who experience uncontrollable events in the laboratory show disruptions in their later thoughts, feelings, and actions.

The theory of learned helplessness claims that there are additional consequences following an individual's expectation of future helplessness, such as cognitive retardation, low self-esteem, sad feelings, lost aggression, immune changes, and physical illness. Studies of learned helplessness have demonstrated that exposure to uncontrollable failure in unsolvable problems impairs performance on a subsequent task and creates both cognitive and emotional problems.

The previous literature review traces the constructs of psychopathy, victimology, and learned helplessness from their basic definitions to their applicability to the question of victim vulnerability. This research refutes the mainstream view, which tries to neatly describe the victim and the criminal into predefined categories, using predominantly behavioral and psychodynamic perspective. As an alternative approach, the existential perspective can be inserted into the research questions in this book to show that the distinction between the victim and the criminal may be more blurred than previously believed.

Chapter 3

THE EPISTEMOLOGICAL PERSPECTIVE OF THIS STUDY

DEPTH PSYCHOLOGY, PERSONOLOGY, AND EXISTENTIAL-HUMANISTIC PSYCHOLOGY

Depth psychology posits the reality of the unconscious. Freudian, Adlerian, and Jungian theories are the classic examples. For instance, external shocks or prolonged intrapsychic conflict can be converted to external symptoms. Fixation is a term broadly utilized throughout many areas in psychology: learning, perception, cognition, personality, and social psychology. An abnormal fixation implies a persistent idea in the unconscious, leading to compulsive behavior seemingly without rational motivation.[28] Alfred Adler (1924; 1927/1998) placed psychopathological vulnerability in the domain of fears of inferiority and its compensations, which are assumed to be driven by conscious forces. The primary concept of individual psychology is that of inferiority and its compensations, which are assumed to define the struggle at the crux of the human condition. The unconscious, according to other authors, contains repressed experiences and other personal-level issues as well as transpersonal forces. It is not reducible to either neurochemistry or pure spirit. The psyche spontaneously generates both symbolism as well as natural instincts. "Primitive man impresses us so strongly with his subjectivity that we should really have guessed long ago that myths refer to something psychic" (Jung, 1969, p. 6).

There are different theories of depth psychology regarding vulnerability. These help to understand the specific nuances of victim vulnerability as they deal with important aspects of the personality structure. Freud's (1961) theory of fixation to traumas related to the unconscious can help describe and explain the construct of vulnerability. It can be recognized most clearly in neurotics suffering from obsessional thinking or obsessional states, people who are often of high intelligence that superstition derives from suppressed hostile and cruel impulses. Freud (1961) described traumatic neuroses as follows: "The traumatic neuroses

[28] The principal investigator was initially biased that the pilot's arduous quest for vindication was obsessive, but, after evaluation of the facts of the case, he has gained an appreciation for the internal need of the pilot to continue his efforts as he deems necessary as part of his journey of life. It was further discovered that only those who have their careers wrongly truncated can truly understand the effects of being harmed this way.

give a clear indication that a fixation to the moment of the traumatic accident lies at their root. These patients regularly repeat the traumatic situation in their dreams" (p. 274).

As is the case with the subject of this research, patients who have not finished with the traumatic situation continue to face it as though they were still faced by it as an immediate task, which has not been dealt with (Freud, 1961, p. 275). Freud referred to an economic view of mental processes applicable to:

> . . . an experience which within a short period of time presents the mind with an increase of stimulus too powerful to be dealt with or worked off in the normal way, and this must result in permanent disturbances of the manner in which the energy operates. (p. 275)

Anger can be a source of superstition in obsessed neurotics. While the term *neurosis* has lost most of its coherent meaning, in the case of this research, it is used to indicate a causal role played by unconscious conflicts that evoke anxiety and lead to the use of defense mechanisms that ultimately lead to symptoms. In the case of the pilot, his extreme focus on his case investigation and his quest for vindication demonstrate a form of obsession, though an entirely appropriate one. Early on, the way in which he managed the barrage of threats made against him also point to an obsession to find the truth about what was happening.[29] The victim, through no fault of his or her own, is inextricably involved in the crime. The victim is, in the majority of cases, the one who suffered most. The victim has good reasons to want, and certainly deserves, vindication (Whiteley, 1998, p. 48).

Transference is the unconscious misapplication of the unfinished internal adjustment related to one's parents (but also siblings or a spouse) onto the therapist. Countertransference is the therapist's unwittingly foisting of his or her own neurosis onto the patient.

There are notable differences in how Robert's mother and father responded to Robert's career choice. Robert's father was quietly supportive of his interest in learning to fly small planes, then in Robert's early decision to embark on a career, which would hopefully lead to his becoming a commercial airline pilot with a major airline. Robert's mother was (and is) a somewhat nervous person. Though outwardly supportive, she was quite apprehensive about her son becoming a pilot. The subject's uncle added to the fear of the subject's mother by expressing to the subject that Jews do not often become pilots because this type of job, in his view, the airline industry was closed to those who were not white, Anglo-Saxon males due to the anti-Semitism existing at that time and other biases.[30] The subject confided to the principal investigator that his mother, while supportive of his becoming a pilot, would have preferred that Robert enter a more traditional career for Jewish males, such as medicine, law, or finance.

Jung's work on symbolism and archetypes is applicable to significant aspects of the victim's life history and will be applied to the pilot's dreams. Jungian concepts are closely relevant to understanding the personality of the subject, especially mythological symbolism. Symbolism is a way of conveying meaning in an artistic form, such as mythology or represented in the form of an allegory (Jung, 1969, p. 289). An allegory is a paraphrase of a conscious content, whereas a symbol is the best possible expression for an unconscious content whose nature can only be guessed because it is still unknown (p. 6). "Knowledge of

[29] Perhaps, as an airline pilot, the subject was trained to focus and to be exact in his decisions and diagnosing of problems. Speculatively, this may have added to his vulnerability.

[30] The subject's uncle was a survivor of the Nazi concentration camps.

the symbols is indispensable, for it is in them that the union of conscious and unconscious contents is consummated" (p. 289). Within psychoanalytic theory, symbolism is the unconscious process whereby repressed desires or wishes are transformed or disguised so as to be dealt with on a conscious level with minimum psychic disturbance.

Jungian psychology is presented as background to the existential perspective with references to the pilot. Jung wrote that the collective unconscious can be negatively distinguished from a personal unconscious because it does not, like the latter, owe its existence to personal experience. The contents of the collective unconscious have never been individually acquired, but owe their existence exclusively to heredity. "Whereas the personal unconscious consists for the most part of complexes, the content of the collective unconscious is made up essentially of archetypes" (Jung, 1969, p. 42). Archetypes are used to describe primordial images and consist of mythological motifs. Mythology is the richness and wisdom of humanity played out through symbolic storytelling (Pinsent, 1969).

Archetypal images include those of animals, people, anthropomorphic beings (such as the vampire or gods and goddesses), objects, abstract ideas, and patterns such as the hero's journey. The central therapeutic concept of Jung's analytical psychology is the concept of the need for balance to gain psychic health. Therefore, when an individual is troubled, he or she will dream archetypal, as opposed to merely personal, dreams whose aim is to right an imbalance in the psyche of that individual. This is the concept of compensation. "Compensation means balancing, adjusting, supplementing" (Jung, 1976, p. 418). Jung viewed the activity of the unconscious as a balancing of the one-sidedness of the general attitude produced by the function of consciousness (p. 419). "In the individual the archetypes appear as involuntary manifestations of unconscious processes whose existence and meaning can only be inferred" (Jung, 1969, p. 153).

Personal symptoms and conflicts contain a transpersonal and archetypal core that, when interpreted, can reintroduce the client to the meaning of his or her struggles. In the process of development, conflict arises between the conscious and the unconscious. "The harmonizing of conscious and unconscious data is an irrational life-process which expresses itself in definite symbols" (Jung, 1969, p. 289). Jung called the union of opposites the transcendent function from which emerge new situations and new conscious attitudes.

Work on the personal level is a prelude to work on the transpersonal level, thus requiring psychological initiations into adulthood. Jung's method of symbolism has been applied to the dreams of the subject in this case study.

Jung, Freud, and others, believed that dreams can serve as vehicles to process subconscious thoughts. These thoughts as well as regular thoughts are all imagined. The images presented by dreams, visions, and mythic experiences may reveal a loss of balance or control over one's life in the unconscious (Jung, 1969). Such revelations form the symbolic space for the psychotherapeutic patient to do the work to make the unconscious conscious. The symbolism in a person's dream parallels his or her life and can be used in the search for unconscious complexes.

Complexes, originally intended to be descriptive devices, have pathological connotations because they are often repressed and in conflict with other behaviors. This unconscious was assumed by Jung to be inherited and transpersonal and "a fringe of consciousness, as William

James put it" (Jung, 1960, p. 95).[31] Its components were archetypes. The symbols are necessary because the person cannot tolerate looking directly at the problem.

Freud (1952) believed in the significance of the meaning of dreams, which relate to the "prediction of the future and which can be discovered by some process of interpretation of a content which is often confused and puzzling" (p. 7). Freud postulated two classes of instincts, one of which are sexual instincts or Eros. These comprise the uninhibited sexual instinct and also the self-preservative instinct (Freud, 1961, p. 37). The second class of instincts is the death instinct, the task of which is to lead organic life back into the inanimate state (p. 38). "The emergence of life would thus be the cause of the continuance of life and also at the same time of the striving towards death; and life itself would be a conflict and a compromise between these two trends" (p. 38).

Certain aspects of the subject's life history can be explained through Murray et al.'s (1938) conception of the Icarus complex. The heroic action of the subject as well as his vivid dreams and childhood interests reveal potential rich diagnostic material. Murray et al. was interested in the psychodynamic elements involved in "the proclivity or penchant of some persons for ascension, rising, floating, or flying in air, in fantasy or dreams or in reality, along with several other covert personal qualities including narcissism and a craving for immortality" (p. 412). Murray et al. called this combination of attributes the Icarus complex—from the myth of Daedalus and his son Icarus, in which they used wings that they had fashioned from feathers and wax to escape from the Minotaur's Labyrinth in Crete.

In the myth, Icarus, against his father's exhortations, flew too close to the sun, the wings melted, and he perished. In the myth, the boy disobeys his father. The myth relates to the existential connection to the subject in this research in terms of how the subject used his freedom. The transition between the subject's fantasy of the hero-rescuer to a state of learned helplessness is an example of someone who flew too high (vulnerable) and became hurt (victimization).

Myths can be metaphors for states of consciousness beyond the merely rational in depth psychology. One of the participants (Grope) in Murray et al.'s (1938) study recalled "*f* dream of flying through the air on a maid's rump and a story of a modern Pegasus fertilizing from the sky a poor farmer's barren fields" (p. 541). Grope's major recurrent fantasy involved landing on a desert island in the Pacific, and then becoming king of a new civilization. He often dreamed and daydreamed of self-propelled flights and of jumping off a high place and floating gracefully and gently to the ground. Grope imagined himself in many occupations, but his more immediate intention was to enlist in the Air Corps and become a pilot.

Murray et al. (1938) coined the term *ascensionism* to describe

> . . . the wish to overcome gravity, to stand erect, to grow tall, to dance on tiptoe, to walk on water, to leap or swing in the air, to climb, to rise, to fly, or to float down gradually from on high and land without injury, not to speak or rising from the dead and ascending to heaven. (p. 548)

Murray et al. viewed ascensionism as a diagnostic component of covert personality. They described their analytical opinion that "in its most mundane and secular form, ascensionism

[31] William James referred to a transmarginal field of consciousness and identifies it with the subliminal consciousness of F. W. H. Myers, as cited in Jung (1960).

consists of a craving for upward social mobility, for a rapid and spectacular rise of prestige" (p. 548).

Murray et al. (1938) formed a tentative opinion, concerning Grope, that

> . . . the Icarus complex is the immature (perhaps perpetually adolescent) form of what might be termed the Solar complex, a complex which is characterized by the same genetic components but, in addition, by a relatively strong ego structure supported by tested abilities, which serves to constrain the reckless aspirations of youth within the bounds of realizable achievements, and thus to neutralize the dread of falling" (p. 555).

Murray et al. surmised that an Icarus or Solar complex might be objectified on the physical and technical levels by such cynosural and ascensionistic enterprises, which include high diving.[32]

The present research involves an examination of the inner life of the person, particularly the subject. As background material for this exploration, the historical views of personality theorists are highlighted, especially the views of Henry A. Murray and Gordon, W. Allport. The study also evaluates the personality of the victim using existential-humanistic concepts. These theorists are included because the history of modern personality theory and research demonstrates that Murray et al.'s (1938) system of personology and the macro-personality theory of Allport (1927) were the progenitors of the existential-humanistic tradition (Nicholson, 2003; Taylor, 2000).

The works of several key existential philosophers contributed to the modern existential-humanistic perspective. Soren Kierkegaard (1813-1855), a Danish philosopher and father of modern existentialism, argued that human beings needed to turn towards their own subjective truths and make a personal leap of faith towards God. Freidrich Nietzsche (1844-1900), a German philosopher, preached an atheistic gospel of aspiration towards the autonomous superman who creates his or her own values and morality, and lives an earthly life of passion and power. Martin Buber (1878-1965), a Jewish philosopher and theologian, emphasized the relational nature of human existence, and the distinction between I-thou and I-it modes of relating. Karl Jaspers (1883-1969), a German psychiatrist and philosopher, developed the concept of the unavoidable boundary situations that human beings face. Paul Tillich (1886-1965), a German Protestant theologian, advocated courage in the face of the anxiety of non-being, and distinguished between existential and neurotic anxiety and guilt. Marcel Gabriel (1889-1973), a French philosopher, emphasized the mysteriousness and immeasurability of existence, the importance of fidelity and openness to others, as well as the primacy of hope. Martin Heidegger (1889-1976), a German philosopher and follower of Husserl, emphasized the freedom at the heart of human existence and the *angst*, meaninglessness, and nausea that it evokes. The philosophy of Jean-Paul Sartre (1905-1980), a French existentialist, encompasses the dilemmas and aspirations of the individual in contemporary society. Sartre saw ". . . the biological and social not as prime determinants, but rather as coexistent givens—marks and resources of the existential condition—with, by, and through which one's authentic engagement could be realized" (Arons and Richards, 2001, p. 132). Maurice Merleau-Ponty (1907-1961), a French philosopher, emphasized the embodied nature of human existence. Albert Camus (1913-1961), a French philosopher, emphasized the absurdity of human

[32] The subject enjoyed high diving as a youth because it provided a sense of weightlessness at the apex of the dive.

existence but the possibility of creating meaning in a meaningless world. Of these, Kierkegaard, Buber, and Marcel were deeply religious, whereas Sartre, Nietzsche, and Camus were atheists.

Kierkegaard and Nietzsche emphasized the need for individuality; Buber, Marcel, and Jaspers emphasized the need for relationship; Marcel emphasized the primacy of hope; and Sartre and Camus considered existence to be meaningless.

Existential philosophy is a difficult, contradictory and ill-defined field of inquiry. Existential philosophy takes as its primary concern the existence of human beings (Ellenberger, 1958). From an existential perspective, a human being is inseparable from his or her social context. Existential therapies "orient themselves around a shared concern: human lived-existence" (p. 1), and have origin in existential philosophy, an already diverse field. Yalom's (1980) existential psychotherapy encourages clients to face up to four ultimate concerns of existence: death, freedom, isolation, and meaninglessness. Van Deurzen's (2002) existential psychotherapy encourages clients to explore four dimensions of worldly being: the physical, personal, social, and spiritual dimensions. Bugental's (1978) existential-humanistic approach encourages clients to focus in on their subjective experiences.

Frankl's (1963; 1988) existential analysis frequently focused on meaning through suffering. R. D. Laing (1927-1989), a Scottish psychiatrist, used the principles of spontaneity as the core of his therapeutic outlook. Laing (1965) acknowledged being influenced by the existential tradition. He followed Husserl's phenomenological idea that to fully understand another's lived experience, one must avoid all attempts at categorizing, labeling, or diagnosing subjects, and, instead, to merely describe them."In the existentialist view, there are always loose ends" (Macquarrie, 1972, p. 1). While most of the existential philosophers have found value in some of the metaphysical systems, there remains no common doctrine to which all existentialists subscribe. The existentialist position holds that "the subject is the existent in the whole range of his existing" (p. 2). This means that the subject should not be interpreted solely from one or a few aspects of his or her life, but from a holistic view of the entire milieu of the person's existence. The effect of this approach is to discern a much deeper understanding of a person by examining his thoughts, dreams, aspirations, fears, hopes, longings, passion, creativity, anguish, dread, and other aspects rather than merely behaviors or actions.

"The themes of freedom, decision, and responsibility constitute the core of personal being" (Macquarrie, 1972, p. 4). Thus, it is through decisions made in freedom that man becomes authentically himself. The tragic elements of human existence, such as guilt, alienation, suffering, and death, are also under the domain of existentialism. Because of the notion that life ends in certain death, the tragic side of existentialism is already acknoJcedged. In general, at some point in a person's life, he or she may need to hide a part of themselves, a sort of emotional fig leaf, which covers the true nature of the person (Andrew D. Decker, M.D., personal communication, June 27, 2005). This refers to persons who needs at any moment in their life to put on a mask and cloak their true thoughts and feelings. The pilot kept secret much of what was happening in his life. Only after great harm was done to him did he confide in his parents and others.

"Most existentialists are phenomenologists, though there are many phenomenologists who are not existentialists" (Macquarrie, 1972, p. 8). Phenomenology seems to offer the existentialist the kind of methodology needed to investigate human existence. "Phenomenology is not a method of proof. It describes what is seen" (p. 11).

Dadaism is a way to understand the existential experience. Dadaism is a post-World War I cultural movement in visual art as well as literature, theatre, and graphic design (Wikipedia, 2005). "The movement was, among other things, a protest against the barbarism of the war and what Dadaists believed was an oppressive intellectual rigidity in both art and everyday society" (Wikipedia, 2005, p. 1). Dadaism, a French word meaning *hobby-horse*, strives to have no meaning with interpretation of Dada dependent entirely on the viewer. The basis of Dada is nonsense. After World War I, Dada was a way to express the confusion that was felt by many people as their world turned upside down. Disorder was accepted as the nature of the world.

Dadaism is a nihilistic movement that was based on the principles of deliberate irrationality, anarchy, and cynicism and the rejection of laws of beauty and social organization. The word *Dada* was chosen at random to be used by followers of this new movement and seen as appropriate for their antiaesthetic creations and protest activities, which were engendered by disgust for bourgeois values and despair over World War I (Peak.Org., 2005). It was a negation of everything previously considered to be normal and, essentially based on the ideas of Nietzsche, it became nihilistic in practice. This reflection of negativism seemed inherent in the Dadaist philosophy of absurdity. The feeling of despair and disillusionment that many felt as a result of the huge destruction of the war increased the number of Dadaist followers.

The Dadaist philosophy of meaninglessness was exemplified in its sound poem, which were nonsense words put together at the whim of the poet (similar to scatting performed by jazz artists). In art, the Dadaist movement took form as the collage, finally leading to the development of surrealism.

The surrealists were in direct revolt with all 19th-century ideas: In response to the war they became antipatriotic, antinationalistic, and nonpolitical. Influenced heavily by Freud, the surrealists attacked their parents' and society's value systems. During the 1920s, surrealism came to stand for revolt against society and the norm.

In its search for universal truths about existence, traditional philosophy, or science, has attempted to find fundamental laws and components. In this view, the existence of an entity conceals its true reality. The essentialist viewpoint has been applied to the understanding of human beings, leading to the development of essentialist psychologies as behaviorism and psychoanalysis, where an individual is broken down into constitutive parts such as stimuli and response, id, ego, and superego (Freud, 1923; Watson, 1925).

The existentialist objects to the study of human beings from the essentialist perspective, stating that such humans are irreducible to a set of essential components. Instead, existential philosophy looks for a deeper understanding of this existence.

Drawing on the phenomenological method, as the existentialists do, it is important to look at the lived experiences of a person, setting aside our initial biases and suspending our expectations and assumptions (Spinelli, 1989). Husserl (1960) suggested that we suspend our assumptions and develop a deeper understanding of how we actually experience our world.

Existential philosophers moved toward a focus on embodied, practical, concrete involvement in the world and attempted to describe some of the inescapable, universal features of the human condition (Cooper, 2003).

At the heart of existential philosophy is the assertion that human existence is fundamentally free (Macquarrie, 1972). Such freedom is an integral part of human lived experience (Guignon, 2002). Jaspers (1986) stated that human experience runs up against numerous limit-situations such as death, suffering, struggle, and guilt, which cannot be transcended, avoided, or resolved. "From an existential perspective, we cannot fully control our beginnings, our endings, or much of what happens in between, but what we can choose is how we face these ontological limitations" (Cooper, 2003, p. 17).

The mood of anxiety is an existential concept (Heidegger, 1927/1962). This is because choices create *angst*, that the person choosing against something else may consider the possibility that the other choices might have been better.

Anxiety and guilt, as well as other negative feelings, are responses to the reality of our human condition. We self-deceive by turning away from these feelings. "At the heart of such self-deception is a denial of our freedom and responsibility, and we may do this a number of ways" (Heidegger, 1927/1962, p. 23).

Human beings have a tendency to hide from the reality of their existence. In doing so, we have only half a life rather than a full one (Guignon, 2002). This is problematic in that it prevents us from a life infused with passion, creativity, and vitality.

Heidegger (1927/1962) emphasized resolutely facing our mortality, suggesting that we should live every day in the knowledge that we are moving towards an inevitable ending. He felt that, in doing so, we cannot defer choices and projects, but must go about the business of living.

Frankl (1959/1984) developed a version of modern existential analysis, which he called logotherapy, a meaning-centered psychotherapy. He found that the central theme of existentialism—to live is to suffer—and to survive is the achievement of meaning through the actualization of values, as opposed to meaning through suffering. Frankl's theories arose from his work with people (as well as his own experience) who had been victimized in the concentration camps.

Frankl (1959/1984) distinguished several forms of neurosis, and traced some of them to the failure of the sufferer to find meaning and a sense of responsibility in his existence. "According to logotherapy, the striving to find a meaning in one's life is the primary motivational force in man" (p. 121). He found that a person can find meaning to his or her existence, which can be accomplished through resolution of the existential crisis, growth, and development. Logotherapy helps people face the phenomenon of the feeling of total and ultimate meaninglessness of their lives. Logotherapy deviates from psychoanalysis in that it considers the importance of fulfilling a meaning rather than simply seeking gratification and satisfaction of drives and instincts. Values are important to help shape how a person responds to the challenges of everyday life. "Man, however, is able to live and even die for the sake of his ideals and values" (p. 121).

Frankl thought that the true meaning of life is to be discovered in the world rather than within man or his own psyche. Thus, each situation in life challenges man to be responsible for his own life and solve his own problems as he faces them. Frankl termed this characteristic *the self-transcendence of human existence*. He proscribed that we do not strive for self-actualization because that is possible only as a side effect of self-transcendence. It is partly due to the attitude we take toward unavoidable suffering that we can discover the meaning in life.

"A helpful impetus for resolving the existential crisis and finding meaning is therapy wherein the patient is assisted in finding meaning in his life" (Frankl, 1959/1984, p.125), through an analytical process. Frankl proscribed "a certain degree of tension between what one has already achieved and what one still ought to accomplish" (p. 117), leading to mental health. Tension is inherent in the human being and, thus, is necessary for mental well-being. Frankl thought that the struggle to achieve goals is a need of man in order to achieve meaning in life.

Frankl's logotherapy is a therapeutic approach that specifically aims to help clients discover purpose and orientation in their lives. Klingberg (1995) traced the roots of logotherapy back to around 1929. Frankl was influenced by the work of Alfred Adler and also applied the work of the phenomenologist Max Scheler. "Logotherapy is the result of an application of Max Scheler's concepts to psychotherapy" (Frankl, 1988, p. 10).

Frankl was interested in several of Scheler's ideas: that values are intuitively experienced qualities of things, such that people can discover the true meaning of a situation; and the idea that human reality could be stratified into body, mind, and spirit. Frankl preferred the will to meaning as the driving force behind all human thought. This is in opposition to Freud, who adopted the pleasure principle, and to Adler, who professed the will to power.

Frankl asserted that each human being has a spiritual core and, as such, is called to a particular task in his or her life. During World War II, Frankl was interred for 2½ years in concentration camps, including Auschwitz. He struggled with experiences of total and ultimate nihilism. His theories of helping people overcome despair were put to the test during his time in the concentration camps. He found that, there, those who were able to transcend their immediate circumstances and hold on to something meaningful were more likely to survive than those who saw their situation as hopeless and futile (Frankl, 2000).

Frankl found evidence that human beings can always choose how to respond to their circumstances, regardless of how tenuous they are. For Frankl (1959/1984), a human being's most basic motivation is to find meaning in his or her life. Frankl argued that a lack of direction or goal in life can lead to a deep sense of frustration, emptiness, and depression. He pointed to people today living in a degree of existential vacuum, and that this sense of meaninglessness may be particularly prevalent at certain periods in an individual's life, such as after a crisis of some sort. Thus, the existential frustration can develop into neurosis, whereby the individual turns to self-destructive behaviors, including addiction and compulsions, in an attempt to fill his or her existential void. Logotherapy helps individuals to rediscover a sense of meaning, purpose, and hope in their lives. Frankl (1986) suggested that there are creative values that can be actualized through work or artistic activity. Losing one's job may present an individual with the opportunity to discover a new career path.[33]

Another type of value that may lie dormant in a situation involves attitudes. Attitudinal values can be actualized through changing one's attitude to a situation. By changing one's attitude and finding meaning in the suffering, the person is less likely to fuel the original difficulty, thus avoiding a pattern. Frankl (1986) found that each human being has an unconscious knowledge of the meanings lying dormant in his or her situation.

The American existential-humanistic approach focuses on the struggle of the individual to be true to his or her own subjective existence. This approach is in contrast to the analytic approach of *Dasein*, which emphasizes the worldly nature of human beings. Existential-humanistic therapists have been influenced by the writings of the existential philosophers, for example, through the teachings of Rollo May's mentor Paul Tillich. As well, there has been interest in the works of Kierkegaard and Nietzsche (Cooper, 2003). The focus tends to be on

[33] This is clearly relevant to the suffering of Robert in terms of the loss of his career and the freedom to explore alternative careers.

the "more individualistic elements of existential philosophy: those that emphasize the need for the human being to stand alone, and courageously face the anxiety of existence" (p. 64).

Maslow (1962) and Rogers (1959) emphasized the sovereignty of individual, subjective experiences, and the need for human beings to be true to their own needs rather than conforming to the needs of others. Both were influenced by existential writers.

Two overriding cultural influences on existentialism are that of the lone individual searching to find his or her way in a chaotic and uncertain world, and the spirit of pragmatism, as developed by such American philosophers as William James.

The so-called Third Force can be attributed to major figures such as Abraham Maslow (1954), Carl Rogers (1963), and Rollo May (1961). "This force follows the other two dominating psychological forces, classical Freudianism, and positivistic behaviorism" (Maslow, 1962, p. 1). Under the influence of positivistic behaviorism, psychology became defined as the measurement of only the stimulus and response. Under the influence of psychoanalysis, psychology was defined in terms of the study of the unconscious. The existential-humanistic view defines psychology in terms of a growth-oriented psychology of the whole person.

May (1961) stated that "every psychotherapist is existential to the extent that he is a good therapist, i.e., that he is able to grasp the patient in his reality" (p. 19). May felt that we repress the sense of being, the ontological sense. Potentialities are unique to each being. To understand an individual, it is necessary to examine what he chooses to "block off from his awareness" (p. 23). May found that there is evidence that daily anxiety arises out of a patient's fear of his own powers and the conflicts that arise from that fear. "It involves a complex struggle of the individual's being against the possibility of non-being, which cannot be adequately comprehended in ego and not-ego terms" (p. 24). Within this lies the individual's responsibility for himself.

Rogers' new approach to psychotherapy was designed as a contrast to the behavioral and psychoanalytic theories dominant at the time.

> Client-centered therapists say that their clients have a natural tendency toward growth, healing, and self-actualization. They act self-destructively or feel bad because of an environment that distorts this tendency. But they can find their own answers to their problems if the right therapeutic environment is provided. (Harvard Medical School, 2006, p. 1).

Similar to psychodynamic, cognitive-behavioral, and family systems theories, various existential-humanistic theories can be used to describe the importance of the human being as a source of data, incorporating his or her thoughts, aspirations, fears, hopes, and dreams. May (1961) referred to "the only real source of data I have, namely, this experiencing human being" (p. 26). Applying the construct of phenomenology, as the endeavor to take the phenomena as given, requires the disciplined effort to clear one's mind of the presuppositions or to see someone in the context of only our own theories. May stated further, "The existential psychological position is, in my judgment, not at all antiscientific" (p. 37). He viewed that the proper unit of study is two persons existing in a world: the patient and the therapist, a dyad. This forms the basic foundation for the existential approach to science. "No matter how great the forces victimizing the human being, man has the capacity to know that he is being victimized, and thus, to influence in some way how he will relate to his fate" (p. 41). May saw a person's existence as consisting of his freedom, whereas Martin Heidegger (1927/1962) defined truth itself as freedom.

Existential ideas, questions, and ways of philosophizing have been identified in the teachings of such notable figures as Socrates, Jesus, and the Buddha (Macquarrie, 1972), as well as in such ancient philosophical systems such as Stoicism (Van Deurzen, 2002). "From an existential perspective, bias is unavoidable" (Cooper, 2003, p. 4).

How a person responds to life's challenges and dilemmas provides a way to reveal and understand his or her uniqueness. By delving into the depths of a person's personality, key elements of how a person finds meaning in life can be better understood. Heidegger (1927/1962) suggested an existential ontology of selfhood as *Dasein* (being-there), the concretely existing human being who is there, as part of a world. Ontology, generally, is an aspect of metaphysical inquiry concerned with the question of existence apart from specific objects and events. Heidegger was primarily concerned with the question of Being (*Sein*) rather than the nature of beings (*Seiende*).

The concept of *Dasein* includes the philosophy that Being-in (around-world) an environment (*Umwelt*) and Being-with (with-world) others (*Mitwelt*) and with-oneself (own-world) (*Eigenwelt*) underlies all participation, engagement, and concrete involvement with the world that is given in a person's immediate preoccupations and concern (Heidegger, 1927/1962). Translated from the German, *eigenwelt*, or self-world, in existentialism, is the relationship between each person and himself or herself.

This concept of the individual's personally constructed reality is best understood when juxtaposed against the others used within this theory: *mitwelt* and *umwelt*. For Heidegger, the question of authenticity becomes intimately associated with the existential character of *Dasein* as concern and solicitude (Mills, 1997). Due to the penchant of persons to fall into inauthentic modes of Being-in-the-world, *Dasein* will inevitably engage deceptive practices or result in the false self. This leaves open the question of what would it be like not to know who you are, to be alienated from your true sense of self?

R. D. Laing (1967) stated that despite the apparent pathology of a person, he or she is working towards a healthier existential end than just adjustment to a sick society. Laing's interpretation is as follows: "When two (or more) persons are in relation, the behavior of each towards the other is mediated by the experience by each of the other and the behavior of each" (p. 25).

In this research, the unusual nature of the relationship between the subject and the predator, as well as the subject's relationship with fictitious identities, created by the predator provides information concerning the subject's progress moving towards a healthier existence through his experiences. He found that a person might treat another as though he were not a person, as well as act himself as though he were not a person. Laing felt that our behavior is a function of our experience, where it follows that "if our experience is destroyed, we have lost our own selves" (p. 28).

Laing said that we are not able even to think adequately about the behavior that is at the annihilating edge. This edge refers to the present limit of our understanding. Laing (1967) felt that "what we think is less than what we know; what we know is less than what we love; what we love is so much less than what there is" (p. 30). He found that it is possible to regain lost ground. This concept refers to the renewal of possibilities each time there is a new soul born. The dissociation of a person from his own action results in someone who no longer experiences himself fully as a person but as someone who has been a helpless victim because of destructive psychological mechanisms. "The person going through ego-loss or transcendental experiences may or may not become in different ways confused. Then he might legitimately be regarded as mad" (p. 138). We all live under constant threat of our total annihilation.

There is a contrast between Laing's statements that persons experiencing pathology may need such experience in order to grow into healthier beings. In order for a dissociated person to move from Laing's position of needing to go through the process of turmoil of an event that may lead to helplessness and victimization towards the previous statement that apparent pathology may include working toward a healthier end, conscious intervention may be needed. This could come in the form of traditional psychotherapy or a meditative technique that might bring the participant to a state of greater enlightenment and interpersonal growth.

Metanoia is a Greek word meaning a change of mind or new mind. It involves a radical revision and transformation of our whole mental process. This process is something whereby a sense of the divine or a sense a sense of something larger than us takes center place in our consciousness, in our awareness, and in our minds (Laing, 1967). *Metanoia* allows the sense of a higher power to enter into our lives and teach us how to see ourselves and how to come to the true self. This can be seen as an act of contrition, leading to repentance, a completely changed perspective on life.

Most of us act out of unconscious fear of our annihilation (Tillich, 1952). Tillich postulated, "Fate, guilt, and the fear of death were the three anxieties that bedeviled the modern spirit" (p. xxii). Death, absent any meaning in life, was the ultimate experience of meaninglessness. In response to these anxieties, Tillich suggested the courage of confidence, especially during times of hardship or crisis. Therefore, courage is the self-affirmation of being in spite of non-being, with spirituality at the core of this power. Applying Tillich's thinking to the present research, because of the severity of harm victims endure, how they find the courage to adapt and grow from such different encounters speaks of their internal courage, resiliency, and spirit.

The concept of non-being has been important as a means for philosophers to describe their various doctrines of the loss of self of the human soul, human sin, evil, and of God. "Courage can be described as the power of the mind to overcome fear" (Tillich, 1952, p. 34). Even Shakespeare's *Hamlet* provides an existential example of this struggle. Dying, Hamlet reaffirms the tragic dignity of a basically decent person in a bad world. This play leaves us with the message that life is indeed worth living, even by imperfect people in an imperfect world. While the story of *Hamlet* is full of talk of death, the message is ultimately one of hope when being a hero is possible. The famous poetic lines from Hamlet (Act III, Sc.1), "To be or not to be . . . " (Black, 1972, p. 1,145) revolves around the nobility of suffering and of non-being.

Being can be described in terms of non-being. Non-being depends on the being it negates. Non-being is always present and produces anxiety even in the absence of the threat of death. For example, the anxiety of death is in our awareness. "Anxiety is existential in the sense that it belongs to existence as such and not to an abnormal state of mind as in neurotic (and psychotic) anxiety" (Tillich, 1952, p. 41). Those who are courageous enough to confront their annihilation run the risk of neurotic and psychotic anxiety. However, such people may also discover their courage to be in the face of death, despite the diminishing of hope the closer one becomes aware of it.

In the case of the subject, towards the end of the long series of criminal acts committed against him, he felt as if he could be physically harmed due to the serious threats levied against him. His attitude was initially tough and resilient, but later became depressed in the face of the danger. Actual death threats against his young nephew served to reinforce his anxiety and also contributed to his decision to not report these events to local law enforcement. The structure of the scam involved supposed members of corrupt law enforcement. This served to keep Robert from approaching the police. His fear was that the extortion and threats were coming from members of actual law enforcement and that if he fought back, he would be harmed. Alternatively, he also feared that the threats were brazenly coming from dangerous criminals, impersonating law enforcement. In fact, it was the unknown that resulted in the greater fear.

According to Herman Feifel (1959), "To be alive is to face the possibility of death, of non-being" (p. 114). Fear of death is a universal reaction by all peoples, resulting in the importance of time. Existentialism is preoccupied with dread and death.

The experience of victimization can be expected to lead to anxiety, even thoughts of annihilation. Feifel (1959) found a "psychological barrier between the living and the dying" (p. 123) in the treatment of terminally ill patients. He observed that when anxiety about death is discussed, it is often interpreted essentially as a derivative and secondary phenomenon. "Attempts to expel death or not to take death into account are a deception committed by man on himself" (p. 124). Positively, by embracing the inevitability of death, a person can be pushed forward in terms of enhanced creativity and accomplishment. This information concerning accomplishment in the face of annihilation can help illuminate the experience and psychology of the subject. By examining his responses to threats made against him and his family, we can understand the subject on a deeper level. Certainly, the willingness to take risks (e.g., driving in heavy traffic or taking an airplane trip) is, to at least some degree, a form of renouncing life.

The experience of being a victim can lead a survivor to question the meaning of existence. How the subject responded or did not respond to the existential question of the meaning of his life will help us view his personality and behavior on a deeper level. Van Dusen (2001) wrote about the design of existence in terms of the total ordering of all levels of existence from God down to the material universe: "Our bodies are part of the material universe, but our minds an inner experiences transcend the material world" (p. ix). Understanding the design beyond our present life is critical because it explains and gives meaning to every aspect of our existence.

Van Dusen (1958) examined the fertile void in psychotherapy, leading to its relation to psychopathology. "The voids are a type of defect: blankness, loss of memory, failure of concentration or loss of meaning" (p. 253). Within the void, one can lose one's sense of self, thus feeling out of control and weak. This can result in the fear of disintegration. The subject felt a loss of control at the point he permitted the predator to enter his home. This, and other events, will be explored as paradoxical existential moments in his life.

"Many have deliberately used the void to find creative solutions to problems, but the neurotic and psychotic struggle against it" (Van Dusen, 1958, p. 254). It is the emptiness of the void that could be a creative source of ideas. Thus, the feared empty space is the fertile void. The exploration of the void, in the face of fear, is a turning point towards therapeutic breakthrough. As the void is evaluated, it becomes less fearsome, with change occurring spontaneously.

The perspectives of the various depth psychologists show that a person's interior self can be explored to reveal the intensity of dreams, visions, mythic experience, and the struggles of everyday life. It is in how a person copes and deals with life that can be reflective of how the person thinks and feels about his or her world. This view of the inner life of a person is seen in the exploration of the person's unconscious made known in the form of dream interpretation or analysis of the lived experiences of the person, most notably in his or her suffering as well as spontaneous reactions to events and circumstances.

These concepts apply to the understanding of the subject's interiority. By doing so, the vulnerability of the subject can be seen more vividly, particularly in his hero-rescuer archetypal behavior, his suffering, which leads to opportunity to derive meaning, and in his quest to reach a sense of self-actualization.

In summary, a person can be evaluated using selected criteria from the existential perspective. The theories of Frankl, in particular, show that an individual who suffers from negative life experiences has the potential to derive great new meaning of his or her existence. The Third Force allows an individual to be evaluated using his or her entire life history as potential data. Thus, information concerning an individual's conflicts and challenging life experiences can be useful in understanding the person's inner life-world.

Kreuter's Previous Research: A Cognitive-Behavioral Perspective

Kreuter (2002; 2003a; 2003b; 2003c; 2004; 2006b; 2006c) investigated the victim in the present research as well as a cohort of other victims. This collective research explored the theories of psychopathy, learned helplessness, and victimization, as well as the etiology of the nature of the crimes committed against the cohort by a psychopathic criminal. Also explored were many of the details of the predator's behavior as well as the way the victims responded.

This previous research showed that the victim and the cohort of victims were all vulnerable to the actions of the predator. Most victims were either too young to speak or elderly, and a number of the victims did not realize that they were being victimized at the time. One victim was an 18-month-old child. Another victim was elderly and suffered from dementia. Many victims did not realize they were being victimized until much time had passed.

Through an exhaustive evaluation of how the victims responded to the predator, as well as exploration of the predator's techniques, the principal investigator discovered common factors that led to victimization of the cohort. These included gullibility in the specific sense that a few of the victims were enamored by the illusion that the predator not only knew, but was having a serious relationship with famous actors and sports figures. In addition, many of the victims were fooled by the predator and tried to help her because they were under the impression that she was in danger and needed their help. The subject's personality, particularly, revealed several key aspects that resulted in the need to continue the research into vulnerability. These included his good-natured trust of people and the fact that he had a history of rescuing people. At several moments in his life, the subject made c' tain decisions, perhaps unconscious, about how to respond or not respond to specific events and turning points in his life in the period of time he was exposed to the predator. These can be seen as moments of crisis.

The subject's life history also revealed a number of prior involvements at crime scenes where he was a passerby. He acted in the role of hero-rescuer when the crimes took place, effectively terminating the crimes. His reflections on why he allowed the predator in his own case to remain in his home environment, despite his awareness of the theft of his money through the extortive efforts of identities later discovered to have been set up by the predator, demonstrated the rescuer component of his personality. Because of this tendency, he accepted inordinate risk and exposed himself to greater harm.

The subject was shown in previous research to be quite trusting with respect to his dealings with the predator. Interviews of the subjects were used to corroborate the findings that the subject and the cohort possibly have elements of suggestibility and lack of skepticism within their personalities that made them more vulnerable to harm. The present research explores the issues of personality at a deeper level.

In the previous case study (Kreuter, 2002), the subject is known to have experienced feelings of fear and of being terrorized and trapped. The psychopath created an illusion of the involvement of persons in law enforcement. This pseudo-conspiracy, coupled with reported threats of physical harm to the subject's family, as well as extortion, compromised the subject's ability to respond. He was reluctant to report the crimes to the police due to intimidation and, ultimately, death threats against him and his family, and he explained very little about these events to his immediate family or to coworkers. Furthermore, it is important to note that in the airline industry, pilots often choose not to disclose personal problems to their peers; otherwise, they may be subject to inquiry.[34] This phenomenon may also be true in other professions or fields.

The relationship between the principal investigator and Robert is best categorized as multidimensional. Though the initial relationship began over 4 years ago within the context of consultant-client, it has evolved to researcher-subject. Robert agreed to submit to the principal investigator's protocols for gathering data and tendered a large volume of information referred to herein as the archive of data.

During the many lengthy interviews of Robert, the principal investigator became aware of potential avenues of recourse for Robert, which he saw as problem-resolution strategies. Robert's affect in the beginning was generally low, but he was very willing to share his thoughts and vivid recollections of the events described in this research.

As an example of transference, Robert's negative experiences with professionals who stated they could help him, but failed to do so, were extended initially to the principal investigator in the form of expressed doubt that anything could be done to resolve Robert's dilemmas.

A possible limitation in the form of countertransference is the penchant of the principal investigator to be steadfast and proactive in solving problems, projected onto Robert in the form of advice. Robert accepted much of the advice offered.

The results of the involvement of the principal investigator and Robert have been varied and dramatic. Because Robert's money was stolen, the principal investigator was able to

[34] Due to the crew concept, there is a built-in check and balance system. In a sense, every flight may be considered as a check-ride, where the pilots observe each other's actions and behavior. Should there be any suspicion of a problem, the concern is reported and action may be taken by the airline. Thus, it is rare for highly personal problems to be discussed in the cockpit of commercial aircraft.

convince the Internal Revenue Service to allow Robert's claim for a significant retroactive tax refund by declaring a casualty loss. Robert's prior tax preparer failed to recognize the opportunity to claim such a loss.

At the encouragement of the principal investigator, Robert severed his relationship with a psychologist who was mistreating him. After several meetings with various law firms, one firm accepted Robert's case and filed a professional malpractice claim against the doctor. This complex suit resulted in a rare and substantial recovery.

After a disability insurance carrier arbitrarily suspended payments to Robert, the principal investigator initiated an appeal inclusive of assisting Robert's therapist in the writing of a report on Robert's current psychological condition. The principal investigator was successful in debating Robert's eligibility for a settlement of his disability claim based on being severely harmed by the predator, then by the FBI, and then by a forensic psychologist.

Throughout the process of investigating this case, the principal investigator has encouraged Robert to consider new career possibilities. Additionally, after reasonable efforts to encourage the FBI to reopen Robert's file have not been successful, Robert has been encouraged to move on with his life as best he can. Some efforts to engage the FBI in dialogue are continuing.

Robert has been helped by the publication of the principal investigator's two articles on the case (Kreuter 2003c; 2004) and a book chapter (Kreuter, in press) and Kreuter's (2006b) doctoral dissertation. He finds them useful to give to others to read as a way of informing what has happened to him.[35]

As a creative and perhaps cathartic approach to help Robert find some form of closure, outside of FBI vindication, the principal investigator was effective in establishing a connection with film producers, who have contracted with Robert to make a feature-length film out of Robert's story. In doing so, Robert has been able to better externalize his feelings about the events in his life while also being encouraged by the respect for his integrity accorded him by those involved in the project.

Since meeting Robert, his life course is changed. He has regained his composure and self-confidence in public settings. He has made substantial changes in his daily routine. Most importantly, he is in the process of resuming normal life activities and sleep patterns.

As a way of protecting against unwitting harm to Robert due to the involvement of the principal investigator, consultations were held with both the principal investigator's therapist and Robert's psychologist. Both independent clinicians have stated that they feel the involvement between the principal investigator and Robert has been completely positive for Robert, with no expressed concerns for his well-being.

Despite the cited examples of benefit to Robert, it is important to disclose admission of at least some potential bias on the part of the principal investigator. However, the depth of facts uncovered in the investigation would not have been possible absent a high degree of trust by Robert. Such trust was developed over the last 4 years and helped by the multidimensional involvement.

---

[35] Of particular importance is a meeting the principal investigator and Robert attended in Springfield, Missouri, with the Board of *The Forensic Examiner* and its independent psychologist, to present the first article, requiring demonstration of Robert's credibility. Because the case involves claimed misjudgment by the FBI, the Board was additionally cautious. Following a presentation of the case and questioning, the article was accepted as well as a second article submitted the following year.

EMPIRICAL CONCLUSION: CRITERIA FOR EVALUATION OF THE SUBJECT FROM THE EXISTENTIAL-HUMANISTIC PERSPECTIVE

A selection of seven themes from the existential-humanistic literature were used to help illuminate the lived experience of the subject. One of the possible reflections on the psychology of individual descriptions is the "use of existential-phenomenological concepts to guide reflection" (Wertz, 1985, p. 177). The principal investigator might use a general theoretical concept to guide thinking about the case. Wertz discussed another concept used in research—the self-world-others structure—which is believed to be involved in every psychological reality. This study will attempt to describe the inner experience and psychology of the subject.

From this brief survey of the literature on the existential-humanistic tradition, certain criteria have been selected as the approach to evaluate the psychology of the subject. The collective set of criteria represents a broad view of the person. The deeper elements of the subject's personality have been evaluated. This was done through analysis of identified aspects of the subject's personality juxtaposed to the specifics of the criteria. Thus, the criteria serve as separate platforms upon which to construct a partial picture of the subject. In aggregate, these components are hoped to form a reasonably complete composite of the total person in relation to his quest to find meaning through his suffering and the greater purpose of his existence.

While the principal investigator did find connections between the subject's personality and the existential criteria, he remained open to the possibility that they would not show up, for whatever reason. Any existentialist might have chosen a different set of criteria. These predefined informed themes, or tools, were methodically applied to an analysis of the subject's life experiences and his personality. The principal investigator's interactions with the data may have led to the conclusion that some of these criteria did not apply, resulting in the possibility of substitution of different criteria. However, no substitutions were ultimately deemed necessary. These criteria are:

1. The interior life world of the person (*eigenwelt*): the relationship between each person and himself or herself (Heidegger, 1927/1962; Becker, 1971).
2. Self-actualization need versus adjustment to social norms: despite the apparent pathology of the subject, he is working towards a healthier existential end than just adjustment to a sick society (Laing, 1967).
3. Meaning through suffering: to live is to suffer; to survive is to find meaning in the suffering (Frankl, 1963).
4. Being in the face of non-being: courage is the self-affirmation of being in spite of non-being, with faith at the core of this power (Tillich, 1952).
5. Attitudes toward death and annihilation: most of us act out of unconscious fear of our annihilation (Feifel, 1959).
6. Dreams, visions, and mythic experience: Dreams and visions can serve as vehicles to process imagined thoughts. Myths are metaphors for consciousness (Jung, 1969).
7. Existential use of the void: understanding the design of existence beyond our present life is critical because it explains and gives meaning to every aspect of our existence (Van Dusen, 1958).

Chapter 4

METHODOLOGY

OVERVIEW

Gordon Allport called the study of large groups the nomothetic method and advocated, instead, the study of the individual, which he called the idiographic method. The nomothetic method of investigation deals with the abstract, the universal, or the general. This method includes assessment of rates of prevalence.

The prevailing method to assess the rates of prevalence, which the principal investigator has not used, of repeat victimization is to use victimization surveys. These surveys can be criticized, as they are retrospective in nature, therefore prone to errors in recollection as well as distortions on the part of the responders. These designs may erroneously suggest a strong relation between multiple victimization and coping failure. In these surveys, victims are asked about the types and frequencies of criminal exposure. A survey finding was that people in a negative mood more easily retrieved prior negative life events than participants who are in a more optimistic psychological state (Winkel et al., 2003). Thus, in a victimization survey, the former participants are much more likely to be classified as repeat victims. In a study by Winkel and Vrij (1998), highly susceptible victims exhibit a relatively unfavorable (psychosocial) risk-profile.

Contrary to exploring victim vulnerability by the use of these nomothetic methods, this research explores the topic by performing an in-depth investigation of the psyche of a single victim. Such ideographic methods have the advantage of dealing with the concrete and unique individual.

The emphasis on measurement and psychometrics in the history of psychology has resulted in useful tools, such as Alfred Binet's intelligence test, the MMPI, and the Strong Vocational Interest Blank. This technology has been used extensively to classify people by government and large corporations, among other users. However, this demand constrained the scope of investigation and explanation to that which was easily measured, thereby neglecting more subtle and complex personality characteristics and processes.

From the beginning, personality psychology involved the study of individual persons as unique, integrated wholes (Murphy and Kovach, 1949/1972). The method employed in this research is the single-case study because the principal investigator has determined that this method is the most appropriate to explore the in-depth aspects of the subject's vulnerability due to its focus on the entire person. This perspective has not previously been applied to the study of victim vulnerability. The existential perspective will add to the understanding of the victim.

Instrumentation included additional interview protocols of the subject as well as numerous other people who have knowledge of the subject and the predator.[36] Archival data include extensive written records and tape recordings.[37] The written archive has been carefully organized and segregated by type and chronology of event. All data in the custody of the principal investigator is maintained in a secure area and will be returned to the pilot either upon his request or at the completion of this research. The data provided essential background information as well as corroborated the interviews.

The new interviews were semistructured and recorded where possible. Some were in person, others by telephone due to logistics. These interviews consisted of predetermined questions (planning was done before each interview to organize a progression of ideas in the form of questions as a guide for the principal investigator) useful in gathering basic details. As the responses were given, additional questions were added extemporaneously. The types of questions included topics covering the interviewees' relationship to the subject or the predator, their knowledge and recollection of key aspects of the subject's life and impact due to actions of the predator, as well as solicitation of the opinions interviewees had concerning various aspects of the subject's personality. In order to understand the subject's experience, questions were asked regarding specific events encountered by him to gather descriptions of how he responded to them.

The data were evaluated as a collective pool of information. The principal investigator sorted the data by type (i.e., e-mail, court transcripts, audio-tape transcriptions, and other documents) compiled into tabbed binders with pages numbered. The documents were sorted chronologically within each binder. The written archive of data was analyzed to determine aspects of the subject's personality juxtaposed to his various experiences. Interview data served to provide greater detail and also to corroborate findings in the archival data.

The archival data is assembled on the one hand and the seven existential criteria on the other hand to be compared. The existential themes each provide a vehicle for which certain aspects of the data can be explained. The original data are followed by analysis. The criteria are then used to isolate important elements of the subject's personality through a view of his experiences analyzed through the existential perspective.

Rationale for the Case Study Method

In *Explorations in Personality: A Clinical and Experimental Study of Fifty Men of College Age*, Murray et al. (1938) wrote of their mission: "Personalities constitute the subject matter for psychology, the life history of a single man being a unit with which this discipline has to deal" (p. 97). Murray et al. considered the personality to be the main element of the total structure of a person worthy of complete analysis. "The study of human beings and the factors that influence their course may be termed 'personology' instead of 'the psychology of

[36] For example, both daughters of the predator as well as the predator's ex-husband, brother, and sister were interviewed.

[37] The subject was very comfortable tape-recording discussions of events in his life. Some of the research material contained herein is based on those recordings.

personality,' a clumsy and tautological expression" (p. 97). Personology was a label applied to the efforts of Murray and those of others who were primarily concerned with a full understanding of the individual (Hall and Lindzey, 1978).

In this approach, a single segment of behavior is not to be understood in isolation from the rest of the functioning person. As a further contrast to other theories, the environmental context of behavior must be thoroughly understood and analyzed before an adequate account of individual behavior is possible.

Murray's fascination with the profound experiences in people's lives led to his vision to create a full-length, full-depth, dynamic, scientific account of human personality (White, 1987). Because personality is a dynamic process, it must be studied over periods of time, which Murray referred to as the study of lives. Kurt Lewin's field theory was compatible with Murray's theories. Field theory suggests that thoughts, feelings, and actions most often take place in a social environment and have to be understood as interactions with others.

Murray et al. (1938) felt that a personological theory can be tested best by utilizing it in the writing of biographies with the history of the personality being the best way to depict the personality. They studied opinions as integral parts of every person's attempts to bring needs and realities into a workable relation. This was important in determining how a subject sized up the world around him and placed it in relation to himself.

The raw materials used for case studies consist of autobiographies, recorded interviews, observations of behavior, and test protocols. The task is to make sense of the voluminous raw data of personality study. Murray et al. (1938) encouraged real analysis that implied going back and forth over the material, annotating it, making sure that all important items were captured. Analysis meant working with the material and patiently extracting what it contained.

Whereas Allport (1961) found that there is an "extraordinary diversity of adult motives, unique in each particular personality" (p. 203), Murray et al.'s position was not quite as extreme. "There is no elementary variable which is not possessed and manifested, at least occasionally to a slight extent, by everyone" (Murray et al., 1938, p. 252).

To explain the personality of an individual, an analysis of the life history is required. Murray et al. (1938) expressed interest in "the adoption of the whole history of an organism, the entire life span of a personality, as the macro-temporal unit that requires formulation" (p. 15). Murray et al. were influenced by the findings of biologists, such as Darwin, McDougall, and Freud with reference to his theories on aggression and anxiety, and Jung, whom he knew personally. Murray defined a number of dispositions, which were termed needs or drives. In following the biological principle that no two individuals are exactly alike, "the study of personality is in part the study of individual differences" (White, 1966, p. 7). People who study biological principles often look at traits.

Murray et al. (1938) contrasted general traits, such as "reactivity, speed of movement, impulsiveness, emphasis, discordination, emotionality, endurance, and expansiveness with the diagnosis of automatic or unconscious social acts and the diagnosis of latent inhibited tendencies" (p. 243). Murray et al. explained empathy as "an involuntary occurrence whereby an observer experiences the feelings or emotions which in his personality are associated 1, with the situation in which the subject is placed or 2, with the forms of behavior that the subject exhibits" (p. 247). They found that personological diagnosis is an apperceptive process, requiring inferences. Through critical empathy—the combination of empathy and projection—the principal investigator can identify with the subject. Reliability is enhanced "when the experimenter is observing an event that falls within his personal experience" (p. 248). Such personal awareness also serves to minimize interference of the subject by the researcher.

The approach taken in this present research is to examine one person's life completely, then discern from certain events relevant personality characteristics concerning his vulnerability. "Personality cannot be completely set forth as an integration of complexes at a particular point in time" (Murray et al., 1938, p. 282). Thus, examination of a short segment of the life history requires the investigator to know "to what extent the observed segment is a progression or a regression from previous periods. The more points we can obtain on the life curve the better can we extrapolate beyond the present" (p. 282). To understand why a person acts the way he or she does cannot be resolved until the researcher pushes his inspection further inward or backward in time. Though the starting point could be a significant event in adulthood, it may be more prudent to consider events dating back to childhood. This research can be done through direct inquiry, observation, and a review of archival data.

Personality is important to study because of the value of philosophical individualism.

> The modern psychological study of personality, which began to flourish during the early decades of the twentieth century, has roots in three nineteenth century intellectual themes: a deep belief in individualism, a pervasive concern with irrationality and the unconscious, and a strong emphasis on measurement. (Winter and Barenbaum, 1999, p. 4).

Abramson (1992) recommended that many aspects of the participants' lives be considered in case study research, including varied descriptive data, for it to be credible. These aspects might include: culture, upbringing, community, beliefs, attitudes, and biases. Due to the diversity in an individual's learning, processing, fears, and repressions, without consideration of the context of the participants' lives, a case study should be questioned in terms of being complete.

Wertz (1985) wrote on the phenomenology of the victim. He found that this phase of descriptions involves understanding and draws implicitly on the special intent of the researcher. The limits of the individual phenomenal descriptions are that the psychology of the descriptions has not been expressed. Thus, the researcher reads each description and considers their psychological meaning.

In his study, Wertz (1985) arranged for a Pittsburgh police department to conduct a telephone solicitation of a representative sample of persons (by type of crime and other factors) who reported crimes during the past 3 years (p. 161). Victims were asked to describe the crime in full detail, including what it was like to be victimized. This study is important because it delved into the issues of what it is like to live through victimization. Wertz's rigorous exploration of the meaning of responses by the victims is an example of the value of how a psychology that is oriented in a phenomenological manner can be used in research of a complex everyday event.

Allport (1960) was influential in the efforts to establish personality as a subject of mainstream psychological research. Allport wrote, "Psychology, it is often said, is destined to become the science of the twentieth century" (p. 3). His 1922 dissertation is considered as the first psychological dissertation on personality. "For much of the nineteenth century, character, rather than personality, was the category of choice for discussions of human experience"

(Nicholson, 2003, p. 5). The gradual shift signaled a change in values and altered the way Americans made sense of each other and themselves.

Allport (1937) saw the total personality as being informed by previous events and motivational sources, but it was also potentially independent of those factors. Early experiences contribute to later development.

Allport placed transcendence at the heart of personality. He felt that the individual had a spiritual existence that was related to the material world. Robert Fuller (1988) described Allport's psychology of personality as "psychological religiousness" (p. 146). Allport's spiritual ambitiousness provided a link between himself and what Eugene Taylor described as a distinctly "Jamesian tradition in psychology" (Taylor, 1992, p. 3). Part of the goal of this study was to search for ways in which the subject can go beyond his bleak and trapped situation.

Allport (1933) maintained that personality could be illuminated by such notoriously unscientific means as intuition and by the study of "case-histories and diaries, ratings, biographies, correspondence . . . expressive behavior, drama, and fiction" (p. 264). He felt that the experimental method is preferred where possible. He further suggested that greater attention be devoted to development of psychometric technology rather than pursue other methods like understanding. But he later said that measuring traits gave an "incomplete and frequently misleading picture" and neglected the "really significant levels of personality" and that it failed to explain the relationship between individual factors and the "total personality in which they are set" (Vernon and Allport, 1931, p. 231). This self-contradiction seems to suggest Allport's reluctance to embrace totally the detailed case study approach that looks at a whole person. Over time, Allport changed his view.

Allport was ambivalent about the *Geisteswissenschaften* (humanities). The *Geisteswissenschaften* brought with it a demand for detailed case studies. He was concerned that "the psychologist had to rely primarily on the strength of his literary skill and the depth of his clinical insight" (Nicholson, 2003, p. 181). In the case study, the investigator's forms of expression, choices of events to emphasize, and analytic ability are clearly displayed. Despite Allport's ambivalence, Rogers's call for the study of a whole person establishes credibility for its use in this research.

THE SINGLE-CASE STUDY

This case study is organized partially in chronological order and partially using a series of questions. Multiple narratives are provided to depict the many and varied nuances of the case presentation. The presentation begins with a variation of Meyer's life chart followed by a detailed case history. Psychological evaluations done on Robert's mental functioning served to provide a clinical perspective of him.

Research findings are analyzed in chapter 6, using the seven chosen existential criteria. Each of the criteria will be evaluated as either a question to answer or a statement to apply to Robert's life.

The single-case study was selected as the preferred methodology to answer the following research questions: (1) What is the psychology of the victim from the existential-humanistic perspective? and (2) What are characteristics of this subject that made him vulnerable to selection as a victim? However, mainstream psychologists were critical of case study methods. Allport and Vernon (1930) found that while the method may seem unsatisfactory, it also suggested that "the concrete individual has eluded study by any other approach" (p. 700). Yet, Allport (1933) refined his definition of traits, leading to a renewed emphasis on trait as the fundamental unit of study for personality. Allport's focus was on "the manifest individuality of mind" (p. vii), which supplied both ideographic and nomothetic methods. "For almost all personality psychologists, traits were viewed as a major element of personality" (Winter and Barenbaum, 1999, p. 13). But, philosophically, it is important to view the whole person, not the analysis of the parts.

The case study method, alternatively, "involves the presentation and interpretation of detailed information about a single subject, whether an event, a culture, the case study of an individual life" (Runyan, 1982, p. 121). Adherents argue, "The case study method is the traditional approach of all clinical research" (Bolgar, 1965, p. 28). This case study provides new information to add to the extant literature and other case studies dealing with this subject matter.

Robert White (1966) studied individual lives based on the "intensive case study, using a variety of methods designed to disclose the individual patterns of personality" (p. 1). Allport also was involved in the discussion of the methodology of how a life history should be written (Taylor, 2004). He recommended the use of personal documents in psychological research.

Runyan (1982) further developed the case study approach, referred to as psychobiography. Runyan added "a psychodynamic interpretation across the life span" (Taylor, 2004, p. 3). "There is no single life history method . . . and life histories may be studied through phenomenological self-reports, archival research, prospective longitudinal research, and experimental research" (p. 6). According to the nomothetic view, the primary goal of psychology is "the development of generalizations of ever increasing scope, so that greater and greater varieties of phenomena may be explained by them" (Levy, 1970, p. 5). White (1966) wrote, "The initial facts of personality are the lives of people, and lives cannot be adequately understood unless they are described at considerable length" (p. iii). White found that personality does not stand still, that the person evolves and "is not always a passive victim of the forces that influence him" (p. iv).

Allport (1965) found that the real test of psychologists comes when they attempt to explain "a single concrete life" (p. x). His only published full-length case study on Jenny Masterson left Allport feeling uncomfortable and "wishing that he could have, instead, used vague generalizations" (p. x). He eventually chose to maintain his phenomenological attitude, preferring a conceptual system that would admit both evidence of experience and a hypothesis in behavioral terms. The approach used by Allport is applicable to this dissertation in that the phenomena of the subject's behavior can be evaluated in existential terms.

Murray (1955) challenged mainstream experimental psychology in favor of psychoanalytically informed case studies and theoretical discussions. He wrote that the study of individual lives, as presented in case histories, provides the only possible way of obtaining the amount of data with which to build a science of human nature. Bromley (1977) viewed life histories as necessary in any serious attempt to explain, predict, or influence behavior. Thus, a complete evaluation of a person's life course is necessary in order to improve the general level of understanding of victim vulnerability.

The case study method provides the completeness needed towards a fuller picture of the human being. The use of a case history is a way of dealing first with an entire life, then a deeper analysis of important life segments. Allport's theories provide useful and historical support for this approach. Runyan (1982) described how particularistic information about Adolf Eichmann, who was involved in the execution of an estimated 6 million European Jews in World War II, was gathered through interviews, cross examination, and analysis of personal and historical documents. In doing so, a more complete picture of Eichmann was possible.

Runyan (1982) argued that personality psychologists want to understand the psychological mechanisms and processes which regulate the expression of impulses, the satisfaction of needs, and the contents of consciousness. They also seek to identify and measure the major dimensions of personality and to understand how phenomenological awareness and self-concepts affect behavior. In contrast, life courses, according to Runyan (1982):

> . . . have more explicit temporal and ecological dimensions and are concerned with questions about the causal structure of sequences of experience, about the processes through which persons and situations interact over the course of time, and about the movement of persons through social and historical worlds. (p. 83)

Some theorists view the case study method as inferior or defective, useful more to generate hypotheses that will be more rigorously tested later (see, for example, Campbell and Stanley, 1966; Lundberg, 1926). Kratochwill (1978) found that case study methodology is characterized by uncontrolled variation, inadequate description of independent and dependent variables, and is difficult to replicate. Disadvantages of case studies include smaller number of cases and potentially less representative ones. According to scientific reductionism, one person's case cannot be reasonably expected to generalize to a larger population.

However, the existentialist position is that the entire meaning of being human is encapsulated only in the single case.

The single-case study, as presented in this research, reflects the interpretive skills of the principal investigator based on his understanding of this lineage. The criteria chosen by the researcher was used to infer an idiosyncratic understanding of the lived experience of the subject. The existential findings can be communicated as the principal investigator's understanding of the case, but the actual method of existential analysis remains unique to the study and is not bound by the quantitative strictures of so-called rigorous and repeatable criteria of analysis demanded of other, less qualitative methods. In this way, it will remain true to the existential point of view and still be able to inform about the personality of the subject in terms of his vulnerability as a victim based on the principles of existential-humanistic psychology.

While this method is prone to attack on the basis that it may include possible errors, biases, and inaccuracies, case studies often contain findings gleaned from the collection and interpretation of original letters, contemporaneous observations, and archival data. Case studies, using life histories, have been "praised for their value in providing information on the subjective side of social experience" (Runyan, 1982, p. 124). They are the only way to evaluate the phenomenology of the subject's internal life world.

Historical and Archival Methods

Two types of data (interview and archival documents) were used in this research. Documents included written and transcribed audiotapes. Collection of data for this research took place in a conveniently located setting that provided both privacy and safety to the interviewees and the principal investigator. Data were collected during lengthy interviews, sometimes over multiple days. Interviews of witnesses who are familiar with facts involving crimes committed against the subject were arranged in a similar safe setting or by telephone, depending on logistics.

All interviews were conducted individually and in person, where practical. Kvale (1996) referred to the research interview as a "specific form of conversation" (p. 19). This follows the phenomenological approach, drawing on the founding philosophy of Husserl, where the understanding of social phenomena is taken from the actors' own perspectives, describing the world as experienced by the subjects, along with the assumption that reality is what people perceive it to be (Taylor and Bogdan, 1984).

Archival data from the principal investigator's prior research was incorporated. Additionally, arrangements were made for subsequent personal interviews or telephone calls to clarify and verify this data, where questions arose.

A significant amount of new archival evidence has been made available to the principal investigator for review. These documents include court transcriptions, personal correspondence, e-mail communications, and instant message dialogues, as well as photographs, tape recordings, and psychological records. They were given to the principal investigator by the subject, presumably unscreened and complete, as the principal investigator has never had reason to believe any documents were omitted. This data provided ample background for a full understanding of the facts and intrigue of this case. Available data related to this research are substantial, varied, and verifiable. The written materials consist of thousands of pages of documents, including original communications, over 20 prior personal interviews, court transcriptions, psychological reports, and transcribed audiotapes.

The printed e-mail dialogues and audiotapes are being maintained by the principal investigator in a secure cabinet. The credibility of the collected data is readily corroborated by comparison to other data within the pool of available information. Thus, its value in supporting research conclusions is enhanced due to these attributes. The new data supplement the previous archival information and were used to address the research questions discussed herein. "Some evidence can be used to sequence events, determine locations and paths, establish direction or establish time and/or duration of the action" (Chisum, 1999, p. 81). Data lead to clues when they point to aspects of research questions. Clues are evaluated as well. As the data are evaluated within the context of the existential themes, the principal investigator comes across sections that may serve as examples of the themes, restate the themes in particular ways, share aspects of meaning or context with the themes, or in any other way relate to the themes.

The subject's candor and trust has increased since the preliminary study. As an example, he entrusted the principal investigator with the only set of his lengthy taped monologue, done in 1997, describing numerous relevant events. The researcher has transcribed these extemporaneous and informative recordings, which have been used to highlight events in the subject's life from his original perspective at this important earlier time.

Subject Selection

The principal investigator first met the subject in this research several years ago in a business setting. They formed a relationship of trust, which led to the subject's full disclosure of the events that described his victimization. Subsequently, it was discovered that the subject possessed an enormous quantity of contemporaneous documentation and was also quite receptive to ongoing interviews. The subject has issued a written release to the principal investigator, covering all aspects of the archival data.[38] He presented his facts in a logical, coherent manner and allowed a forensic study by the principal investigator, who determined that the subject's report of harm done to him was accurate and worth additional study.

The Interview

The involvement of the researcher with the interview protocol is important. Eisner (1991) referred to the self as the instrument to describe the capacity for resonating with experience. "The self is the instrument that engages the situation and makes sense of it. It is the ability to see and interpret significant aspects. It is the characteristic that provides unique, personal insight into the experience under study" (p. 33).

Extensive interviews formed the primary data, while the archival documents formed the supporting data. The interviews have varied in duration. They have ranged from 10 minutes to many hours, depending on the importance of the interviewee, and have sometimes been conducted over several consecutive days. Altogether, approximately 300 hours of interviews have been conducted as of the writing of this research.

Witnesses who are familiar with facts involving crimes committed by the predator, harm done by the FBI, and an unethical forensic report issued by a forensic psychologist, all committed against the subject were also interviewed as a way of obtaining additional data. "The research interview is based on the conversations of daily life and is a professional conversation" (Kvale, 1996, p. 5). The postmodern philosopher, Rorty (1979), emphasized the constitution of knowledge through a conversation. He suggested that "conversation is the ultimate context within which knowledge is understood" (p. 389). Using this understanding, interviewees were asked to search their memories and mentally return to the time where their experiences of the subject, or the predator, took place. The objective was much more on the recall of useful data and less on the opinions and attitudes of the interviewees unless it related to the research questions.

"The qualitative research interview aims at obtaining uninterrupted descriptions" (Kvale, 1996, p. 32). Descriptions, or the subject's relevant themes, should be as complete and as free of presuppositions as possible. Then, the investigator evaluates the question of why the subjects experience and act as they do.

In the process of interviewing, the investigator seeks to describe specific situations and sequences of action, from the subject's world. The focus of the qualitative research interview for this research was on certain themes in the world of the interviewees. It was neither to be rigidly structured nor completely nondirective. Thus, the entire milieu, regarding the themes

[38] As previously mentioned, the data will eventually be returned to the subject.

of the research focus, can be garnered through such flexibility. An analogy is a legal deposition of a witness. The deposing counsel usually follows a prepared progression of content questions, but many additional questions are composed during the session, thus adding a spontaneous nature to the important inquiry.

"To carry out a qualitative study, a variety of methods and technique can be used to identify and gather data" (Piantanida and Garman, 1999, p. 139). Within these strategies, the specific tools, such as interviews, audiotapes, and documentation, may be used to gather and record information about the phenomenon and context under study.

Ambiguous and contradictory statements gathered =pring interviews were clarified and negated the need for subsequent interviews. The archival documents include transcripts of the previous interviews. In this research, the initial interviews have been completed in the previous work and were followed up by a second set of interviews. Because the interview involves an interaction between the dyad, the interviewer and the subject reciprocally influence each other. Interpersonal dynamics may play a role during the interview. Examples are feelings of anxiety, which may evoke defense mechanisms in the interviewee as well as the interviewer.

The interview style employed here was analytical in nature. "It studies the subjects' perspectives on their world; attempts to describe in detail the content and structure of the subjects' consciousness, to grasp the qualitative diversity of their experiences and to explicate their essential meanings" (Kvale, 1996, p. 53). The analysis employed the existential perspective.

Merleau-Ponty (1962) espoused the importance of describing events as accurately as possible rather than to explain or analyze. "Phenomenology is the attempt at a direct description of experience, without any considerations about the origin or cause of an experience" (p. 53).

These general areas of inquiry led to development of an interview guide (Kvale, 1996), which was the main method for the interviews to provide an approach to retrieve valuable insights and information relevant to the case study. Specific interview questions were designed that were based on the particular interviewee and their predicted level of knowledge concerning events in the subject's life as depicted in the life chart of the subject contained in this study. The life chart and ensuing analysis was the primary analytical tool used in this research.

Part of the interview guide encompassed the following content:

1. Relationship to the subject or the predator
2. Depth of knowledge of certain events in the subject's life
3. History of the incident
4. Critical past incidents showing personal patterns and traits, or sensitivity to victimization
5. General past developmental history and relevant family history
6. Medical and psychiatric history
7. Possession of corroborating documents

In contrast to the research interview employed in this research, there is also the clinical interview. The subject underwent several psychiatric interviews with various psychologists and psychiatrists, which are discussed later. Sullivan (1970) viewed the psychiatric interview as an interpersonal situation where the relevant data is extracted due to the interaction itself. He emphasized that in participant observation, it is the interviewer as a person who is the method, the instrument. Sullivan wrote, "The data of psychiatry arise only in participant observation" (p. 3). The principal instrument of observation is the self. This can be extended to include data gathered in the interview. Such data would seemingly include the participant's verbal recantations of past events. It is the role of the observer to develop inferences as a result of analysis of data. However, this analytical process should be conducted after the data is collected, thus avoiding prejudgment. Additional questions will be developed spontaneously depending on the responses to the predetermined questions.

The interview, according to Sullivan (1970) is primarily a vocal communication between the expert and client for the purpose of "elucidating characteristic patterns of living of the subject person" (p. 4). Vocal communications include not only verbalizations but also intonation, rate of speech, and difficulty in enunciation. Sullivan argued that it is important for the interviewer to avoid any intense emotion concerning any issue portrayed by the interviewee. The reactions should be as neutral as possible. Similarly, the attitudes of the interviewee are data. It is important to understand how a patient interacts with society. "If you are to correctly understand your patient's problems, you must understand his dealing with people" (p. 13). To assist in gaining this level of complete understanding, interviewing others familiar with the main interviewees is helpful. Thus, the process of interviewing is a method.

Generally, in research, the subject has some expectation of improvement or personal gain from the interview because it is felt that in divulging facts and opinions, the subject has a new opportunity to understand what occurred and what the lived experiences meant (Kvale, 1996). However, not all interviews lend themselves to helping the interviewee. In this research, the subject was advised that the principal investigator did not intend to fill the role of therapist. In a report written by the subject's current therapist, the therapist felt that the work done by the principal investigator and the subject has helped the subject recover somewhat from the trauma caused by the events portrayed in this research.

In a qualitative research interview, the topic is the lived world of the subjects and their relation to it (Kvale, 1996). "The purpose is to describe and understand the central themes the subjects experience and live toward" (p. 29). The interviewer, then, undertakes a process of interpretation of the meaning of such themes. As the interview seeks to cultivate qualitative knowledge, expressed in normal language, the methodology does not involve any measurement. Instead, the interview attempts to obtain descriptions of different aspects of the actual world of the subjects.

DATA ANALYSIS

Documents were evaluated together with interview data and placed in chronological order by theme. A major strength of case study data collection is the opportunity to use many different sources of evidence (Yin, 1994, p. 91). In doing so, it is possible to develop converging lines of inquiry, a process of triangulation. "With triangulation, the potential problems of construct validity also can be addressed, because the multiple sources of evidence essentially provide multiple measures of the same phenomenon" (p. 92).

The sources of data used in the evaluation of how to best present the case of Robert include interviews of Robert, interviews of others, corroboration of information through documents, and the availability of Robert's audio-taped monologue. The various sources of data did not suggest any type of meaningful contradiction amongst the sources.

With triangulation, the use of multiple sources of evidence provides various perspectives of the same phenomenon. The documents were evaluated in terms of their origin, believability, and meaningfulness. Interview material was based on its corroboration with documents. "Qualitative research frequently involves some circumstances, however, for which a degree of anticipated flexibility also is wise" (Locke, Spirduso, and Silverman, 2000, p. 102). Such flexibility is important in this research, as several sources of data were available for most aspects of the key elements, but when followed up with interviews of the subject or others, new information would often be presented. It was necessary to discern which information was pertinent and which was tangential or irrelevant.

The life chart was used as the basis for a content/thematic analysis of the data. Using a content analysis, the principal investigator looked for themes and sorted these themes into a hierarchy of categories (Kvale, 1996). For this subject, themes were based on certain behaviors in his life, referred to as paradoxical existential moments. These moments were paradoxical in that they reveal circumstances of extreme pressure faced by the subject yet also reveal the potential for discovery of meaning through survival of such pressure. Such moments reveal very precise elements of the personality of the subject. At these crossroads, his documented behavior led to harm, thus his vulnerability is seen through these moments.

The case history of the subject can be depicted in various ways. This research first presents a life chart as a way that allows the reader to look at that part of the person's life being analyzed within the context of his life history. Following the presentation of the subject's life chart, a detailed case history is presented. Analysis of the actions of the subject to the events is presented in connection with the existential criteria chosen for this research.

LIMITATIONS AND DELIMITATIONS

Within the methodology chosen for this study, the principal investigator was sensitive to what the participant did not report directly through responses to interview questions. Indirect analysis was done through interpretation of various dreams the subject has reported and through analysis of the writings of the subject.

One limitation of the study involved the infeasibility of direct personal contact with the predator as a potential interviewee, although the principal investigator has recently been successful in engaging in limited e-mail dialogue with her. Another limitation is the possibility that the subject has either screened the data given to the principal investigator or omitted documents that might alter the research findings. Locke et al. (2000) referred to this type of limitation as a restrictive weakness whereby the "optimal number of observations simply cannot be made because of problems involving ethics or feasibility" (p. 17). During the conduct of the study, the principal investigator and the subject developed a positive working relationship, where the subject believed in the research objectives and was interested in contributing his time and documents for purposes of the study. Because of the nature of the research, the principal investigator discovered several ways to help the subject deal with his situation. Through their established multilevel relationship, the subject provided the principal investigator with extensive data. Thus, there is often a tradeoff between development of a more involved relationship and the ability to obtain data. Accordingly, suggestions were made to the subject to commence legal action against the psychologist, who behaved unprofessionally and illegally during treatment, as well as to file appellate claims to recover disability benefits that were improperly withheld and to file an amended tax return for the financial loss he suffered due to the theft of his money by the predator. The delimitations of this research are the choice of the case using mainly a single person to describe the phenomenon of victim vulnerability and the high level of trust that has developed between the subject and the principal investigator.

Chapter 5

PRESENTATION OF THE CASE

THE LIFE CHART

Taylor (2004) proposed Adolf Meyer's (Meyer, 1948; Leys, 1991; McHugh, 2001) concept of the life chart as a way to summarize the case study method in the context of a person's life history.[39] Meyer (1948) stated:

> Medical psychology consists largely in the determination of the actual life history and experiences and concrete reactions of the patient, and the gaining of a safe and sensible perspective, so as to adapt as far as possible the aims to the means and the means to the aims, and the personality to the situation and the situation to the personality. (p. 418)

In such a depiction, the chronology of major biological, psychological, social, and spiritual events in the person's history are included. "It is the length of the records and their apparent lack of pointedness that make many physicians shun the task. It is, furthermore, somewhat difficult to control the time relations and causal interdependence of the events" (Meyer, 1948, p. 419). This method helps the principal investigator evaluate a picture of the whole person under study in terms of his or her illnesses, deficits, or conditions.

Table 1 is a chronological summary of the significant psychobiosocial events in the life of Robert.[40] This depiction, based on a variation of the Meyerian life chart, provides an entire glimpse of a person. Murray et al.'s (1938) interest in a life segment as a progression or regression from a previous period, as well as depth psychology in general, justifies a longitudinal look at the life history of the participant and his responses to situations. Events described in this life chart are referenced in this study and explained from an existential-humanistic viewpoint. Through this dynamic view and through the portal of his history, assessments of Robert's personality are possible.

---

[39] The principal investigator acknowledges with appreciation Dr. Eugene Taylor's permission to reference his unpublished work in this book.

[40] This presentation is a slight modification of Meyer's original formulation but serves the same purpose.

Table 1 Life Chart of Robert

1954	Born in Brooklyn, New York; parents are Paul (retired in 1992) and Susan (retired in 1985); Robert is oldest of three male children whose siblings were born 1957 and 1960.
1960	Hospitalized 3 weeks with life-threatening spinal meningitis. He fully recovered.
1961	Absorbed with children's television shows: "Sky King," about a pilot, formed favorable impression of pilots who are able to help others, and "Superman," impressed with his ability to fly and save others; enjoyed scuba and high diving for the feeling of weightlessness; fascinated by space stories and World War II movies involving flying; liked watching birds; subscribed to flying magazines; built small planes out of balsa wood.
1962	Inadvertently, stole a small pack of sneezing powder worth under $1 from a novelty store.
1964	Tried to bully another child; realized it was wrong and immediately experienced remorse.
1965	Best friend and schoolmate died of a brain tumor; had bicycle stolen by neighborhood youths; avoided struggle, scrapped up own knee, lied to parents about the incident.
1967	Fascinated watching planes, as a teen, through bedroom screen window; started tracking landing intervals; bought radio device to pick up cockpit communications; developed imagination and identification with pilots.
1968	Ran into a tree face first while playing football; took a glider flying lesson; went to camp to learn about small engine planes; won a swimming award.
1970	Soloed an airplane at age 16; saw F-111 crash and the pilot killed.
1972	Defended himself in a street fight.
1974	Emergency landed a small plane with jammed landing gear, without panic.
1975	Came to the rescue of a victim (stranger) of a street crime.
1976	Rated as a flight engineer on large commercial aircraft (Boeing 727, later DC-9, Boeing 737), then upgraded to pilot (727 and 737).
1977	Brother Joseph died in Robert's presence of asthma; Robert ended serious heterosexual relationship following the tragedy of Joseph's death.
1979	Nearly crashed a plane flying due to conditions of extremely poor visibility with a faulty navigational instrument.
1984	Acquitted of a DUI incident; felt vindicated by supportive judge.
1986	Expressed concern for grandfather's habit of walking alone in a dangerous area, imagining crime, wishing to protect him.
1987	Rescued a crime victim (stranger); earned a police award; had role of hero; hired by major airline as a pilot.
1991	Struck with a bottle by muggers.
1995	Contacted on the Internet; beginning of a scam; start of victimization.
1997	Filed a complaint with the FBI; FBI sent letter of concern about his mental status to the FAA; FAA suspended his First Class Medical Certificate; placed on disability by employer; faulty forensic psychological report issued, began self-directed case investigation. Started seeing psychologist for treatment; treatment lasted 4 years with poor results.
2000	Increased defensive-stalking efforts; led to new investigations of the predator and relentless pursuit of information about her life and activities despite the physical distance of several hundred miles.
2001	Started seeing new psychologist; diagnosed with PTSD; met the principal investigator.
2003	Provided sufficient information to authorities resulting in incarceration of Connie.
2004	Signed contract to have film made on his story; has dreams about death; successfully donated a kidney to his father; wins lawsuit against the initial treating psychologist who also was convicted of Medicare fraud.
2005	Settled dispute with disability insurance carrier; met new female friend.

In order to assemble this story line of the life of Robert, a variety of sources of data were considered. These included personal interviews of the subject as well as others and review of the archival data (documents and audiotapes). The principal investigator found that the multiple sources of data were largely in agreement, though some information on life events were included by some interviewees and omitted by others. There were no instances of factual disagreements concerning the life history of the subject.

The process of triangulation served to corroborate research findings. For example, in instances where the subject made certain statements about how he was treated by the original forensic psychologist, the subject also provided a transcript and the original audiotape of a taped telephone conversation with the psychologist. In this conversation, the psychologist admitted he believed the predator and not the subject, but was unable to cite his basis for doing so. The psychologist also admitted that he would refuse to amend his forensic evaluation. He took this posture despite the additional evidentiary information submitted to him by the subject. This refusal is the basis for the subject's claim that the psychologist acted unethically by refusing to consider amending the report based on new information. An example of data found in one format and not in another is the added authentic expression of real emotion by Robert contained in his monologue, which is not as clear as in the e-mail archive.

This book hopes to contribute a wider perspective in the fields of personology and the psychology of the victim through the use of an existential-humanistic interpretation of a single-case study. In doing so, the current dialogue is expanded from its formerly incomplete treatment found in cognitive, behavioral, and experimental psychology to encompass this missing perspective.

THE DETAILED CASE HISTORY

This discussion begins with an analytical overview of Robert's life, including findings from a forensic psychologist's report on Robert's mental functioning.[41] Then, a detailed narrative, together with excerpts from an audio monologue made by Robert, is presented along with diagnostic perspectives related to the existential criteria chosen for this purpose. In addition, certain events, referred to as existential moments, and Robert's dreams are evaluated.

Robert was born in 1954 in New York. His parents are living. His father, Paul, owned and managed a retail shoe store in Brooklyn, New York. He is now retired. His mother, Susan, is highly educated and taught school for about 10 years, starting her career comparatively late in life. She is also retired. Robert is the oldest of three children. He has one living brother, born in 1957, and a deceased brother, born in 1960 and died in 1977.

Robert described his formative years as being normal and happy, but growing up he had friends from the neighborhood. His upbringing was absent any parental abuse or domestic volatility, and he was routinely in the midst of extended family. He reported a few significant or unusual family events. At age 6, Robert contracted spinal meningitis, causing him to be hospitalized for a 3-week period. His condition was considered serious, possibly fatal.

[41] The names of Robert's relatives have been changed in this study.

Robert grew up in an upscale, mostly Jewish neighborhood, mostly in well-built, attractive houses. He attended public schools. Following the birth of the second child, the family moved to a larger house in Brooklyn, where Robert lived until he turned 18.

Robert was an average student. Interestingly, he underwent an intelligence test in 2003, as part of an insurance company's demand for a full evaluation of his mental status. Robert felt unfairly pressured by the insurance company. Robert was so upset because he felt he was manipulated by the insurance companies, resulting in his being forced to undertake a battery of tests. His score was in the average range of intellectual functioning.[42] Robert feels that his scores might have been higher if he approached the test under a non-risk scenario. There is no record of prior or subsequent intelligence testing of Robert.

One of Robert's closest schoolmates, Michael, died of a brain tumor while both were in fourth grade. Michael's death was traumatic for Robert who was age 9 at the time. Michael had become very sick from treatment and lost his hair. Robert did not fully understand why this was happening to Michael. This was particularly difficult for Robert, who did not understand how he was expected to deal with Michael's illness.

When Robert was in high school (age 16), he experienced a situation in the classroom that involved him being bullied by a boy (Gary) who lived in Robert's neighborhood. They were marginal friends who attended elementary school together. Robert described Gary as wild and wacky as a kid, and that Gary was known to have harmed cats when he was between the ages of 11 and 13. Robert recognized Gary's conduct as deviant, but he did not really understand how deviant such behavior was until he was older. In music appreciation class with a young teacher, Robert sat in front of Gary. The desks were the one-unit type wherein the desk and chair are connected. Robert described Gary's conduct towards him as unpredictable and annoying. Though Robert knew Gary to be this way, by the time they entered high school, Robert had grown tired of Gary's juvenile acts and semi-cruel jokes. In the classroom, Gary annoyed Robert continuously, kicking his chair and poking him. It almost seemed to Robert to be done in a good natured way, or out of boredom.

Robert tried to stop Gary verbally, but the abuse continued. The teacher noticed the situation and handled it by scowling at both Gary and Robert as if Robert were partially responsible. Sometimes, the teacher made idle threats to them. Gary was unbothered by these threats, but Robert did not like hearing them. In retrospect, Robert feels that the teacher or even the school system was not strong enough to deal with people like Gary, that it was unfair for Robert to be associated with the problem with Gary, and that the teacher knew Gary was solely responsible. Robert expected that the teacher should be the first line of defense when a student is disruptive.

Eventually, Robert thought to resolve the situation on his own. Robert wanted to end the bullying. If he had to go to the principal because of what he planned to do, he was prepared to do so if it led to cessation of the annoying acts. Robert determined that he did not want to confront Gary after school, thinking instead that he needed an advantage of some form. So Robert studied the actions of Gary each time Robert was kicked. Robert developed an idea as to how to handle Gary and rehearsed his plan over and over in his mind. One day, Gary again started to use his right foot to tease Robert by raising his foot to push Robert's right elbow off his desk or repeatedly kick Robert's chair. This situation was annoying to Robert and embarrassing to him because the whole class knew what Gary was doing as well as the

[42] Forensic evidence reveals flaws in the testing procedures, which likely affected Robert's test results.

teacher. Robert previously had done nothing to stop Gary's behavior except appear to get frustrated and upset. Robert timed Gary's raising of his foot towards Robert and when Gary's leg was extended fully he took Gary's foot in both of his hands and twisted his leg so fast that his whole body spun around, followed by his desk, which fell on top of him. Gary was rattled and confused, according to Robert, as well as shaken up and very embarrassed. The teacher was outraged and scolded both of them. Gary never confronted Robert about what had occurred or bothered him again, though Robert did not know what was going to happen after his initiated his plan or if Gary's behavior would stop.

Robert felt good after the incident, even victorious. He felt a sense of disappointment in the teacher because she failed to acknowledge that Robert finally did something to protect himself, whereas she was unable to step in and control the situation.

In a sense the teacher was also a victim of the bully in the classroom as the bully was very disruptive. When Robert took care of Gary by sending him twisting and flying Robert would have liked just the slightest acknowledgment from the young female music teacher. This could have been in the form of a knowing look, a nod, or even a smile of recognition that he not only took care of his problem, but he took care of her problem as well. Robert could have informed the school guidance counselor, the principal, even his parents. According to Robert, these were not good options because he felt that in the world of high school it would have just created another problem.

Perhaps Robert's handling of Gary can be compared with his handling of the predator or the FBI. He took care of Gary on his own terms, without the official blessing of the school, but nevertheless, the problem went away. Twenty-five years later, rather than go to the federal government for help, Robert might have been much better off if he had taken certain matters into his own hands and risked the consequences. Metaphorically, if he had done to the predator what he did to Gary, he would not have been as harmed.

From as early as he can remember, Robert wanted to be a commercial airline pilot. As a young child, he remembers lying in bed, looking out his window, noticing planes in the distant sky. As he later learned, his house was in the vicinity of a routine flight path to JFK International Airport in New York. He began to notice that successive planes would intersect a particular point on his window screen. He soon discovered that there was a predictable pattern to the flights in terms of the time interval between planes. He decided one day to test the order that he found and created his own makeshift flight chart, resulting in his first scientific field experiment. He further expanded his thoughts and considered the possibility that on successive evenings he saw the same aircraft and maybe even the same pilots and flight crew that he saw on previous days. This experiment developed into Robert's curiosity about who these people were, and he marveled at the number of people on the planes for whom these pilots were responsible. Despite his intrigue, Robert did not share these thoughts in detail with his parents, his siblings, or his friends.

Robert graduated from a local high school and attended Brooklyn College for one semester. He transferred to an aeronautical University in Florida, to earn a degree in aeronautical science, as he thought this could help him reach his goal quicker. He did not like the fact that the school was comprised of predominantly older male veterans recently released from the military. Robert preferred to be in a more integrated university environment. As a result, he kept to a small like-minded group at school. Robert attended several other schools for various amounts of time, including a semester abroad at the University of Copenhagen.

While attending college, he got a job as a flight instructor in Miami. It was around this time that his youngest brother, Joseph, died (at age 17) from an asthma attack. Joseph was visiting Robert on a vacation and died in Robert's presence. Robert suffered emotionally through this loss for almost 2 years. He felt depressed and tearful, and cried all the time. He sought the services of a psychotherapist, attended three sessions, and focused more heavily on studying aeronautics to get away from the pain. Robert stopped treatment because he felt it was not meeting his expectations. Today, Robert admits that he may have had unrealistic expectations. At age 23, Robert was rated as a flight engineer on the Boeing 727 jet. During that time, he had been dating a girl, but he ended this relationship because he felt she was incapable of providing adequate emotional support for him.

At age 25, Robert moved to Texas to get a job with a small airline, but the company soon folded. In the early 1980s, he was hired as a co-pilot for an oil company to fly its executives to meetings across the country. Because his career aspirations were high, Robert was in this position for 2 years. He was eventually fired from that position. According to Robert, his termination was due to his verbalized doubts that this position was limited because at this point in his career Robert felt he was now ready to work for an airline. The normal progression for pilots is to take lesser desirable jobs in order to gain experience with airlines. Robert was harassed by anti-Semitic jokes, but eventually stood up to the offenders who respected Robert and ceased their insults. His next job took him to Maine to fly for Bar Harbor Airlines. He and the other Jewish pilot got fired within 5 days of each other for no apparent reason. Robert had a DUI arrest after a holiday party where, reportedly, the policemen harassed him. Robert speculates that the company used this event as the reason to fire him even though he was acquitted of the DUI charges after spending several hours in jail, with no repercussions. He reported feeling satisfied that the judge reprimanded the officer in front of the judge.

Several existential moments provide insight into Robert's personality. Following the death of his brother, Joseph, when Robert was a flight instructor, Robert stopped flying and teaching while he was dealing with Joseph's death. Though he ceased actively flying aircraft, Robert did continue taking courses to round out his knowledge of aviation, such as aviation law and the economics of flying. He reports that, due to his low mood, he felt very apprehensive around this time because his original career plans were impacted following Joseph's death.

After 1 year of additional courses, Robert completed his bachelor's degree in aeronautics. Despite feeling inexperienced, he also knew he was on the path to becoming a pilot. In order to develop his skills as a pilot, Robert knew he needed substantial flying time. Thus far, all of his training and experience as a flight instructor were done at low altitude, on a single-engine plane, in good weather, typical of the beginner pilot.[43]

After the death of his brother, Robert started to have doubts about his career because he was heavy hearted and felt wounded. He had diminished enthusiasm for life, including flying. Because his attitude was negative, it was difficult for Robert to function as a flight instructor where he was expected to have an upbeat disposition. Meanwhile, his relationship with his girlfriend at the time ended partly because Robert was dealing with the trauma of Joseph's death and the relationship no longer worked. Robert felt he needed a change in environment.

[43] Robert wanted to obtain sufficient flying experience, including a variety of aircraft, so he could attain a position with a major commercial airline.

After he received his academic degree, he embarked on a course to become a licensed flight engineer on turbo jets (i.e., the Boeing 727), which was a big jump from the small planes he was used to working on.[44] He felt that this was a good time for him to reemerge and begin a difficult process. Robert referred to this step as a quantum leap from an engineering standpoint.[45]

In order to qualify for the move up to jet planes, he immersed himself in his studies. He memorized and understood each piece of technical equipment and how each interrelated.

Robert wanted to get back into the process of becoming a jet pilot. He studied hard, took all the tests, and received his license based on testing in the simulator. This built up his confidence in complex mechanical systems. Robert also learned to rely on instruments. However, he was mindful that he needed actual flying experience. He also needed a job. A friend gave Robert a lead for a job working for a small airline that served corporations with small planes, but the company reduced in size. He did not get any hours of flying, so he quit. He then moved to Texas and took a job with another fledgling airline, but that job ended after his relocation, as the company reduced in size. He then took more courses to become recertified as a flight instructor.

Robert was able to find a job with an oil company that was looking for a pilot for a Cessna twin-engine plane. The company sent Robert for pilot training, and he was able to get certified to fly the small, yet complex, twin-engine plane. However, Robert was concerned about actually having to fly the aircraft because of his overall shortage of experience for that type of plane and the kind of flying that he would be expected to do.[46] But the owner of the company, himself a pilot, had confidence in Robert. Robert flew the plane a few times without incident. His concern was about flying in overly challenging meteorological conditions.[47] The following event in Robert's life is told in detail so as to provide the reader with a vivid picture of how Robert responded to a traumatic event, dealt with fear, and managed to survive.

There came a need for Robert to fly the plane from a small airport outside of Houston to Houston's Hobby Airport. He drove to the airport and the weather was poor. Robert was apprehensive, but also felt he had to take the flight because he needed the job and the experience.[48] Robert described the weather conditions as a low cloud base, which meant he would be flying the plane using instruments. He was certified to do so, but was inexperienced. He took off in the plane for the expected 10- to 12-minute flight and maintained radio contact with the tower. There was a new piece of navigational equipment that was recently installed in the cockpit.

The tower at the arriving airport gave Robert tactical landing instructions, but the new equipment provided erroneous information that he was flying in the wrong direction causing Robert to become momentarily confused and disoriented as to the heading of the plane. Not wanting to distrust his instruments, he turned the plane in the direction that was indicated on

---

[44] For example: much higher altitude, faster speed, and significantly larger numbers of passengers.

[45] He went from being qualified to fly single-engine planes to controlling turbo jets as an engineer. Robert chose this step to see if he would have sufficient mental capability to reach the objective of being able to understand top-level airplane technology.

[46] According to Robert, it is not uncommon for pilots to take a step they may not feel they are fully ready to take.

[47] Robert was interested in challenging himself as a way to break through his concerns in order to accomplish his goals.

[48] Many pilots face this crossroads where they have to choose: fly an airplane at a time or into a place where they would rather not, or risk unemployment.

the faulty equipment because of his trust in instrumentation and lack of awareness that the equipment might be malfunctioning. Then he went into an uncontrolled spiral dive.[49] The instrument giving incorrect directional information caused Robert to be distracted from flying the airplane, and it was during this brief period of distraction that he became unaware that the airplane was gradually getting into a bad situation and if not corrected immediately would deteriorate. Robert noticed the degree to which the airplane was less and less being controlled by him, as it had entered into a low-to-the-ground spiral dive.

Robert reported on how he felt physiologically, describing a condition known as spatial disorientation.[50] Both the visual (eyes) and vestibular (inner ear) systems play a critical role in spatial orientation, assuming good visual cues are available. The primary role of the vestibular system is to enhance vision. It provides angular and linear acceleration information to stabilize the eyes when motion of the head and body would otherwise result in blurred vision. Its secondary role, in the absence of vision, is to provide a sensation of position and motion. However, the vestibular system has evolved for use on the ground, where it is most accurate. Since angular and linear acceleration experienced in flight can be quite different from those experienced on the ground, the vestibular system does not provide a reliable sense of orientation on flight.

The control tower had inquired of Robert why he turned away from the final approach course. This took Robert's attention away from the instruments. The instruments were reflecting the actual situation of the airplane. This was combined with G-forces and a generalized sense of disorientation because Robert expected the instruments to show a familiar scenario of normal, stabilized flight, and instead they were showing what the airplane was really doing. They were reflecting an unusual attitude. At that point, it became very urgent to interpret exactly what all the instruments were saying in conjunction with each other.

There was no additional time to pause and reflect on the problem. The plane was still in cloud cover, so there was no visual reference. Robert knew he was in trouble, but he could not immediately figure out what the problem was.[51] As soon as Robert stopped using his instruments, he was flying blind, gradually losing control of the plane.

Robert reported at this point experiencing sheer terror as sound of the engines was screaming. This, combined with other cues, confirmed that the airplane was descending too rapidly.[52] Proper instrument flying requires that a pilot not rely on just one source of information. This is why instruments are checked and crosschecked against each other almost constantly. This situation is a defining existential moment for Robert. While he thought he was not going to survive the emergency situation, he did not dwell on the terror.[53] He also did

[49] In this situation, the speed of the plane increases rapidly, altitude is lost at an increasing rate, and the g-force is increasing. The spiral dive is the cause of many deaths. A stalled wing situation, unless immediately corrected leads to an uncontrolled spin.

[50] A sensation of dizziness can occur if the pilot moves his head too much during instrument flight. Pilots are also susceptible to spacial disorientation during night flight over featureless terrain or conditions of low visibility.

[51] Robert was distracted by the single instrument seeming to malfunction to the extent that he did not scan and interpret the information from the other instruments. This scenario led to a worsening situation that Robert was unaware of while he focused on the one faulty instrument. The need for Robert to process what he considered to be confusing information from the instruments is similar to his dilemma dealing with all the information he received from the identities exploited by Connie. In both situations, Robert contemplated what inputs he could make to make all this stop happening.

[52] This is referred to in aeronautical terms as exceeding the red line.

[53] Pilots are trained to handle emergency situations. Accordingly, they remain calm.

not pray or think about God or rely on any faith. Robert stated, "I never pray and I never think about God and I never rely on any faith, so it would have been nutty for me to have done that because I'm not accustomed to it. It would not have been a very efficient use of my time, of which I had very little."[54] What he surmised was that he had only a few seconds to determine what corrections to make.

Robert relied on his training and knew he had to first diagnose the problems, then he had to execute a critical recovery effort. He realized he should never trust certain instincts when flying. He refers to those instincts that can be tricked when a person is operating in a three-dimensional environment with loss of visual references. Then he thought to look at a backup instrument dial that depicts the direction the plane)Rs turning.[55] Robert interpreted that the airplane was spiraling and thought to remedy it by pulling back on the power and applying pressure on the rudder opposite to the direction of the turn, which would counteract the rotation of the plane and then he was able to level the wings. This procedure worked and the plane stopped rotating. Some of the instruments could now be interpreted as pointing to normal readings, reflecting accurately what the airplane was doing. The airplane was flying more normally, as was reflected in the instrument indications. However, the plane was still in a fast dive. He was dangerously low to the ground and was able to climb the plane back up to normal altitude.[56] Once back up to an appropriate altitude for the phase of the flight Robert was in, he tried another instrument approach to the runway. The same instrument failure recurred, but he ignored it and was able to land safely.

Robert taxied the plane to the parking area, shut down the engines, and opened the window. He reports that it was suddenly very quiet. It was then that he experienced an existential crisis that he almost crashed and died. He was unable to move his trembling legs and he felt numb. This was the equivalent of paralysis from shock. He kept thinking that he made the wrong decision to fly the plane given the weather and his lack of experience. If Robert had more experience, a failed instrument would likely not have had the same impact. Robert realized at this moment that he had the capacity to use poor judgment, which clashed with his objective to become an expert pilot. This was a humbling moment for Robert. At the time of the event, Robert did not consider that he had the presence of mind and piloting skill to pull the plane out of a precarious situation. When Robert spoke to ground personnel, his voice was quivering and he could not get out of the plane. He sat there immobile for 20 minutes.

Robert thought of the phrase: "If you fall off a horse, get right back on." He knew he had to make a decision before he left the airport whether he should be pursuing a career as a professional pilot. He got out of the plane and his legs felt like rubber. His confidence about being in unfamiliar airplanes he was inexperienced with was shattered. He also knew that the way to rebuild his confidence was by going back to flying single-engine planes and improving his skills. When Robert saw the owner of the plane, it was obvious Robert was in a place he did not belong. He was amicably released by the owner of the plane with some friendly advice to continue developing advanced flying skills and not to give up. Further, Robert was told to go out and get the experience that he needed, then to reapply for the job.

---

[54] Robert considers himself to be an atheist.

[55] This instrument is the turn and bank indicator.

[56] At this moment, had Robert reacted by pulling the plane up too steeply, it might have stressed the plane, resulting in severe damage.

Robert was age 25 when this event occurred. At the time, he did not think the plane was damaged due to the added stress on it during the spiral dive. Had it occurred after Robert gained more experience, however, he says he would have written it up as an incident just in case there was some damage to the plane, even to his own detriment.

Robert's description of the event provides additional insight into his mental abilities and his capacity to cope under pressure: "The terror was compartmentalized in my brain, X amount of brain cells were assigned the task of being terrorized and they were doing a good job, but it was an isolated area of my brain. The rest of my brain was being used to try to get out of this problem. The terror was in me, but it did not overwhelm me. I didn't freeze up." Robert knew that he had to act decisively and correctly and resume control of the airplane. Failure to do so would mean the aircraft would become even more out of control and even harder, if not impossible, to recover. He had only a few scant moments to turn the situation around. While he was trying to solve the problems, he was concerned about where he might crash and was filled with dread at the thought of coming down in a populated area. Thus, the terror did not interfere with the job he knew he had to do, an aspect of mental discipline.

During the few seconds Robert had available to diagnose and correct the problems, he reported feeling a rush of adrenaline and that he became hyper-vigilant. When he was finally on the ground, he remembered before he took the flight that the amount of critical thinking and aeronautical skill needed exceeded his level of experience. He chose to not listen to his inner voice. However, the fact that he took the flight disturbed him, but he respected the great learning experience. He dismissed the notion that his efforts were deserving of any form of commendation because he blamed himself for misjudgment. Robert learned from this experience and never took a flight again on an aircraft that he felt he could not handle or was unsafe to fly, learning to respect the limitations of both the craft and the operator. Thus, Robert experienced defining moments in his life, which have impacted on his manner of handling other emergencies in his life.

Robert soon thereafter decided to take a job flying smaller, single-engine airplanes and built up his confidence through the routine of flying frequently even in poor weather to hone his instrument flying skills. He managed to work his way through a number of smaller airlines, as co-pilot on some, as captain on others, and at age 32 he reached the pinnacle of his career by being hired as a pilot for a major airline. Robert was a highly qualified first officer and flew 727s and other types of jet planes domestically for 15 years with a perfect flight record.[57]

Robert almost immediately went back to flying simpler single-engine planes. He became very comfortable flying, even in clouds and poor weather. When he had the option of flying above the clouds, Robert would intentionally fly in the layer of clouds just to sharpen his skills flying on instruments.

Several months after the near-crash incident, Robert felt he became a smarter pilot, especially when dealing with instrument flying conditions. Robert experienced a second existential moment while flying, this time a positive one.

On a 90-minute flight, Robert was climbing out of clouds and saw the sunlight again. He felt completely rejuvenated in terms of trusting his judgment for flying. Robert stated that it

[57] He was moving up in seniority and likely would have been elevated to the level of captain at his last place of employment within a few years.

was then that he knew he would be alright in flying.[58] In this regard, flying provides a freedom like that experienced by birds. When you are not in a crisis, it feels great.

In mid-August 2005, Robert took his young nephew, then age 12, to an airfield to take his first ride in a glider plane.[59] This was the same airfield where Robert had his first lessons in gliders 35 years before. At the airfield, while Robert's nephew was getting ready for the flight, Robert reported that he felt that the "FBI slammed the bar down" on him. He felt that he had less than full freedom, which caused him to feel a loss of sense of security. Accordingly, he feels that life for him is very restricted.[60]

Over the next several years, he continued to work for several different commuter airlines, some of which went out of business. In 1984, a medium-sized airline hired Robert to fly air cargo on Being 727s as a co-pilot. Robert stayed in this job approximately 2 years. Following that job, Robert moved up to a major airline and was hired as a first officer. When this airline merged with another major airline, he flew the Boeing 737 and various models of turbo jet commercial airplanes for them. In 1994, he moved to Philadelphia. Shortly after this relocation, the events that led to Robert's victimization began.

Robert casually dated since he moved around the country due to his career. At age 40, he was living alone with no nearby family and no immediate prospects, yet he thought it was time to settle down. As he began to become comfortable with his status in life, he thought he would remain in Philadelphia. Robert bought a computer and soon was using the Internet. He was desirous of meeting some new friends and finding women to date. Robert lived a very satisfying and structured life due to his flight schedule. He had a personal policy of not dating crewmembers and wanted to concentrate on building his career and to become relatively affluent before looking seriously for a potential marriage partner. As a result, Robert was determined to continue his success.

Robert went into a chat room, the purpose of which is to draw people living in Philadelphia together. Robert observed the dialogue between the participants, but did not contribute. He was shocked at the tone and level of the conversations, feeling disappointed with the extensive use of sexual innuendo. Robert soon left the chat room.

Shortly thereafter, he received an Instant Message from a woman who said her name was Connie. Robert believes that initially she contacted him with the sole purpose to find someone new to infiltrate his or her life and to victimize. They shared Instant Messages and exchanged telephone numbers. After a few telephone calls, Robert formed an impression that she was acting amorous towards him.

Robert ultimately determined that Connie selected him as someone whom she determined would protect her from a concocted environment of threats and harm. After a year of mental manipulation on her part, she got Robert to allow her to move temporarily into his home. He stated that Connie was forced by others (in retrospect, herself) to move in with him, even though it did not appear as if it was forced.

At the time, Robert believed that Connie's old boyfriend, Max, wrote him letters to gain Robert's cooperation. Connie exploited Max's identity by sending Robert messages allegedly

---

[58] This revelation can be seen as an existential moment of psychological healing.

[59] This is the same nephew who was threatened by the cyber identity set up by Connie when the boy was age 4. Ironically, Robert's actions to protect his nephew from harm were a component in the events that led to the suspension of his license to fly.

[60] In a way, he felt conditioned to live a limited life, the same as if he were behind an electric fence or like an immigrant that does not speak English and does not feel welcome, thus isolated from the mainstream.

from Max, but they were really from her. Before he died, Max was an actual state trooper and reportedly had a long-term extramarital affair with Connie.[61] Connie made it seem that Max was a federal investigator, leading a team of agents who were working on government cases.

By this time in their relationship, Robert had received numerous communications from identities via e-mail created by Connie, but which appeared genuine. He was told by Connie that she was being used without her full consent over 20 years ago and that the government had control over her life. Connie reported her side of the story to the forensic psychologist who evaluated Robert, pursuant to an FAA order. She admitted to the first psychologist that they met on the Internet and that they chatted in this forum for several weeks before she called him on the telephone. Robert maintains that he spoke with Connie on the first night of their immediate contact. She reported that communication in this manner lasted from May 1995 to August 1995. She stated that she finally agreed at the end of August to meet Robert at a hotel in Pittsburgh. Robert says that he was forced into meeting her through statements made by Max.

May 1995, was the time of initial contact. In July 1995, Robert started suspecting that a scam of some sort was taking place. He saved all the e-mail he could in case he needed it at some future point. Because he was concerned, he stored approximately 2,000 pages of material, spanning 9 months of time, in suitcases placed in a closet. He later discovered that much of this documentation was missing. He confronted Connie, who denied taking any of Robert's papers. He eventually received e-mail from the identity known as Max, an alleged corrupt state trooper, who told Robert that the records were taken for his own protection.

In October 1995, Connie drove from her hometown in Dubois, Pennsylvania, to Philadelphia to spend 2 weeks with Robert. She moved in with him in June 1996 after successfully convincing Robert that she needed his protection.[62] The arrangement was non-sexual, though Robert cited a few instances where Connie used a charade of hysteria or suicidal ideation as a way of manipulating Robert to agree to participate in sexual activity. Robert reported no desire to have a consensual sexual relationship with Connie, but reluctantly complied on a few occasions out of fear and intimidation.[63] He was not attracted to her. He only wanted to help her, but as the situation became increasingly threatening for him, he felt he needed to find out what was going on and also wanted to protect Connie.

It seems Connie agreed to meet with the psychologist because she must have thought she could easily fool him. Connie reported to the psychologist that the love of her life was her old boyfriend, Max, whom she had met when she was 17 years old. At that time, Max was in his 30s, married, and a Pennsylvania state trooper. She had an affair with him and felt Max remained an important part of her life. Connie further stated that Max interfered with her other relationships. She said she was engaged to a physician, but Max stopped it. Though untrue, she told the first psychologist that Max had contacted Robert and talked with him about her on numerous occasions. Connie was of the opinion that Robert was obsessed with Max and that he felt intimidated by Max because Max has always been involved in her life. Her lying, diagnosed as psychopathic, was believed by the psychologist despite Robert's

[61] A private detective hired by Robert located the actual state trooper, Max, and asked him about Connie. Max admitted knowing her. When Max was shown some of the e-mail messages allegedly sent by him, he laughed and said to the detective, "Is that what she is doing?" No evidence has been found linking Max to the scheme against Robert.

[62] They slept in separate bedrooms.

[63] Further on in this discussion, the speculation of male rape will be raised.

portrayal of the situation, buttressed by Robert's explanations and a substantial package of corroborating documentation. Robert's parents were also interviewed by the psychologist. They reportedly supported Robert's statements.

Robert had developed several working theories by August 1996: that he was being harassed by corrupt law enforcement officers; that he was being harassed by computer hackers who were impersonating law enforcement officers; or that he was being harassed by members of organized crime, or hackers who were impersonating members of organized crime. The possibility that organized crime could be behind the scam frightened Robert. He did consider that Connie might be behind the scam and was always looking for clues to prove it. Apparently, Connie was able to manipulate Robert into thinking that she was an even bigger victim of the circumstances than he was.

By September 1996, Robert calculated that a large amount of money had been stolen from his accounts. Robert later learned that Connie sent items purchased with his money or from credit taken out in his name and that the items were stored in the basement prior to shipment. Upon investigation, he learned that Federal Express picked up packages from his apartment when Robert was out of town. These packages were sent by Connie to her daughter.

Robert's parents pretended to befriend Connie only as a way to flush out the truth from her. They tried to work together to see if they could catch any inconsistencies or lies.

Some of the e-mail messages were quite lengthy and went into elaborate detail about how Robert has been used to keep Connie as part of the investigation. His mind seems to have been occupied with many new thoughts related to Connie's role in what he was beginning to realize could be an actual undercover governmental investigation into organized crime. Robert deemed all threats he received to be genuine.

An incident involving cigarette burns around Connie's vagina was later confessed to have been self-inflicted "to divert Robert's attention off her as a possible suspect, and to see her more as a victim, as she had always maintained" Robert's e-mail (1998, p. 363). While Connie was in jail following one of her arrests, she was confronted by a detective who Robert hired. The detective asked Connie about the burns on her vagina. Connie told the detective, "Demonstrations like that were effective in controlling Bob and keeping him off guard and confused about what was really going on" (p. 363). It was during one of these meetings that Connie wrote the handwritten confession to the FBI about her creation of the scheme against Robert:

> I [Connie] was called by one of your agents on or about May 1997 – to question and answer about Robert _______ who had come to your office to complain of threatening e-mail he received, apparently by someone who worked for the FBI. – I would like to at this time admit that the e-mail was sent by me, more as a joke to Robert ________ - and it was deemed by the FAA that he was psychotic. [Robert] was in fact reading real e-mail and threats that I had personally sent him under false names. [Robert] is not psychotic – he is as sane as you are. Please take into consideration contacting the FAA and re-evaluating [Robert]. He had nothing to do with this. I was responsible for making him believe I was in danger. I have made this statement on my own free will without any threats or promises.

[Connie] signed in jail. This statement was witnessed by a private detective and a Pennsylvania constable (p. 369).

Connie's confession was forwarded to the FBI, but the FBI apparently ignored it. Robert made an effort to convince the FBI to consider this evidence as well as the documents he found about Connie's prior criminal history. The FBI took the position that it is the responsibility of the Federal Aviation Administration to deal with Robert. This dilemma has never been resolved. During the course of their interaction, Robert considered the possibility that others were manipulating Connie and that they would not let him walk away from the situation for fear they would harm her or him. Robert was not sure at the time, but guessed they were somehow connected with Max and possibly involved with the government. All of the communications were through electronic means. He stated that he had printed hundreds of the early e-mail messages, but many were taken by someone. He was able to save a small portion of the eventually massive printed e-mail archive, which demonstrates that the person who sent the e-mail was threatening Robert and trying to explain why it was important that Connie stay in Robert's home.[64]

One such e-mail read, "One reason we wanted her with you, Bob, because after she had started to know you and you appeared to handle the McCallum thing so well with understanding for her, we knew with everything else that had happened she needed your kind of personality, you were the type of person that would do her good. We didn't know we were going to have to fuck you over at that time" (p. 201). The reference to McCallum is David McCallum, the actor, who played a character in the television show: *Man From U.N.C.L.E.* It was later learned that Connie was obsessed with this actor and used his persona as a cyber-identity in the beginning of the elaborate scheme.

E-mail dated May 12, 1997, reads, "We are who we are; we work for the U.S. government. I am and have been for 16 years, a CIA agent, before that I was a cop, a damn good cop, with top rankings in New York State. So you ask: how can he be a racist cop or a Fed and get away with it, the answer is because he's Max, because he was always allowed and he wanted to" (p. 431). The level of intimidation escalated to the point of direct death threats against Robert and his family.

The e-mail (unedited for the many typographical errors) also discussed Gregg Maddux, at the time an Atlanta Braves pitcher. "Gregg is not the nice mister baseball he wants us to believe. He's a cold-blooded killer who has and I'm sure will do it again to benefit his 'family' and himself" (p. 434). The forensic psychologist who evaluated Robert wrote in his report, concerning these e-mail messages, "The purpose of quoting from the e-mail that [Robert] gave the evaluator is to make two points: one, either [Robert] is so psychotic and paranoid that he wrote these letters to himself to substantiate his delusions; or two, someone else wrote them to threaten or dupe him" (Robert's taped telephone calls, 1997, p. 4).

Robert's mother and father reported that they both saw the e-mail and even saw them on the computer. In a taped telephone call between Robert and the first psychologist, Robert asked him why he believed Connie. He said, "Why shouldn't I believe her?" The psychologist further stated that he understood everything Robert told him was true, although he reiterated that he would not agree to amend his report. Robert attempted to convince the psychologist to correct the conclusions in his evaluation of Robert because they were based on incomplete and inaccurate information. These efforts have failed, despite the large amount of

[64] Robert and his parents even spent an entire weekend taping together bags of shredded printed e-mail correspondence between Robert, Connie, and the cyber identities. They are contained in three binders and comprise 529 pages.

supplemental documentation that was sent to the psychologist. One such document was a Peer Review Forensic Report done by another psychologist, which cited major flaws in technical procedures, challenged the first psychologist's conclusions, and impeached his ethics.

After living with this pressure for 2 years, Robert finally went to the FBI in New York City to report that he had been harassed. The agent told Robert that his report needed to contain serious charges otherwise they would ignore him. Robert then chose to report that someone had threatened to harm Connie even though he was reluctant to sound so extreme. It is not unusual that he chose the FBI, given that his pilot's license and work performance was monitored by another governmental agency and he trusted the government. Robert reported that Connie called him, hysterically, while he was out of town working. Connie also called Robert's mother numerous times in a hysterical manner citing her fears over what might happen to Robert's family. Connie told Robert that while she was out running, two men had been following her to a marina in Philadelphia and threatened her. She stated that she jumped in the marina to separate herself from the two men.

The FBI agents who met with Robert did not believe his story was credible, though they led Robert to believe otherwise. After a very superficial investigation, they informed the FAA that Robert reported a false crime, which started the process of Robert's loss of his license to fly.[65]

Robert had also confirmed that his personal financial accounts had been accessed and his savings were being depleted. He produced several credit card statements for the first psychologist that showed he owed collectively over $25,000. He stated that he did not remember ever having these credit cards, ever seeing the charge slips, or ever seeing the past due notices until the time he received the statements.[66] He believed at the time that these events were connected and meant to control or harass him. After exhaustive efforts, taking years, Robert was able to prove the facts he gathered to many banks that a predator used his identity and that she stole these monies. Ultimately, Robert was relieved of obligations to pay these balances. These letters of vindication served Robert well in his efforts to try to convince others that his report was credible. Upon Robert's review of this text in the form of the principal investigator's dissertation, he expressed his opinion that the first psychologist was motivated to find ways to structure his report so as to support the FBI's concerns.

The first forensic psychologist considered the implications of the river incident with Connie, who told him what had happened, in a similar manner as Robert reported it, except that she did not jump into the river but ran back home to get away from the two men. The first psychologist, in his report,[67] mentioned, "Interestingly, [Connie] did add that she was not wet from the river, but she was 'wet from fear.' This is rather an unusual statement as it almost acknowledges Robert's version of the event" (p. 6). Although Connie told the first psychologist that she was not being harassed or terrorized by anyone, approximately 2 weeks after the conclusion of the psychological evaluation, Connie contacted his office and said that

[65] The United States Constitution provides that each of us will be judged by our peers, but not in the case of a victim falsely accused of making things up. When we put the victim on trial, we ignore civil liberties.

[66] This lack of recollection is because the statements and receipts were hidden from him. This should not be associated with the syndrome of dissociative psychogenic fugue, an inorganic disorder.

[67] This forensic psychological report was sent directly to the airline pilot's association, which convinced the union that Robert was having psychological problems. This misinterpretation by the airline pilot's association resulted in the permanent loss of Robert's career as they chose not to help him.

her life was in danger and that others were threatening her. It is believed that this frantic call was done to continue to amplify her scheme to convince Robert that she was in danger.

Both Robert's parents were very much aware of the ongoing events and threats Robert was facing. His parents felt at the time that he was under severe stress and was being terrorized by someone. His mother felt that someone was attempting to control him and Connie. She cited a contradiction involving Connie. Connie told her that she did not have a daughter; yet, she mentioned subsequently that her daughter had an operation. It was later learned that Connie had two daughters at that time. Robert's father believed that Robert's money was gone, his job was in jeopardy, and he was living in terror.

Robert decided to move back to New York closer to his family. The first psychologist advised Robert to move away. Robert feels that such a recommendation was absurd and was based on incorrect assessment of his mental functioning. This is an example of the inappropriate overlap of the first psychologist's role where the psychologist made recommendations that were not in accordance with Robert's best interest. He informed Connie that he was doing so and that she would have to leave his apartment, as he was selling it and would be having the utilities cut off. She begged him to stay, but despite her impassioned plea, he left. Connie eventually moved out. After moving out, Connie stole monies from subsequent neighbors and landlords. She was able to obtain a government-subsidized apartment. Robert eventually moved to a cooperative apartment in Queens. At this point, Robert began his own investigation of Connie and became a defensive stalker through hiring a private detective and attorneys.

After learning, in 2004, of his father's progressive kidney disease, Robert volunteered to donate a kidney to him. In order to qualify as a donor, Robert was required to undergo extensive medical and psychological testing as well as lose weight and commence a strenuous fitness program. Robert feared that the false psychological reports about him might disqualify him as a donor. He was committed to being the donor and was cleared by the transplant team, including a psychiatrist. The surgery took place in December 2004 and was completely successful. In doing this, Robert faced an existential challenge of risking his life, compromising his future health, and saving his father from the need for frequent dialysis for the expected certainty of kidney failure. Thus, Robert bravely faced his own mortality to help his father.

Robert has successfully sued his former treating psychologist, against whom Robert claimed maltreatment and abuse.[68] He received a modest sum and his legal case took 3 years to finally settle prior to trial. The winning of the settlement represented to Robert a form of vindication.

There are additional avenues being considered by Robert. He is planning on seeking assistance from his pilot's union and may be filing a request for assistance with the American Civil Liberties Union, as he has been building a case that his civil rights were violated based on the improper and misleading way his complaint was handled by the FBI.

Very recently, Robert has shown signs of willingness to explore new career options. He has told the principal investigator that once each possible action reaches a point of closure, he will feel more open to moving forward with his life.

Robert continues to seek opportunities to rescue others. Once he learned of his father's deteriorated kidney function and what life would be like for him on permanent dialysis, he

[68] Supreme Court of the State of New York.

persuaded his resistant father to accept a transplant. Robert has told the principal investigator that he is extremely happy to be the donor, yet accepts no commendation for the noble gift of life. This is reflective of the earlier mentioned incident of robbery intervention, where he opted not to attend the police department's award ceremony.

Robert's newest reported dream (October 2005) occurred shortly after his relocation into a house he purchased. He dreamt that his car had a ticket attached to it for leaving his door partially open. When he reported the dream to the researcher, he stated that receiving a ticket for such an event is absurd.[69] Yet, in the dream he felt that being summoned for this was unfair and that the government was just out to get him. He linked the ticket to his previous sensation of hopelessness. Because of Robert's history of frustration fighting the government, he felt it would be futile to argue the merit of the ticket in court, whereas his former self would surely have gone to battle over the injustice.

Another serious consequence of Robert's victimization is that because his disability benefits enable him to sustain his existence without seeking reemployment, he feels entitled to collect disability benefits while he continues his case investigation and quest for vindication. Also, Robert feels limited in his available choices for a new career. It seems at least reasonably possible that his behavior has been influenced by the abusive legal system in that he is taking full advantage of a generous employee benefit plan by fulfilling the criteria of PTSD. Yet, the PTSD label has become a convenient place for him to survive economically so he can continue his mission under the financial shelter of his disability income. It is likely that he feels entitled to receive this income given his self-perception of what has happened to him.

His case investigation into the ongoing fraudulent activities of Connie against new victims has included monitoring her Internet activities. He was able to do so by successfully guessing her pass-codes and figuring out technically how to review her electronic communications without her knowledge. The data gleaned from this surreptitious action has led to the discovery of felonious activity perpetrated by Connie against an elderly man. Robert has turned over this data to the police and feels even if they question how he was able to obtain the data, he would openly admit to his method as long as they prosecute her for the obvious crimes and potentially save the elderly man from abuse. This mindset points to a jaded view Robert has of the law. While he plays the role of vigilante, he not only exposes himself to possible prosecution, but may even taint any evidence obtained in such a manner. This activity no longer continues, as Robert has lost access to Connie's online account and he also realizes what he did could be considered wrong, but he feels it was right.[70]

Robert had two new missions in life: one, to develop his life story into a documentary film project, which is ongoing, and, two, to donate a kidney to his ailing father, which has been completed. Recently, Robert has been renovating a newly purchased house, including the addition of a rental apartment. His experience working with construction contractors has led Robert to consider acquiring other houses in need of renovation as a way to embark on a new business. These activities serve to spark some new life in his psyche and may pave the way for future success in life. Regrettably, Robert has recently tempered his former disdain

---

[69] Interestingly, Robert stated that in the dream he felt that not too many of these types of tickets were issued. This is similar to the emergency suspension of his medical certificate (grounding), also a rare event.

[70] Robert no longer is able to do so.

for traditional psychotherapy.[71] It may be possible in the future that he will be open to a nontraditional approach.

Robert agreed to be studied by the principal investigator because he felt that his story should be made known so that others would better understand the destructive potential of predators, especially those suffering from psychopathy. Through his relationship with the principal investigator, Robert has become stronger in his sense of purpose, displaying at least a modicum of optimism. He also consistently steps in and comes to the aid of others, including helping his former girlfriend locate and move to a different apartment.

In terms of the power of faith, Robert is a self-declared atheist. Though born Jewish, he does not practice any form of organized religion and does not recognize the presence of a divine being.[72]

THE PSYCHOLOGICAL EVALUATIONS

In 1997, at the time of his psychological evaluation, Robert acknowledged that the more he told the truth about his story, the less credible he sounded. In the forensic psychologist's report, the evaluator determined that Robert was cooperative and eager to talk about his situation. He maintained good eye contact with the evaluator and was oriented to time, place, and person. His sensorium reflected normal processing of information. He denied any suicidal or homicidal ideation or intent. He denied having auditory or visual hallucinations. His recent and remote memory appeared to be within normal limits. His speech was slow, deliberate, and goal-directed. At times, he appeared tangential and long-winded. He denied having any depressive symptomatology. He did not meet the criteria for an anxiety disorder, but was clearly upset, frightened, and anxious due to the events of the past 2 years.

The first psychologist performed most, but not all, of the tests required by the FAA's Emergency Order of Suspension. Two of the tests he administered, which are cited in his report, are the MMPI-II and the Rorschach Inkblot. The doctor commented that it is unclear whether Robert was malingering by presenting a false claim of mental illness, or he was under a great deal of stress that was causing him confusion or a deterioration of personality. The results of the tests indicated to the first psychologist that Robert was impulsive, self-indulgent, and wanted to be the center of attention, but did not want to accept any responsibility for his actions. The first psychologist feels that Robert tended to withdraw and isolate from others and blamed them for his shortcomings. He saw the world as a very threatening and sinister place. He did not trust others, which allowed him to maintain a distance from them and prevented him from developing close relationships. This in turn allowed him to say he did not fit in with others or others did not like him. When pushed further, he could be manipulative and self-centered, which may cause difficulties for people he is around. In retrospect, Robert feels that the first psychologist's interpretations are wrong and were based on a biased viewpoint because it is clear from the evidence that the first psychologist formed his view based on his own misdiagnosis, not believing that Robert had been extorted, etc.

---

[71] Robert only attends biweekly sessions with a psychotherapist.

[72] This is a point borne out in the story of his near-crash experience.

The psychologist found considerable evidence of paranoid thinking. For example, on a particular Rorschach Inkblot slide, one of Robert's typical paranoid responses was that the eyes are the predominant part, which drew him to call it a mask.[73]

During the clinical interview, the psychologist mentioned that Robert tried outwardly to present as a friendly individual; however, behind this façade he tended to be aloof and unapproachable. The report stated that in the clinical interview his paranoid thinking was very evident throughout his recounting of his life story. It is quite likely that he had the diagnosis of paranoid personality disorder and did not meet the criteria for either psychosis or paranoid schizophrenia. Yet, the first psychologist then cited that it was difficult to determine whether he was truly imagining and concocting these delusions, or someone else (maybe the author of the e-mail) was trying to get him to believe he was being harassed and threatened and to have others believe he was paranoid. He goes on to state tritely, paraphrasing an old saying, just because someone was paranoid does not mean someone else was not trying to get them.

A second psychologist was retained by Robert to evaluate the situation and come to his own independent conclusions. Accordingly, he performed a Peer Review of the work of the first psychologist and found that the first psychologist failed to administer the Wechsler Adult Intelligence Scale (WAIS), as required by written FAA guidelines, and he did not follow standardized procedures for the administration, scoring, and interpretation of the Rorschach Inkblot test, thus violating the basic professional requirements for the use of these psychological tests. The counterpoint is that such requirements may be too rigid to apply these rules to projective tests.

Additional information was supplied to the first psychologist. However, this information, though it fully corroborated Robert's report, was ignored. In doing so, the first psychologist failed to meet the ethical guidelines as promulgated by the American Psychological Association for Forensic Psychologists. He failed to make reasonable efforts to resolve contradictory information provided by collateral sources. He did not use established procedures to evaluate the reliability and validity of information contributed by collateral sources. He failed to conduct an organized clinical interview.

Upon learning of the arrest and criminal conviction of Connie, based on Robert's original claims, he refused to correct and withdraw his evaluation, which was obviously flawed. Because his conclusions heavily relied on information presented by Connie, he had an ethical responsibility to change his report.[74] Failure to administer the WAIS renders the report incomplete in relation to the requirements mandated by the Federal Aviation Administration.

In regard to physical and mental health as well as professional performance and competence, airline pilots are among the most frequently tested and monitored professionals in the world. The typical pilot is subjected to a rigorous and thorough screening and evaluation by airlines prior to employment. This includes psychological testing and performance evaluation. The battery typically includes the MMPI-II as well as testing for memory, judgment, and problem-solving ability.

After being hired, airline pilots are subject to at least an annual medical certification. In these examinations, airline pilots are evaluated on broad mental standards that might affect their performance capabilities. Also, pilots routinely undergo checks during flights, by other

---

[73] The report did not mention which inkblot was presented.

[74] Amendment of forensic psychological reports is required under the ethics rules in cases where subsequent information or facts become known to the psychologist.

pilots, to assess their performance. In Robert's case, he last underwent a complete physical and mental examination two months before he reported the situation to the FBI, and he was found to be physically and mentally fit.

Having been placed on total disability, Robert was required to have psychotherapy in order to maintain his benefits. The therapist who treated Robert for several years determined that Robert's reported story was credible. He also found that the first psychologist's findings on Robert's mental functioning were inaccurate, but that Robert was suffering from trauma caused by the actions of the government and the misdiagnosis of the first psychologist. Robert terminated treatment after realizing that this psychologist was mistreating him and that he was also under investigation by the FBI for Medicare fraud.[75]

When Robert first saw the psychologist for treatment, he was assured the psychologist understood what had happened to Robert and that he could help Robert. The psychologist immediately brought Robert's parents into treatment sessions under the guise of family therapy. It was later learned that this was due solely to provide an opportunity for the psychologist to bill the Medicare accounts of both Robert's parents for Robert's treatment. A summary of the invoices issued by the psychologist reveal that Robert was double billed on a number of occasions and billed for sessions that never took place on other occasions.

The psychologist's conduct during Robert's treatment sessions was entirely unprofessional. While in session with Robert, the psychologist often made and took telephone calls with other patients; sessions were held in a car while the psychologist ran errands; the psychologist passed out during a session, speculatively, while under the influence of medication; the psychologist changed clothes in front of Robert and did stretching exercises; the psychologist improperly billed Robert's parents' Medicare accounts for Robert's sessions for which he was found guilty of Medicare fraud.[76] Robert continues to seek ways to force or convince the first psychologist to modify his report, though such efforts have not had any positive result.[77]

Robert has already found closure with respect to his successful suit against the unethical psychologist who treated him, as well as a settlement with a disability carrier.[78] Robert is also beginning to investigate new education and potential career choices. His purchase of a small house fulfills one of his life goals.

Currently, Robert attends biweekly therapy sessions with a psychologist. His new therapist diagnosed Robert as having posttraumatic stress disorder (PTSD) related to the impact various actions of the psychopath, the government, and two psychologists had on his life and career. During his biweekly sessions, Robert uses the time to inform the therapist of his ongoing case inquiries and about his life in general. He is in active treatment, though he does so more to maintain his one remaining income stream of long-term disability benefits than to seek deeper awareness of him and others. Without this monthly income, he would be

[75] The psychologist was convicted of a felony and remanded to prison. He also lost his license to practice as a psychologist. In 2003, the State Education Department accepted the psychologist's voluntary surrender of his license.

[76] The case was investigated by the FBI. Over 30 patient files were confiscated and revealed numerous instances of insurance fraud.

[77] Recently, Robert mailed the first psychologist a copy of the Peer Review Forensic Report, which harshly criticized the procedures and findings of his report. Along with this report is a letter asking the first psychologist to reconsider his original report based on the errors that are claimed to have been made and that Robert's story is true according to the principal investigator despite the overwhelming argument that the first psychologist ignored the evidence.

[78] In both cases, Robert received significant recompense.

forced to sell his home and seek employment, likely very much outside the airline industry. Because his skills enabled Robert to perform a particular task, namely, to operate aircraft, it has been difficult for him to become motivated to start a new career where there will likely be limited transferability of his training.

Robert had a very low opinion of the potential efficacy of psychotherapy as it related to his problems referred to in this book. Currently, he has a better feeling about therapy. Further, he does not feel he has any disorder treatable by psychotherapy.

During one of the many interviews conducted by the principal investigator, Robert reported another disturbing dream. Verbatim notes were taken during the interview and were used as the basis for this presentation of how Robert described his dream and his interpretation. In the dream, he heard a dog yelping in pain. As he is the owner of a miniature Italian Greyhound, this was very meaningful to Robert. However, in the dream, he also acquired a new younger dog of the same breed. He ran into the room where the older dog was, secretly wishing that the dog in pain were the second dog, as he loves his first dog. He approached the dog and saw immediately that it was, in fact, Kali, his first dog. A scary-looking black bird with a long piercing beak was attacking the dog, tearing large pieces of flesh from its body. The bird was a strange combination of crow and crane, nothing he has seen before in his conscious life. He determined that the injuries sustained at this point by Kali would very likely lead to soon death. Robert further thought that perhaps it was better for Kali to allow the dog to be finished off quickly rather than face long-term pain and doubtful recovery. Robert went into a different room and contemplated the terrible situation. Almost immediately he ran in, distracted the bird, picked up Kali, and ran down the street toward the animal hospital. While running, Kali expired.

Chapter 6

RESEARCH FINDINGS AND THE EXISTENTIAL ANALYSIS

The research questions have been reframed so they can be explained through the existential perspective. Seven criteria have been chosen for this purpose: (1) the interior life world of the person (*eigenwelt*); (2) self-actualization needs versus adjustment to social norms; (3) being in the face of non-being; (4) meaning through suffering; (5) attitudes toward death and annihilation; (6) dreams, visions, and mythic experience; and (7) existential use of the void. These criteria, as a cx'lective, are summarized starting on page 87.

THE SEVEN CRITERIA

The Interior Life World of the Person (*Eigenwelt*)

> The basic question a person wants to ask and answer is "Who am I?" "What is the meaning of my life?" "What value does it have?" And we can only get answers to these questions by reviewing our relationships to others, what we do to others and for others, and what kind of response we get from them. (Becker, 1971, p. 70)

Robert reports that he was a different person before and after he became a victim. His internal view of himself was very confident and quite proud of all that he accomplished becoming a pilot. He liked to wear his uniform, proudly displaying his three stripes, indicative of his level of first officer.[79]

When the criminal events occurred in his life, Robert's entire sense of himself changed. He became severely self-conscious of negative things happening to him. Once he lost his pilot's license, Robert began to experience problems, such as people being rude to him. His self-respect was compromised due to his feeling that he was no longer being treated by others with the same level of respect he had known as a pilot. Robert's concern was that his mental state was cast in doubt and he was seen by others with suspicion.

Absent deeper analysis, Robert's belief in the ruses created by Connie subjects him to suspicion of having a delusion. However, when evaluated in context of the entire elaborate

---

[79] The next level (captain) includes a fourth stripe, worn on the jacket sleeves.

fraud, the case history demonstrates how Robert's belief system was manipulated. The research of psychopathy (see, for example, Hare, 1998) and use of identity theft by the psychopathic personality (see, for example, Lucks, 2001; Patterson, 1993) reflects the manipulative techniques. Speculatively, Robert's high reliance and trust of instruments may have contributed to his faith that information coming through his computer (an instrument) might be genuine.[80]

Robert questioned his sense of self-worth. Man's sense of self-worth is constituted symbolically; his cherished narcissism feeds on symbols, on an abstract idea of his worth, an idea composed of sounds, words, and images, in the air, in the mind, on paper. Representations of ourselves are comprised of wealth and power (Becker, 1971). Because Robert feels defeated, he toils in the thought that something has been taken from him. He speaks of what would have been. Robert's dilemma is his notion of the life he lost versus the life he still has and can still have in the future, thus, the tragedy of the vulnerable victim.

Self-Actualization Need Versus Adjustment to Social Norms

The existential perspective claims that despite the apparent pathology of the pilot, he is working towards a healthier existential end than just adjustment to a sick society. A sociological perspective holds that there is an immense range of social or semisocial causations that invite human planning and integration. The bulk of visible and seizable criminality—at least 80% of it—is predominantly society-made (Von Hentig, 1948). Thus, any attempt to control crime and recidivism may require the reshaping of the environment.

Whereas the sociologist views crime as a complex phenomenon due to the variability of human beings, the psychiatrist and criminal anthropologist tend to limit their interest in crime to the innate traits and tendencies of the perpetrator of a crime. Social forces remain underestimated among psychiatrists and anthropologists. These social forces test the resistance of the physical and mental constitution.

Before Robert was targeted by Connie, he was enjoying a thriving career and all the benefits associated with it. His curiosity and being new in town, in part, led to his departure from his normal pattern of existence.

Societal influences would suggest that Robert should have abandoned Connie very soon after seeing how bizarre the situation was becoming. Robert did try to abandon her, but he found that for the first time in his life he was unable to do so. This influence is reflected in Ugolini and Kelly's (2001) statement that prevention is the most effective way to manage stalking cases. To apply this concept, it is necessary to recognize that it is a case of stalking. Gross (2000) found that victims are sometimes unwilling to impose limits for fear of hurting or disappointing someone. However, his willingness to subject himself to harm through exploitation might speak to his internal rebellion against the societal norm or it could indicate that he might have overlooked some facts. Robert genuinely wanted to help Connie and tried to do so, which led to his own peril. Through his suffering, he became even more tragic, having assumed the role of defensive stalker, mimicking Connie in many ways. Yet, in doing so, Robert is fulfilling his quest for redemption.

---

[80] The principal investigator discussed this speculation with Robert who does not agree with the possible connection.

Robert now is fully aware of many elements of the scheme perpetrated against him. While he has been frustrated in his attempts to gain vindication by the FBI, his investigation into the life of the predator has resulted in her incarceration. Following Connie's escape from a correctional facility, Robert was notified by the probation department. He devoted several months of intense effort and eventually tracked down her location via research on the Internet and through telephone calls. He notified the local police, who arrested her. She was re-sentenced for the escape. Later, Robert was able to access Connie's Internet account, where he discovered that she was committing identity theft against an elderly man. Robert forwarded this information to the authorities, who issued a search warrant for her apartment and confiscated her computer. Connie was never prosecuted for these crimes due to the dementia of the elderly man who she carefully chose due to his weakened condition. Robert also forwarded evidence of Connie's violations of parole to the authorities, which led to her re-incarceration for 6 months.

Robert is attempting to gain closure and healing, which could lead him towards self-actualization. During the many interviews of Robert, he has routinely expressed his strong desire to move past the feeling of being the victim. An example of his manner of expressing this desire is when he talks about finding a way to restore his identity, which for him would ideally happen after his record at the FBI is corrected.

While Robert's defensive stalking behavior could be viewed as revenge (a lower motive), he has said that this behavior was necessary so as to discover more facts about Connie and what she was doing. There is an important and practical reason for Robert's desire to understand more about Connie's activities. Connie owes Robert almost $100,000 based on a civil judgment and interest. Connie may accrue money one day, either by working, receipt of an inheritance, or winning a lottery. The law allows Robert to request seizure of Connie's assets. The only way he would know if she accumulates assets is to periodically look at her life. Thus, Robert's conduct can be viewed through a more understanding lens as depicting a normal person seeking to recover from harm done to him.

Robert's objective in reporting her subsequent criminal activity to the police was to hopefully lead to her further admission of culpability for crimes committed against him. Robert also has expressed continued fear that Connie might still attempt to harm him, which added to his desire to investigate her.

Perhaps only those who have experienced inappropriate loss of their career could comprehend the need to do what Robert is doing. Thus, Robert has not given in to societal demands that he simply moves on with his life and accept that he was victimized. His courageous fight speaks of his need to self-actualize his way.

Robert's eventual discovery of Connie as the mastermind behind the scheme led to his realization that he could be victimized and that his behavior and life choices contributed to his vulnerability. McClurkin (2001) also found that individuals wû6 seem to attract this kind of abuse often suffer frequent victimization. This phenomenon is supported by the work of Drapkin and Viano (1975), who noted that following victimization, a loss of faith in the justice system with correlated alienation may further the experience of victimization. A reactive behavior of Robert as investigator is his way of searching for vindication even though it could be viewed by some as stalking and others, including the principal investigator, as normal. Robert's activities have been limited to non-physical investigation, using Internet resources and other legal means to gather information

Now that Robert understands more about what Connie did and how he responded to her pretenses, he has been going through a long process of self-evaluation of his trusting personality and has become more guarded. He can be said to be self-actualizing in the sense that he does accept responsibility for being victimized, which will allow him to grow as a person instead of continuing in the role of victim. He does not feel hate towards Connie, which would be a heavy burden for him to carry. His conclusion is to continue his efforts to achieve vindication by the FBI. His awareness of the past and his efforts to accept what he has been suffering are all facets of Robert's journey toward self-actualization.

Recently, Robert had been dating a woman, who he met at a party, for about a month. As soon as they started dating, she informed Robert that she is seeking a husband who would agree to have a child immediately and who will be very motivated to work hard to support their family. Robert has accepted her life plans, although he felt immense pressure from her to develop an immediate plan to secure suitable employment.

They saw a lot of each other and they seemed quite compatible. Robert again faced potential manipulation as he struggled through his issues on an accelerated basis to try to appease her. He spoke of her desires and that she is Type A personality (and a social worker). Robert is not Type A. Robert has even begun to help with her other issues, spending time finding ways to help her deal with them, which is a normal thing for people who are involved to do.

Some new information about the subject is included as a way of illustrating key points about his vulnerability. Interestingly, Robert's newly purchased house had the potential to become the venue for another round of change stimulated by an influential person. What could have worked better in terms of moving their relationship to the next level is if Robert drew from the ego-strength of his new friend. He could have aggressively explored new career options, using fear of loss of her as a motivator. In doing so, she did not become a type of debilitating force. If he could make life decisions on his own accord and felt comfortable with them, he might have been able to settle in to a different lifestyle and resume an active and productive life coupled with a mate, possibly experiencing and accepting the responsibility of parenthood. His case is similar to allowing the woman to assume the lead in a dance but he becomes a great dancer in the process. He may be better able to orchestrate a life plan with the support of an outside and trusted influence.

This new situation provides a very current impression of Robert's vulnerability. His rescuer approach to people, combined with his long-stated desire to date only somewhat younger women mostly because of the possibility of his starting a family, leads to him becoming potentially manipulated into changing his life course very quickly in order to prevent upset or hurt in another person. An important ingredient of this pressure is her telling Robert about her own fear of becoming vulnerable should their relationship progress only to later discover that Robert was either unwilling or unable to move forward with a career plan that meets her approval. Ironically, this left Robert in a position as a vulnerable person to abandon his own concerns about his vulnerability to focus instead on doing all he could to protect her from becoming harmed. This situation presents as a pattern: vulnerable man meets aggressive woman with issues, who also vocalizes fear of victimization, sending the hero in to save the day.

Robert's saving device is his collective conscious of personal experiences of having gone through the morass of rescuing a false victim and being abused by a powerful agency. If he was able to apply his learning to his current situation, he might have figured out that it was possible that two people in a relationship could have very different approaches to solving the same dilemma and that each person must retain sovereignty over his or her own life so as to feel positive about him or herself. From this platform of self-esteem, ideas could have been considered for Robert to use to resolve the paradoxical situation. In this case, Robert can find meaning from his suffering and continue to grow in awareness of his own internal vulnerability. In doing so, his propensity to the rescue approach may yield to a more balanced method of dealing with people, particularly a determined woman facing her own biological clock who is headstrong in finding a suitable life partner. It was she who first announced the impossibility of the relationship. Robert respected her opinion on this matter and agreed with her on many levels. Later, as the friendship continued, Robert saw the wisdom of her foresight and ultimately he was glad she recognized the incompatibility factors so early.

Since his problems began within a poorly perceived relationship with a psychopathic criminal, which destroyed a thriving career, perhaps if he established a more effective method of handling a relationship he may then be able and willing to embark on a new career, thus possibly leading him to meet his need for self-actualization. Additionally, new skills and awareness may help Robert's discernment when he is faced with overwhelming circumstances.

One new, albeit short-lived, idea Robert has for a new career is to approach his former airline and seek a position as a flight dispatcher. He has realistic concerns, however, that his FBI file will harm his chances of moving to that job classification. Robert's concern is valid that his record of suspicion of having psychosis will bar him from any job classification that involves FAA clearance. This reinforces his persistent effort to get the FBI to reopen the case and accept the evidence that is available, which the principal researcher hopes will result in the clearing of his name.

One idea he is considering is asking the pilot's union to help him find a new career within the airline industry. When challenged about his efforts to at least consider other occupations outside of the airline industry, he is quick to decline such consideration because of his concerns over the potential effect of his FBI record. Thus, Robert's prior victimization has left him fully committed to his persistent efforts to clear his name.

His recent relationship, however, may catalyze Robert to resume some command over his life and find new direction suitable to himself, while also working though his issues in terms of responding to his female friend's needs without compromising his own preferences. The relationship ultimately became a basic friendship. Perhaps Robert has been on the sidelines too long and can now go down the runway of life at an accelerating speed.

One month into the relationship, Robert's friend told him that she did not feel he would be able to develop an acceptable plan to form a family with her. She further told him that even if they did stay together and she was unable to conceive naturally, she would want to adopt a child and she would then be concerned that Robert's FBI file might inhibit them from qualifying. So, she changed the nature of the relationship to one of a platonic friendship.

Robert explained this development to his psychotherapist, who offered to Robert an alternative solution that in the event they wanted to pursue adoption, she could apply as a single person, adopt a child, and then Robert could marry her. On hearing this suggestion, Robert reacted quite negatively and reverted to feeling like an outcast. He stated that he felt his therapist should have known that Robert would react negatively to any suggestion regarding working around the system because of Robert's case history. His reaction to the suggestion of the therapist is indicative of Robert's long-held feeling of the role of perpetual victim. Robert viewed it as not only unhelpful, but yet another example of being misunderstood.

Meaning Through Suffering

Frankl (1963) distinguished between finding meaning through suffering versus the actualization of values. To live means to survive; to survive is to find meaning in the suffering. Several experiences of Robert address how he has had the opportunity to find meaning through some pain and trauma.

The event of bullying in Robert's young life is meaningful and demonstrates the formation of a feature of Robert's personality suggesting vulnerability and the ability to suffer for long periods of time before taking action. This reveals some abnormality in that Robert endured the actions of the bully until he evaluated the situation and discovered a way to stop it. Where he could have told his parents or the school authorities, he chose to keep silent. Certainly, in this scenario he had options. He could have informed the school guidance counselor, the principal, or his parents. He chose not to report the bullying to anyone. His action plan involved a certain amount of risk, and he accepted the risk. His feeling after his action was satisfying, yet he was deflated when he did not get the approval of the teacher (a type of vindication). This need is contrasted with his need for vindication by the government for errors they made in handling his complaint. Robert's need for vindication from the government is borne from the fact that the government created this need.

The suffering he endured provided meaning for Robert in that he became very self-reliant. It also served to isolate him from others as he chose to keep his concerns hidden from others who were in a proper place to help. Robert ultimately sought help from the FBI; then from several psychologists. He behaved similarly during the 2 years Connie was harming him. He again chose not to inform his parents, the local police, or co-workers because his parents were threatened.

Schneider (2004) stated that people, having free will, choose their responses. "The degree to which a person or society experiences choice within their particular center, largely determines their extent of discernment, solidity, and depth" (p. 11). Discernment can be negatively impacted if, by example, an individual is "paralyzed by unpredictability," or "to the extent that one is inured to vulnerability, hateful to accommodation, or aghast at limitation" (p. 12).

Schneider (2004) suggested that "there is scant room for soul-searching in our culture; crises are relegated to the "inconvenient" (p. 40). Those suffering or in pain could seek a modern remedy involving drugs or binge therapy, or engaging in self-help. Rather than avoid the notion of suffering, another approach is to "recognize that the capacity to tolerate ambiguity, discord, and strife is one of the hallmarks of maturation and that without such a reserve, there is almost no chance to thrive" (p. 40).

Finding health through trauma—while it is possible to develop strength and hardiness through the experience of trauma, it may also be possible to achieve the equivalency of traumatic illumination by taking advantage of the many opportunities to transform (Schneider, 2004).

"Among prisoners in concentrations camps it has been observed that the accumulation of bad treatment led to a saturation of the guilt feelings and the unleashing of criminal impulses" (Lagache, 1950, p. 18). Often it is the law that decides who shall be considered guilty and who is the victim. Certain courts in Switzerland, in cases involving a precociously perverse child who seduces his seducer, begin by ordering an expert psychiatric examination of the victim (Ellenberger, 1955).

Hanns Gross (1901) wrote about the reflexoid crime, which is committed semiconsciously. The subject feels he or she has to do the act, but does not take time to reflect on it. Thus, some people who acted fully within the bounds of the law previously are capable of committing a reflexoid crime if a particular situation presents itself in an unexpected way. While Gross focused largely on criminal actions, there are also reflexoid acts of a heroic kind. The subject provides the example: He chased a mugger through the streets of Philadelphia, placing himself in danger. He reported to the principal investigator that he did not think about what he was doing; he just had to act. Ellenberger (1955) found that a great many individuals, perhaps all of humanity, are endowed with hidden predispositions and latent capacities that can carry them, according to the circumstances, to fill the role of criminal or victim (p. 266). The potential victim, or latent victim as Von Hentig (1948) refers, exerts a peculiar attraction upon the criminal. These people can also be referred to as born victims.

Von Hentig (1948) referred to the blocked victim, the individual who through accumulation of errors finds himself or herself in a situation so involved that there is no way out. The criminal, however, finds this situation ideal. The recidivist criminals, as Von Hentig suggested, are people who have the curious habit of being deceived or robbed repetitiously and who play always in one way or another the role of victim.

Being in the Face of Non-Being

Courage is the self-affirmation of being in spite of non-being, with faith at the core of this power. Schneider (1999) spoke about a process of fragmentation, leading to a sense of smallness, meaninglessness, and insignificance. This process is caused by the plight of many workers who must follow routines and precise movements and protocols, yet other workers can be seen to be nervous about keeping their jobs.

The routine existence has become increasingly common. Some break out of this routine through adventure. In the case of the pilot, given that the Internet for home use was new in 1995, he decided to keep up with technology and obtain a personal computer and hook up to the Net.

William James (James, 1920) wrote in a letter dated May 6, 1906, to W. Lutoslawski:

> Most people live, whether physically, intellectually or morally, in a very restricted circle of their potential being. They make use of a very small portion of their possible consciousness, and of their soul's resources in general, much like a man who, out of his whole bodily organism, should get into a habit of using and moving only his little finger. Great emergencies and crisis show us how much greater our vital resources are than we had supposed. (p. 253)

Greening (2003) considered four existential challenges in the human condition: life and death, meaning and absurdity, freedom and determinism, and community and aloneness.

Robert's life world changed dramatically following the fraudulent events, the mishandling of his complaint by the FBI, the report of the first psychologist about him, the improper and unethical treatment of Robert by a psychologist, and the insensitive and upper-handed treatment of Robert by an insurance carrier. As Greening (2003) suggested, this "creates a confusing and sometimes chaotic world that offers many meaning systems and also denies meaning" (p. 1).

Robert is constricted in his freedom as this refers to his career. Due to the label of suspected psychosis in is life, Robert feels that any attempt to gain employment in the airline industry will be frustrated because of his record.[81]

Importantly, because Robert receives disability income barely sufficient to cover his living expenses, he is at least, to some degree, compromised in finding alternative employment. This situation results in the principal investigator's conclusion that Robert uses the disability income stream as at least a partial barrier to moving forward with his life. While he may be justified in his quest to clear his name, by continuing to rely exclusively on disability insurance, he mutes any self-effort to reestablish himself in another occupation. Robert justifies his stance through his view that his career was taken away from him, thus he is entitled to rely on the disability income. Further, he has not yet accepted the concept that he will, one day, need to secure a replacement income source. His disability income ceases in about 10 years, but he feels inhibited by the overwhelming obstacles he feels he needs to deal with due to the FBI report, etc.

Robert felt a sense of loneliness in his life. He does go out, spends time with family, and he has a few close friends. He feels alienated from his former pilot peer group. Additionally, he often experiences conflict and a lack of respect with people in everyday life pursuits in situations where people are aware of Robert's history. This rarely occurred when he was a pilot.

Robert responded to the life events that harmed him by embarking on a long, drawn-out mission, one that persists and which seeks vindication. In essence, Robert's quest is to convince the FBI to correct his record, which indicates suspected psychosis.

The recovery of monies from Robert's malpractice suit against his former treating psychologist seemed to bring a sense of vindication to Robert. When Robert first saw the psychologist for treatment, he was assured the psychologist understood what had happened to Robert and that he could help him. The psychologist immediately brought Robert's parents into treatment sessions under the guise of family therapy. It was later learned that this was due solely to provide an opportunity for the psychologist to bill the Medicare accounts of both Robert's parents for Robert's treatment. A summary of the invoices issued by the psychologist reveals that Robert was double billed on a number of occasions. The psychologist also conducted Robert's treatment sessions in an unprofessional manner.

Robert's ongoing efforts to have the first psychologist held accountable are proving frustrating for him. The state board of licensure has agreed to receive new information about alleged ethical violations, but for now has decided not to bring charges against the psychologist. This psychologist currently holds an important position on the state board.

While some of Robert's responses are simplistic, overemphasizing on the negative aspect of the paradox of how to respond to the existential challenges (Greening, 2003), some aspects

---

[81] Robert is considering applying for a job requiring a federal license, and if he is declined due to his FBI record, then he may request the assistance of the ACLU (American Civil Liberties Union).

are more confrontational and creative. An example of how his actions are confrontational is the way Robert investigates Connie's past and current life. Although Robert never physically monitored her, he has monitored Connie's movements for years and found ways to read her e-mail communications over a six-month period in 2002. His explanation as to why he is justified in doing this is that he continues to feel threatened by her. Even Connie's daughters and siblings have all expressed to this researcher how fearful they are of Connie reentering their lives. As a defensive posture, Connie's relatives have put metaphorical walls up, preventing her from reaching them.

Greening (2003) discussed how each of us experiences "pleasure, pain, security and danger, vitality and vulnerability" (p. 2). As a result, people can feel weakened by life events, especially traumatic ones. Robert's responses can fit into Greening's second category, involving resignation. His mood has shown signs of melancholy and utter frustration in dealing with the significance of the challenges he faces. Robert's frozen state: remaining in the vigilance of seeking redemption regardless of time or cost exemplifies his sense of preoccupation with the daunting tasks he faces (i.e., fatalism). Robert can choose not to accept a fatalistic view of life and, instead, work toward building a more effective existence. This would include learning to respond to the actions of others appropriately and with a level of prudent skepticism. Yet, the principal investigator, having evaluated Robert's life history, is of the opinion that Robert should be found justified in vigorously pursuing vindication. Simultaneous with this effort, the principal investigator consistently advises Robert to also seek a new source of income. Robert feels as if he cannot compete in the world due to the false record. He feels like an undocumented worker and perceives unusual obstacles in this regard.

In a very real way, Robert's situation results in the conclusion of vulnerability based on how he responded to Connie in the first instance, then, in how he handled the FBI and the psychologists. Because his career was abruptly ended absent justification, his past and present actions should not be deemed inappropriate, but relentless. Speculatively, only someone who has had their career end in such a devastatingly abrupt manner can really understand what that actually feels like. This research reveals the history of Robert's life events in a way that demonstrates how he responded to crime and injustice.

"From the victim's perspective, the sentence should serve as an appropriate, public expression of his resentment and associated condemnation of the wrongdoer. It can and should communicate in a strong way his demand for at least a minimum degree of respect" (Whiteley, 1998, p. 44). The victim's reaction to the sentencing of the wrongdoer often involves resentment, which is a moral sentiment. "Resentment has, in addition, an affective component. It arouses in the victim desires or feelings directed at the wrongdoer. Those desires motivate the victim to act in ways characteristic of the emotion" (p. 46).

Robert's response to the challenge of meaning and absurdity reveal some degree of despair and meaninglessness in terms of how he views psychologists and the legal system. He has become quite ridiculing of law enforcement.[82] His reactive choice is to become active and also to state how there is some dysfunction in certain systems in society.

Greening (2003) pointed out, "No one has exactly the same existence that I do, and, therefore, cannot fully share my experience" (p. 4). Thus, the explaining of a person's life

[82] Recent data from the ongoing investigation and research shows that often when victims or witnesses file complaints with law enforcement, little is actually done and sometimes the reporters are criticized.

history is idiosyncratic to both the person's life as lived and the researcher's unique point of view.

Greening (2003) suggested that at a particular point in a person's life, one of the four existential challenges may predominate. In the case of Robert, his experience of being victimized led to a prolonged and still uncompleted crusade to achieve complete vindication. Vindication would be, to Robert, inclusion of the truth of his report by the FBI and correction of any reference to his file that he reported a false crime in which they cite suspicion of having psychosis.[83] Along with an FBI file correction, Robert seeks a retraction or amendment of the forensic psychological report as submitted by the first psychologist who diagnosed Robert as being delusional. His earnest efforts have been judged by some of Robert's relatives, attorneys who declined to accept his case against the forensic psychologist, and a number of people who have been made aware of the essence of this case as being excessive and potentially serve to re-traumatize himself. Interviews with Robert, however, reveal that what he is doing is necessary in order for him to reach a satisfactory point of closure. If he simply abandons his quest, he would feel like a failure. Robert's treating psychologist is supportive of Robert's actions and feels they are necessary steps for Robert to take even though this endeavor is now in its ninth year. Even a family friend, a psychiatrist, stated that Robert is following a most healthy path in not giving up.

The principal investigator finds that the payment of long-term disability benefits to Robert serve as the motivational inhibitor to his seeking a new career. Robert may jeopardize his disability income if he becomes reemployed. This concerns him, as he likely will not earn even half of what he used to earn as a pilot. He considered suggestions of additional education, but feels he is past the age where this would suit him.[84]

Attitudes Toward Death and Annihilation

Most of us act out of unconscious fear of our annihilation. The unconscious does not know death or time: in man's physiochemical, inner organic recesses he feels immortal (Becker, 1971). Only humans understand and contemplate the concept of death because the ego fixes time. "For the lower animals, the id is a timeless storehouse of fleeting emotional meanings. A deer cannot know yesterday from today, or tomorrow from next week: its world is a flow of 'external' sensation, punctuated only by a fearfully pounding pulse, a flavorful berry, and the unanticipated annihilation of sudden death" (p. 16).

Ellenberger (1955) wrote, "Some people can attach themselves to some form of Nietzschian philosophy or oriental fatalism. For such an individual, the fact of being a latent victim is nothing but the equivalent of being practically ready to commit suicide" (p. 277). The psychological reports on Robert's mental functioning did not refer to any suicidal ideation. In the dialogue with the principal investigator, Robert has not ever spoken of suicide or seemed so despondent that it raised this concern. There is, however, a consistent fatalistic undertone in much of Robert's thinking. He is very discouraged about the future and remains quite distrusting of certain psychologists, lawyers, and members of law enforcement.

[83] Robert filed for and received copies of his FBI file pursuant to the Freedom of Information Act; however, some references in his file were redacted.

[84] Recently, Robert has begun looking into college courses.

Interestingly, Robert did not share his near-crash experience with his peers, his friends, or his family.[85] In the years that followed that incident, Robert came across pilots who also made errors in judgment worse than his own. This served to partially lessen his self-condemnation. Robert wanted to maintain the imprint because it reminded him of the importance of maintaining his focus. His decision not to tell his family about the incident is similar to his decision to keep the actions of Connie secret from his family and his professional peer group. Robert did not want his parents to worry about his occupation. He also did not want his peer group to question his ability to pilot aircraft safely and competently. He felt he should just work independently to solve the problem with the experience in the plane. He felt he could not ask for help. In the situation with the predator, he felt he should not divulge what was happening to him. He had a lot of experience thinking his way through situations. Thus, he relied on logic to solve all the problems he faced. Robert felt he needed to be smarter than the people who were hurting him. He noted a parallel between facing death in the plane and the possible outcome of the death threats he was receiving. Just as he worked his way through to resolve the plane problem using cognitive skills, he applied this same approach to determining exactly who was behind all the confusing messages he was receiving and the infiltration of his savings accounts. In both situations, he wanted to figure it out. He "wanted to come out on top," as Robert stated.

Because of Robert's training, piloting skills, and reliance on instrumentation, he developed a characteristic that, absent adequate information, he was unable to diagnose and solve problems even more than the average person. The regimen a pilot undergoes to become instrument rated can leave the pilot feeling very secure when flying in challenging weather conditions. It may also cause pilots to become very reliant on facts and instruments when faced with a crisis. On an instinctual level, perhaps this learned reliance interferes with innate feelings that something may not be right and protective decisions need to be made. In a situation where someone is faced with a psychopathic predator who falsely claims to be a victim, the predator fools the normal protective instincts in the target.

This near-crash existential crisis can be connected to how he responded to Connie's actions. He has been often questioned why he did not simply contact the local police. He reports that this simple step was short-circuited because he was led to believe that the people whom he was dealing with were purported to be the police, even higher up than law enforcement.[86] Robert's dilemma was in not knowing who those people really were. Yet, Robert still perceived the threats to be real.

Robert's current and long-standing effort to investigate the crimes committed against him can be equated to the diagnosing phase of the turning, rapidly descending airplane in that he methodically evaluated every detail until he understood the problem. In the plane, doing so enabled Robert to survive. In the situation with the predator, this approach was too slow for Robert to prevent the harm done to him. Even his decision to go to the FBI was, to him, a reasonable step. However, this decision proved disastrous. The fact that he relied on instruments can be equated to his lack of complete skepticism concerning the information that he was reading in the Internet messages, especially from the cyber identities. He saw the computer as an instrument, and, although he did report that he had some doubt as to the

[85] Robert did not share because he felt it was negative or would cause his family to worry. His parents were supportive and proud of what he accomplished but always worried about his career choice.

[86] The fact that his young nephew was threatened if Robert went to the police was also a factor in Robert's decision not to do that.

authenticity of the e-mail, he had no way to know that the personas sending him messages could be other than genuine. Robert was hesitant to act because he could not unmask who the perpetrator was during the scheme. Robert felt the e-mail messages were not genuine, as he felt they lacked certain logic. But, this did not make them any less frightening to him because the threats were real to him.

Because these events occurred in 1995 when the Internet for home use was very new, there was nothing Robert had read or heard about to warn him of such possible danger.[87] Thus, Robert learned to rely on the veracity of what he saw on the computer, correlated to numerous physical clues and corroborating information. His reliance can be linked to his career and training, possibly contributing to his vulnerability. Additionally, by 1995, Robert had been flying in two- to three-crewmember cockpits for over 15 years, where there was always another pilot in the cockpit to discuss situations. At home, Robert was alone and had no means to ask for immediate assistance from any trusted peers. Perhaps this isolated Robert from reacting in a more defensive manner. Further, because of his near-death experience in the air, he may have felt less threatened on the ground, certainly in his own home.

Robert stated that in subsequent emergency situations, he was able to declare a few emergencies and calmly handle the situations. Thus, he derived great meaning in his career from the experience of the terror (suffering) and his decision to resume his flying career. In the opinion of the principal investigator, what he is in the process of doing is gaining a sense of empowerment in his life in general because of the historic event where he nearly crashed over 25 years ago, but was able to hold on and prevent disaster. Thus, a decoupling of the events leading up to the incident are warranted: first, his poor decision to fly the plane given how he felt about the conditions, and his lack of experience, and his heroic handling of the crisis, leading to survival. Robert's existential dilemma was in thinking back, had he walked away from his flying career and started a different path in life, would he now be in the midst of a traditionally 30-year career?

Robert spoke of self-annihilation:

> We're both on the very brink of our destructions, suicides, insanity, who knows. At this point, I haven't entertained thoughts of suicide, but I think she has. I have felt as close to the edge mentally as I ever want to feel in life and I blame these people bringing me there. I think I'm gonna stop for now. I guess I'll just deny their [the tapes] existence or maybe they'll be turned over to an attorney, just so somebody knows something, because I'm tired of trusting the feds (Robert referred to them as feds in this dialogue solely because whoever they are referred to themselves as feds. Robert had no independent knowledge that they were actually members of law enforcement). They've had me for well over a year and all I want to do is crawl into a hole and go to sleep and never wake up. So how can things be worse? The thing is, they could make things worse. But I'll have to deal with that if I choose to go public or choose to go to an attorney or hand these over. At least someone will watch me and watch my life and know there is something terrible that is happening to me and maybe it's not a coincidence, maybe it was made to happen. (Robert's monologue, 1997, p. 67)

This is an indication of Robert's fatalistic attitude towards his situation at this point.

The ongoing experience of the residual effects of the trauma of losing his career unjustly results in his penchant to attain vindication so he can feel free and resume "flying in smooth

[87] Identity theft, stalking, and cyber-stalking had not become thought of as specific types of crime until years later.

air." As stated by Robert, what he really is seeking from the FBI is a simple acknowledgement that they made a mistake and should not have done what they did to him.

Schneider (1999) suggested that all human experience exists along a constrictive-expansive polarity. At the constrictive end of the pole is the experience of smallness, confinement, and is associated with words such as *diminishing* and *falling*. At the expansive end of the pole is the experience of greatness, of feelings and sensations. It is associated with such words as *gaining, ascending*, or *accelerating*.

Schneider (1999) argued that in cases of psychopathology, individuals tend to restrict themselves to only one side of this polarity, or shift widely between expansive and constrictive extremes. Schneider suggested that people develop dysfunctional states as a defense against the opposite extreme and the dread that they will be annihilated if they experience ultimate constriction or ultimate expansion.

This theory is applicable to Robert who, at first, experienced falling in the near-crash event. Several months later, he ascended through the cloud cover and felt a sense of euphoria that he would be able to fly without a feeling of residual lack of confidence. While neither state of Robert presents as pathological, they serve to demonstrate the polarity of thinking that occurred in Robert's mind with the stimulus of two different types of events.

Dreams, Visions, and Mythic Experience

Dreams and visions can serve as vehicles to process imagined thoughts. In Jungian theory, myths became one of the units for analysis of the collective unconscious. Myths are metaphors for consciousness. These thoughts occur at a deep level of the subconscious. Robert's dreams are illustrative of his inner struggle.

Freud (1952) wrote extensively about interpretation of dreams. Anagogic interpretation, having a spiritual meaning or a sense of referring to the heavenly life, reveals the more serious and often profound thoughts, which the dream work has used as its material (p. 75). In the work of interpreting, one is opposed by the psychic forces that are responsible for the distortion of the dream (p. 525).

Freud (1952) felt that the method of interpretation of dreams consists of transforming the content of the dream as it is remembered, either by replacing it in accordance with a fixed key or by replacing the dream as a whole by another whole to which it stands in a symbolic relation (p. 7). In addition, waking life shows an inclination to forget any dream that has been formed in the course of the night. "The agent chiefly responsible for this forgetting is the mental resistance to the dream which has already done what it could against it during t· night" (p. 526). To support the fact that during the night the resistance loses some of its power, Freud wrote, "The state of sleep makes the formation of dreams possible because it reduces the power of the endopsychic censorship" (p. 526).

Jung (1960) was critical of Freud for "over-emphasizing the pathological aspect of life and for interpreting man too exclusively in the light of his defects" (p. 335). Jung preferred "to look at man in the light of what in him is healthy and sound, and to free the sick man from just that kind of psychology which colours every page Freud has written" (p. 335).

Jung viewed Freud's psychology as that of strictly neurotic states of mind and not a psychology of the healthy mind. "It was a great mistake on Freud's part to turn his back on philosophy" (p. 335). Jung felt that philosophical criticism helped him to see that every theory has the character of a subjective confession. "Anyone who descends into the unconscious gets into a suffocating atmosphere or egocentric subjectivity" (Jung, 1969, p. 20). Jung felt that "if we are able to see our own shadow and can bear knowing about it, then a small part of the problem has already been solved: we have at least brought up the personal unconscious" (p. 20). Jung also believed in the combination of natural instincts with the phenomenon of the spirit. He saw that his patients guided by their own insight or inspiration sought the right way to deal with the forces of psychic life.

Jung challenged Freud's view of the father-complex as "a piece of mysticism pressed in terms of biological and family relationships" (p. 339). He also felt that Freud's concept of the superego is a "furtive attempt to smuggle the time-honoured image of Jehovah in the dress of psychological theory" (p. 339). Thus, Jung respected the advance of individuals toward a spiritual life.

Robert's dreams reveal his vulnerability. The following interpretations are from the principal investigator and by the subject himself. Robert's own interpretation: The two dogs represent his parents. The black crow-like bird is death. The innocent victim of death is his father. (At the time of this dream, Robert's father was experiencing major kidney failure, and Robert had volunteered to donate a kidney to him; however, Robert was required to first improve his own health in order to be approved as the donor.) Robert felt responsible for the potential death of his father.

The principal investigator's primary interpretation: The attacking animal is the predator, in a two-dimensional personality: the overt psychopath and the masked gentle woman. Kali represents Robert in his vulnerable state, being victimized without apparent cause. The new dog is a vision of the hoped-for life ahead, following attainment of vindication he has been searching for, concerning the veracity of his claims. The issue of his momentary vacillation represents the hero-rescuer component of his inner personality as he always considered what was best for the hurt animal. Surely he recalled Westerns where riders sometimes would shoot their fallen horses to put them out of their misery. Yet, he attempted a rescue despite the formidable odds (reflective of his previous intervention with the mugger).

A secondary analysis: The older dog represents the kidney that he plans to donate to his father. The rescue is the planned donation, itself. The attack symbolizes his father's kidney disease. With the death of Kali (metaphorically, the donor kidney), he then experiences in a dream state the potential element in organ donation when the recipient dies soon after the transplant. Robert admitted to the principal investigator such concerns and that he had not shared these fears with anyone.

This dream points to several personality factors useful in interpretation of Robert's vulnerability. He has subconscious fears concerning failure. These fears point back to his formation years where he studied diligently to be a pilot, all the more fervently after the death of his youngest brother. He became a qualified pilot at an unusually early age (16) and rose to a high level rank prior to his victimization.

Robert reported having disturbing dreams periodically. Most of the dreams involve interviews for various positions as an airline pilot, where he receives a very welcoming response, but his FBI file suddenly appears, and he is told that he is just the type of person whom the company wished to hire but that because of the file, it would not employ him. He also has had upsetting dreams that directly involve Connie.

Robert felt defeated by the unusual ticket he received and had no energy to even attempt to have it corrected. He also said in the dream he felt the system made no sense to him. Such a dream, occurring at this stage, could also point to his realization that he is coming to terms with his past trauma and that by being able to link his dream containing an absurd event with a conscious awareness of its absurdity, he may be building a stronger psychological armament, which will aid him in the future. It was precisely his inability or unwillingness to see Connie's actions as absurd and criminal that contributed to his victimization. Therefore, his dreams can be viewed as a form of self-healing were he able to be influenced by their potential instructive authority.

Robert has exhibited some degree of naiveté, though he strongly objects to the use of that term in relation to his behavior. Even his visceral reaction to such a mild term leads to the conclusion that character aspersion is anathema to his self-esteem. His focused, lifelong quest to fly aircraft expertly resulted in his repudiation of any negative impression that reflects on his character. His reluctance to date flight attendants or female pilots points to his guardedness over his career interests. However, amazingly, he risked everything to save Connie (and in doing so, save himself and his family), though, ironically, at the time, he did not perceive that Connie was the enemy and that his entire career could be at stake.

Robert's extension of trust for people exposed him to the early portion of the psychopathic invasion. His trusting nature is partly the result of being raised in a safe, calm household with loving parents, as well as his faith in his piloting instruction and reliance on instrumentation, information from air traffic control, and weather reports. There are no childhood experiences of mistrust in Robert's life. Today, his trust in others is severely compromised, especially as it relates to the government and therapists. He has growing disdain for the legal system and feels insurance companies put the health of the insured second to profitability.

Robert questions his existence today in the sense that he feels his life was taken away, more than he appreciates his current health and future. Robert often laments over what he has lost, mostly a career he cherished. When challenged to view his current life as potentially dynamic, full of new potentials, he balks at the notion and speaks in a muted fashion. Even at the recent milestone of his fiftieth birthday, his pleasure in the possibility of a celebration was greatly diminished because he was unwilling to experience this type of happiness until he regains his life. Thus, his personality is stuck in times past with his energies devoted to finding his way back home, almost similar metaphorically to Dorothy in *The Wizard of Oz*, where she is lost due to trauma and tries to find her way back home, when all the while she had the power to do so through her own volition.

With Robert, his lamenting attitude is the main culprit, which keeps a stronghold on his forward momentum. His concept of a life well lived involves doing what is right. This causes him to feel emotional pain when others behave badly. As a person who has been severely taken advantage of in life, he uses his resiliency to fight battles in retrospect instead of choosing to accept life, move on, and gain strength to take on future challenges. Thus, he is not thriving, but acts merely as a wounded survivor.[88]

In terms of Robert's inner creativity, he grew up building a career in a single-minded fashion. With his career tolled, he does not use his energies to create a new life. Thus, he lacks courage in the sense that any new world he chooses to face will require risks. One risk is financial in the event he losses eligibility for his disability income. By maintaining an

---

[88] Even when challenged to accept Nietzsche's notion that we are strengthened by that which does not kill us, Robert holds the opposite view that it weakens us.

active case investigation, he attempts, perhaps valiantly, to recapture lost momentum. He has stated that he wants the life that has been taken from him. Sadly, even if one day he is fully vindicated, he may still not be able, or desire, to return to flying. At the point that he does achieve vindication, he may relinquish his understandable obsession with the past and face his deeper issues, rebuilding a healthier proportion of risk and self-protection. In parallel, as he ages, he may face new challenges and limitations on capacities.

Existential Use of the Void

Understanding the design of existence beyond our present life is crucial because it explains and gives meaning to every aspect of our existence (Van Dusen, 1958). Psychology is best viewed as an inquiry (Koch, 1993). Inquiry is necessary if we are to discover the meaning of our lives.

Schneider (2004) wrote, "The starting point of consciousness is awe" (p. xv). This concept is found throughout religion, philosophy, and spirituality. Awe includes a combination of dread and wonder. The purpose of writing about awe is to point out that human beings are typically overwhelmed by the world, yet, if we succumb to hopeless feelings of cynicism, despair, and meagerness, we have problems. At the opposite end of the spectrum is placing too heavy a notion of our greatness, leading potentially, to self-destruction. Therefore, acceptance of the absurdity of our human condition leads us to live an active and productive life.

A more fully existential-humanistic psychology, or science of humanity as Schneider refers, avoids the commonplace reductionistic thinking found in most paradigms of mainstream science. Even the fields of psychology and psychiatry are prone to reductionistic categorization, as evidenced by the bland descriptions of psychopathology found in the Diagnostic and Statistical Manual (American Psychiatric Association, 2000).

Schneider (2004) discussed the importance of discernment when an individual is faced with overwhelming circumstances. An awe-based psychology draws upon various sources to verify experiences. "It is not content with mere cognitive or behavioral inquiries, but with inquiries that embrace the whole person or whole subject matter" (p. 10).

Schneider (2004) proposed the concept of the fluid center, which he defined as "any sphere of human consciousness which has as its concern the widest possible relationships to existence" (p. 10). Thus, the resilient attitude uses a sense of awe to overcome despair through an awakening of the wonderment of life. "So much emphasis is placed on mechanized learning in our culture, and that speed, instant results, and overt knowledge are so highly prized" (p. 15).

Robert presented the principal investigator with his 7-hour taped monologue, which he made in 1997. At the time Robert made the tapes, he still did not know the truth about the source of severe and constant threats and extortion, now known to have been caused by Connie. The tapes were then transcribed. This material was used as one source of data to evaluate the vulnerability of the subject of this research. In the following section, commentary is included with verbatim excerpts from Robert's monologue (shown in quotes) and fit, at various points, certain elements of the criteria.

Contrast Between Hope and Hopelessness

Robert expressed his sense of hopelessness:

> I feel manipulated and angry that I was used not necessarily against my will, but against my own knowledge. And I guess I became very sad, despondent and have this feeling of hopelessness all the time now because I have become aware of that, that everything that has happened was a manipulation. (Robert's monologue, 1997, p. 58)

This represents Robert's attitude toward the void. Instead of making other choices to address the problem and trying to respond more effectively, Robert became depressed due to death threats, extortion, and loss of savings. He became unwilling to face the void and see Connie for who she really was, though Robert had no real way of doing so.

"I don't believe I'll ever be able to express the full story in this format, but I do hope that by the time I'm done that I've put down on this tape or tapes enough information to draw some conclusions or these can be used in some way to help me or others" (Robert's monologue, 1997, p. 1). At the time he made these tapes, Robert did not know how he could help himself by making this recorded story. His terrifying experiences made him feel frightened and very hopeless. Yet, he managed to create an audio archive of the events of this experience. He did not mention the existence of these tapes until after 2 years of work with the principal investigator on his case investigation. Robert explained to the principal investigator that he finally felt complete trust and wanted these tapes to be heard. They were delivered secured to a piece of cardboard with notes that these tapes were made by him and contained information about what had happened to him. Robert considered the possibility that he might not survive this situation, as the tapes were made prior to his discovery that the psychopath was responsible for the crimes.

Discussion

The existential conclusion reached in this case study by the principal investigator is that in the end it is Robert's heroism that fails him. His inability to integrate that truth creates an unbearable disappointment that compels him into such obsession that it threatens to keep him from moving past his shattered life. While it is true that fate is a mysterious force that confronts us, some of the contact is temporary; it uses internal capacities that we cannot join necessarily. Regardless of whether Connie, as a force of fate, is brought to justice, some of Robert's problems remain. However, it is ultimately the *noir*-infused force reaching out of the night of our unconscious to cause us harm and shatter our lives, which has the more meaningful and lasting impact. If we do not respect such contact or give it its due, it will ruin us in a way that no fateful agency can, whether a psychopathic predator or a bureaucratic monolith.

Against his good judgment, the desperation of Robert's unconscious need for relevance drives him into a territory for which he is unprepared, not that anyone could ever be truly prepared for such a catastrophic meeting. It is this need, which we all share on varying levels and in varying intensities, that can, at certain points in our lives, fall prey to the malevolent force of fate.

Was Robert Raped?

While the main element of Robert's suffering involves the use of his identity, leading to the loss of a large portion of his savings as well as the eventual loss of his career, there is also evidence of crimes against him of a sexual nature. He discussed in his monologue that his story involves, in part, rape. But when he discloses the sexual interactions he had with Connie, he never considered it male rape at the time. However, the times he shared sexual intimacy with Connie involved subterfuge, fear, and threat. This can easily be labeled at least coercion. In one situation, Connie stood on a balcony of a tall building and threatened to jump if Robert did not have sexual relations with her. He complied out of fear and has never stated that this was consensual.

The rape of men is not a recent phenomenon but has historically been overshadowed by the public attention received by rape of women (Struckman-Johnson, 1988). Because the study of male victims has been neglected, little is known about adult men who are raped outside of an institutional setting (White and Robinson Kurpius, 2002). Men are reluctant to report assault, owing to the stigma associated with being labeled as homosexual (Scarce, 1997).

Robert reported that Connie would become very irate and extremely irrational as a means to manipulate Robert. Connie appeared dangerous to Robert during these moments. Speculatively, Connie used the device of intimidation to coerce Robert into having sexual relations, but only on a few occasions.

Uncertainly of Illusions Based on Monologue

> A lot of what I know, I cannot say I know first hand. Much of what I know I believe is not factual. I think that I have been made to believe certain things were true. And, in fact, I have believed these things. Other things I believed actually are true and I have always had the problem of sorting out the fact from the fiction (as it relates to the extortion). (Robert's monologue, 1997, p. 1)

This is a self-disclosure of his being overly-trusting. Robert always knew he was being victimized by someone, but it was unclear by whom. Eventually, Robert figured out that he was being victimized by Connie. But his admitted inability to decipher the evidence was an aspect of his vulnerability, even though he has not used that term in self-labeling.

Robert was vulnerable to his own belief in how things appeared because he could not disprove them. His belief that things were plausible further contributed to his vulnerability. As an example, Connie told Robert that she got sick, lost her one remaining ovary, and was having a rough time. He believed her when she first told him. However, when he taped his monologue, he was confused and had no reason to believe her assertions. Robert felt that he and Connie genuinely liked each other in the beginning during their telephone and e-mail dialogue. However, this changed even before they first met. He said that in the very beginning she seemed nice and easy to talk too, though eccentric. At the time he made the tapes, he said he no longer cared about her. Although he did not hate her, she brought him trouble, even though he did not know she was responsible for creating the situation.

Robert began receiving e-mail messages shortly after meeting Connie online. Robert said that, often, when he and Connie were having a difficult time in the formation of their relationship, he would receive e-mail from a persona, Max, supposedly an FBI agent who knew Connie and knew about their relationship.[89] The persona, Max, would send Robert an encouraging message. Robert stated, "I'd get an e-mail from Max, and in a very persuasive way, he would encourage me to give her a chance or to understand that she was going through certain problems and she is worth the effort" (Robert's monologue, 1997, p. 4). In this regard, Max became pseudo-paternalistic in Robert's mind, offering wisdom and advice concerning Robert's relationship with Connie, albeit he did so in a bullying manner.

Robert reported, "As time went on with hindsight being 20/20, it is clear to me now how (the persona of) Max was aware of what was happening and that is because as it turned out he might be connected with the Department of Justice, and I believed he is part of the U.S. Marshals office" (Robert's monologue, 1997, p. 5). Robert's pertinent questions were not answered although he tried to understand what was going on.

The false personas almost caused Robert to develop a sense of fear, as he stated, "There is a lot to this. I later learned that all my e-mail and phone calls were monitored. At the time, I did not know it. But over the course of time, it did become revealed to me that I was being watched and surveilled" (Robert's monologue, 1997, p. 5). There is ample circumstantial evidence that Max was somewhat involved.

This played on Robert's emotional need to be a rescuer, which has been argued here in this research. Robert became actively involved and began questioning the treatment of Connie, which served to cleverly distract Robert from questioning the credibility of the situation.

Robert often questioned why Connie was telling him all these stories involving famous people. Currently, Robert explains that his purpose in taping many of his thoughts was to jog his own memory in the future about the events because the scam had so many elements to it. If the tapes were discovered by the wrong person, Robert and his family would be in greater danger. Therefore, some of Robert's raped monologue involved minor distortions so as to protect himself and his family. He reported:

> I found that a little strange. She just came off a devastating experience with David McCallum, there was me, a guy that was available to know, who was interested enough. And it was always very shocking that she was segueing from one celebrity to another in record time. I didn't like that and I felt that that is not what I was looking for in somebody. And I had a lot of reason in my mind to back away from her in this situation. (Robert's monologue, 1997, p. 6)

Yet, Robert continued to be pressured to remain involved with Connie despite the danger and the oddity of the events. There were times when Robert thought of getting out of the situation. As he spoke about the manipulation:

---

[89] Max was, at the time of the origination of Connie's scheme, a state trooper. Investigation shows that Max and Connie did have a long-standing affair. Max was probably not involved in the actions involving Robert, and Max died in 2003. Connie used Max's persona to create a high-level secret government operative, capable of enormous influence and capacity to invade the private worlds of ordinary citizens.

> And again, every time I was doing it or felt I was or believed that would be the way to go, once again along would come a very well-written note, e-mail if you will from Max, friendly enough, saying things in just such a way to keep me motivated enough to make me want to continue to get to know her. I must say that it did work. (Robert's monologue, 1997, p. 6)

Robert's suggestibility became a way for Connie to gain a foothold over his defense mechanisms. Max became the dominant male figure, almost a bully and a substitute for Robert's misplaced self-consciousness. Robert felt forced to rely on Max as a source of information because he, himself, could not figure things out. Robert continued to question all information he received.

Connie told Robert about how she met Max when she was 17 and he was 32, and they formed a close, physical relationship. Robert learned of this, but it did not serve to lower his opinion of her because at that point Robert was not interested in the relationship and Max had not yet contacted Robert.

Connie explained to Robert that Max died under bizarre circumstances. Robert believed that she was genuinely devastated by the loss of Max. Robert felt that Connie was sad and this, in turn, made Robert sad because he felt she lost another person close to her. Robert was then also stuck with her. He was also concerned that Connie would focus all her attention onto him. Robert stated, "Max was gone and there was that loss. We did a few things; we went shopping and tried to occupy the time" (Robert's monologue, 1997, p. 7).

Even though Max reportedly died, Connie tried to convince Robert that he was still alive:

> When she went back to Dubois, she was kind of glum and depressed. On a couple of occasions, she would go to his house in Rochester Mills.[90] She had the keys, and she would be there just to be in his house. Things started to get mysterious at that point. She thought she was losing her mind. One day she called me that she thought she smelled his scent in the house. (Robert's monologue, 1997, p. 9)

Robert was very disturbed by all of this. But he accepted that at least Connie believed it to be true that maybe Max was still alive. Robert's voice on the tapes seemed as though he was experiencing emotions in the telling of the story.

Robert listened to Connie slowly describe an intriguing idea of the deep undercover agent with a new identity. Connie went to Max's house one day and told Robert she found a letter addressed to her, allegedly from Max. It told her effectively that he was not dead and described details of Connie's visits to Max's house.[91] His letter discussed that he had to have people think he is dead. Robert was told this story by Connie and had no way to disprove it:

> Max is involved with high levels of the government or law enforcement. I suppose when you are at that level, and you need to go under cover, you can't have a life, you have to lose your family, people have to think you are dead; you don't have an identity anymore. When he came back after a few weeks, I'm not clear about that. But he was back. It was eluded to that he was part of a witness pool or a sting operation where certain parties of organized crime were being tried in that part of the state and he was going to testify against them. We were led to believe that he had in some way been on the take or been a bad cop if you will, got found out and then

[90] It seems unusual that after a person's death, his or her house would be accessible to non-relatives.

[91] In retrospect, it is obvious now that she would easily be able to write such a letter herself or there was no such letter.

> chose to testify against the organized crime people and in exchange for his testimony would have a new life, his freedom back. (Robert's monologue, 1997, p. 10)

This was particularly troublesome for Robert and it would seem very unlikely that a person could testify against organized crime and resume normal life activities. Robert spoke about Max's finances: "Max, by the way, was reportedly wealthy. Connie said he had family money, but possibly money came to him in a dirty way too" (Robert's monologue, 1997, p. 10).[92] The presumption of wealth added to the intrigue for Robert.

Connie used the cyber identities to create personas with varying demeanors. The fact that the identities were real people does not matter because she decided what personalities she would give them. In effect, she made the various identities differ from each other in terms of how they interacted with Robert. Connie seems to have been very successful in maintaining separate personalities for each of the identities she controlled despite the lengthy exchanges that often took place between them and Robert. Throughout the time Connie had Robert convinced these identities were real, she was able to maintain a consistency with respect to the pattern of dialogue and level of aggressiveness of each personality.

Connie convinced Robert that Max had killed himself.

> She called me and told me that some cops came to her door in the morning, told her that Max had killed himself. He put a gun in his mouth and shot. This upset her a lot, naturally, but she was once fooled by this guy who claimed to be dead once as a result of a car accident. And so she needed to see the body. (Robert's monologue, 1997, p. 12)

According to Robert, Connie went to the morgue and asked to see the body.[93] The mortician allowed her to see the body. "She looked at him and it was Max. Max was dead. She spent a few minutes with the director and asked if she could be alone with him" (Robert's monologue, 1997, p. 12). Connie insisted she be allowed to be in the room alone, and the mortician agreed to give her a few minutes alone. "This time, [Connie] examined the body, looked at every intimate part of the corpse to get final closure, full closure that the man before her was Max: dead; dead; dead" (p. 12).

"With Max out of the way, a few things happened. David McCallum attempted to reestablish contact with [Connie]." In addition, Gregg Maddux reentered the picture.[94] Connie began to become increasingly erratic. "She sounded confused most of the time, as though she were drugged. And Gregg would communicate with me as well, telling me to back off, telling me I'm not interested in her and he is so back off. It was sort of threatening" (Robert's monologue, 1997, p. 13). Connie, in fact, was often influenced by heavy use of narcotics, obtained illegally.

Robert became increasingly interested in becoming a rescuer of Connie, though more on the subconscious level. Robert was also trying to rescue himself. Robert felt that he should try to help Connie fight off those whom she claimed were harming her. His vulnerability is that

---

[92] Presumed wealth seemed to serve as a way of adding believability to the situation. In fact, Robert thought that Connie also had money, as she seemed to be able to make many long-distance telephone calls to Robert and never seemed to be working. Connie later concocted a story about inheriting a lot of money from a relative who died. This proved to be untrue. She was also prosecuted for running up a large telephone bill using her older daughter's billing account.

[93] It is very unlikely that Connie would have been allowed to view the body given that she was not related to Max.

[94] As part of the manipulation, Connie used and reused various personas to suit her pruposes.

he senses someone is in trouble, so he steps in to help, but fails to protect himself in the process. The persona of Maddux sent Robert messages that he was using a drug (Rohyphol) to rape Connie. Robert would call Connie about the e-mail and she would seem upset and would tell Robert details of being drugged. “It bothered me and hurt me. And I felt I needed to protect her in some way and I pleaded with Gregg to use his common sense and not be that way, but it didn’t matter to him when he was with her” (Robert’s monologue, 1997, p. 13).

Connie convinced Robert that his actions were counter-productive. Connie told Robert to stop doing things to upset Maddux, such as threatening to say what he knew about him to the Atlanta Braves organization. “She said every time I told her that, he would treat her worse. I was in a bind” (Robert’s monologue, 1997, p. 14). This establishes how Connie tried to control Robert’s sensibilities. Connie was able to get Robert to fear for her safety, thus inhibiting a normal response of how to manage a threatening situation. “I felt if I didn’t try to protect her in some way that he would totally try to dominate and hurt her and I didn’t want to turn my back on her. It felt like I had to protect her” (p. 14). Robert’s misplaced trust in the falsified scenario suggests that he might have felt somewhat guilty if he abandoned her and then discover that she was truly hurt. Robert did, in fact, make several attempts to abandon her, but Connie always persisted with dramatic portrayals, which demonstrated extreme physical harm to her due to the abandonment.

Connie convinced Robert that Max was still alive. Robert stated:

> I kind of did resist thinking along those lines as [Connie] did see Max’s body in the morgue. I got an IM from this person: Hamlamḍun. It was a two-hour session and at the end, I was convinced that I was talking to the same person I knew as Max (Believability that this persona was not Connie was enhanced because of what Max was saying). Now you might say: How does that work? And that’s what I said. Didn’t you kill yourself? Weren’t you dead twice in the past four months?[95] I fought him on this. I initially said, “You can’t be who you want me to think you are, so tell me who you are,” and he said, “You know who I am.” I said, “You’re not Max because we all know Max is dead. In fact, [Connie] viewed the body.” There were a number of other things that were said that left no doubt in my mind that it was him. I was relieved because we needed somebody to help us. We needed somebody. Gregg was getting way out of hand. His threats to me and his harm on her were something I’d never seen before. And so, this Max metaphorically comes back from the dead. He didn’t explain very much about where he had been or why he needed people to think he was dead, but he did convince me that it was all a very elaborately staged production for the benefit of all, to believe that Max ____, state trooper, killed himself. (Robert’s monologue, 1997, p. 16)

It is interesting to note the paradox that Robert needed proof of lies to believe that he was being lied to, yet he believed this was Max, with only dialogue through e-mail. Because Robert could not rescue himself, a disabled hero, he needed someone such as Max to become his own hero-rescuer, according to the interpretation reached in this research.

A careful analysis of Robert’s monologue, combined with many interviews of him, reveals a pattern that Robert was slowly and methodically lulled into a belief and trust that what he was being told was quite possibly true. Robert routinely admitted to the principal investigator that he gave Connie ample room to show him that these things that were allegedly happening were true. Because Robert developed a cautious alliance in the persona

[95] At this point in the scheme to fool Robert, his practical senses were shattered. He actually did consider that he was now talking with a person who had faked his death twice.

of Max, he relied on Max to be their protector because Robert did not have a better option. This shift in responsibility caused Robert to feign acceptance of what was happening while continuing to ask questions and demand proof. Proof was sent to Robert slowly.

Robert and the Max character discussed Robert's threatening the Maddox character with going to the owner of the team with what Robert felt was incriminating information. Robert was left to feel he could handle the situation, but that it would not be the correct method. Robert acquiesces to Max's point of view:

> Glad you're not dead. It was obvious that you just can't make yourself be dead and get away with it unless you are connected to a powerful government agency that supports this type of thing. I always did at that time believe he was with some higher law enforcement agency. I didn't need to know. Just the very fact that he can be dead twice and do it so convincingly, even people seeing his dead body. I was ready to trust this guy and I needed to trust somebody. (Robert's monologue, 1997, p. 16)

This demonstrates the illusion that Robert's desperate need to find someone to trust blocked his good judgment. Robert was now living with a situation where he was somehow teeming up with one fictitious character (Max) to handle the issues with another fictitious character (Gregg).[96] Robert often questioned how he knew everything about Connie's past relationship with Gregg:

> Gregg visited [Connie] many times, got into her house; became aware of Max. In those days, Gregg was still trying to figure out who Max was. Max followed Gregg around the next few months. I am sure others did too. From what I know now, I can say dozens and dozens of people probably did. (Robert's monologue, 1997, p. 16)[97]

Robert knew he was being told lies, possibly including Connie. However, the following is an example of how Robert spoke on the monologue as if Connie herself might discover the tapes:

> This is all becoming a little bit too surreal to me. I knew I was being lied to, but I never did think [Connie] was lying to me, so from my perspective, I tended to believe that [Connie] was being seen by Gregg and hurt and she was terrified. She'd call, crying, depressed, suicidal, after he'd leave. These calls lasted for many hours. All through the night, one, two, three, four o'clock in the morning sometimes. I was losing sleep. Because my lifestyle was being upset, I never refused a call from her. I was told she was forced to have sex with Gregg and, at gunpoint, made to say my name, Bob. Gregg, I think, could never understand her interest was in me and why I was involved with her when after all he is Gregg Maddox and he should be able to have what he wants. (Robert's monologue, 1997, p. 17)

Connie was clever in her methods regarding the computer subterfuge. A type of void resulted from the extensive use of the Internet in that Robert was shielded from knowing the true identity behind the fictitious personas set up by Connie. Robert held the belief that

[96] It is important to reiterate that these individual characters are, in fact, real identities, some of whom may have been involved in the scheme with Connie at any time.

[97] Robert explained that his reasoning for this belief had to do with the fact that he was led to believe that all this was about an investigation into organized crime.

Maddux was able to monitor Robert's e-mail and even use Robert's e-mail account. Connie told Robert that she received a nasty message apparently from Robert, but that it was really from the Gregg character. Robert stated:

> I had some e-mail correspondence with Gregg a few times and somehow I was able to get Gregg to admit the truth to her and admit that he did it. And it was a time that showed me that anything that you put in e-mail can be read by anybody and not only that, somebody can use your accounts and send somebody else e-mail and make it look like it is coming from you. (Robert's monologue, 1997, p. 18)

Connie was adept at exploiting various e-mail accounts and manipulating perceptions. In this case she wrote a very vile e-mail from Robert to herself, using Maddux as the voice, but making it appear to come from Robert. She reacted hurt that Robert would send such an e-mail. It is very interesting that this awareness went unapplied to what was being done to Robert. Robert never considered the possibility that he was receiving messages from multiple people, but really all from Connie as part of a fraudulent scheme:

> I gotta say there is a lot of stuff that, even though they are my perceptions, I don't bank on them a hundred percent. We've been fooled too many times to trust in anything. I mean once somebody we believe is dead and who you are told and [Connie] has said she saw this body and examined it and it was definitely Max, and then you find out it was a hoax, staging some magical government illusion. Once they fool you at that level, you know you can be fooled at every level. (Robert's monologue, 1997, p. 18)

Robert became increasingly aware that there was more to the situation than he could figure out. "So, I've got to interject that a lot of what I know I don't know if I know it factually. But I have experienced a lot, seen a lot. And I can't say definitely if it is true, although a lot of it does feel true" (p. 18).

Robert did not understand why the people whom he thought were involved with Connie allowed the situation to go on for so long. "Did anybody not see the wear and tear on [Connie], the pain that she was going through?" (Robert's monologue, 1997, p. 18). Connie took advantage of the rescuer part of Robert by challenging him with personas for him to try to figure out and protect her from.

Robert establishes his desire to provide a clear story with enough information for others to follow:

> I guess what I hope to do is just put enough of a rough and dirty story out there. A million parts are going to be missing. Hopefully I'll include enough names, places, and dates to form some sort of a structure for anybody who ends up with these tapes to sort of begin putting some of this puzzle together. (Robert's monologue, 1997, p. 20)

Robert remained confused: "Of course, things are happening in real time; there is no way to know anything when you are being fooled by such professional, confident tricksters, who employ every trick in the book" (Robert's monologue, 1997, p. 22). Ironically, Robert was looking at the situation and asking relevant questions, but the scam was so well orchestrated that Connie had Robert looking at the wrong people.

Connie stole Robert's credit card:

> I think it was maybe February 1996, not sure. [Connie] did come to visit, went out for a dinner. I got a little bit drunk, not too. Accidentally, I dropped my credit card and I think she said she wanted to pay and somehow these cards got switched. By that point in time, [Connie] had hired a private detective. The method she used to pay him, she gave him her bank card and told him he could access her ATM in the course of his daily doings. One day I got a statement from my bank, which I had about $4,000 to $5,000 in, and I noticed that I had almost nothing in it. I looked at all the transactions that occurred, there were many and they all took place in Dubois, in that area. I called [Connie] and asked, "Do you know why my checking account is almost empty?" We talked about it. We determined that what must have happened . . . we might have switched cards and that she told me she gave this card to the detective who was doing some work for her about her father, in West Virginia. [98] That would mean he would have to know my personal identification number, which was at the time (3333). Coincidentally, [Connie's] personal identification number was 3333.[99] You'd think that would be a suspicious thing. But I had 3333 for years since I opened a bank account when I got hired by a major airline in 1987, and I used 3333 on different other occasions. I use 3333 for the lock on my flight bag, telephone answering machine codes. (Robert's monologue, 1997, p. 24)

"[Connie] figured this out. She said, 'Bob, your ID number must be 3333.' I said, 'How did you know?' She said, 'That's what I use, my mother's date of birth: March 3, 1933.' This seemed to answer the question. This was one of many weird coincidences of things that happened" (Robert's monologue, 1997, p. 24).

Robert accepted these types of coincidences and added up the various examples. However, there was nothing he could do about the enormity of the scam. Had he been able to slow down the barrage, he might have become more suspicious of Connie and done more for self protection. Connie took advantage of Robert's inability to pinpoint the blame on her, because for Robert, for it was hard to grasp that the entire scam could have been perpetrated by one person.

Connie used her cunning to pretend to back away from the idea of temporarily staying with Robert for two weeks. This drew Robert further in to where he lost all perspective on the topic. It was agreed she would move in with him, so he went to help her pack up her belongings. Robert agreed to do this under the pressure of threats from Max. Robert reported strange events:

> There were a few Max interventions with e-mail, he saw her a few times in Dubois as well. I didn't trust Max.[100] Something was so up. Something so big [was] going on behind the scenes that we weren't allowed to see (Robert referred to "we" because Connie made it seem he and her were fighting a common enemy as co-victims. And things were being played out in such a way that we only saw the little part that affected us, our lives, that is us moving in together, those kinds of decisions. Those types of decisions were all affected by powerful, unseen forces and powerful manipulation by Max, by his people, because of the phone taps and the spying and using information in ways to get people to do things. (Robert's monologue, 1997, p. 30)

---

[98] An additional story Connie told Robert was that she was trying to track down information about her supposed biological father.

[99] The probability of this is statistically remote.

[100] Yet, his insistence on meeting Max never resulted in an actual meeting.

Robert felt that people were in and out of his apartment because his dresser drawers were ransacked and cash was taken. "I knew that they were in my apartment. They had broken in. I guess they have a right to do that" (Referring to the government) (Robert's monologue, 1997, p. 30).[101] Robert felt that his apartment was being bugged.

> But I had no doubt that they were in my apartment, maybe to put bugs in, maybe to sort through my things, maybe to intimidate. Subsequently, since [Connie] moved, the feds routinely come into my apartment, that's the least of it. I've lived a life of intimidation for many, many, many months. (p. 31)

Before Connie moved in with Robert, they had a fight. "She wasn't always rational. She was highly drugged. I felt I had to save her. I was against them, those who were hurting her, forcing the decision for her to move to Philadelphia with me" (Robert's monologue, 1997, p. 31). Robert had some tough instant messaging sessions with Max over the issue of Connie maybe not moving in with him. The Max character put heavy pressure on Robert not to interfere with the government's high-level investigation into organized crime and professional baseball. Robert, showing a rare tirade, said to Max:

> I'm sick of you, sick of your intimidation, sick of your phone taps, sick of your breaking in to my apartment, sick of you fucking up her life, sick of not understanding what this is all about. I quit. I quit. I don't want any part of this anymore, so fuck you, fuck your organization, but I can't do it. Max countered by suggesting Connie would be killed if he did not cooperate. Max said, "Want me to send the obituary notice to you? Yeah, it won't be long before she's dead. (Robert was told that his participation was critical and if he withdrew he would be putting Connie in jeopardy) (p. 31)

In May 1997, Robert insisted he was not going to cooperate any further, which is a major turning point in the story. He was then threatened. Max said, "If you don't do it, we will forever be in your life and you will never rest" (Robert's monologue, 1997, p. 32). Robert felt he had no choice and realized he should go along with their plan and cooperate. Robert begged Max to give him another chance:

> Listen, Max, give me another chance. Let me see if I can change her mind about moving in with me. You gotta remember, there was more than one thing running through my mind at that time. I didn't want her hurt. I think I did believe that he would let her be hurt. He let her get raped, drugged, why not killed? (p. 32)

Connie used her cleverness to take advantage of Robert by pretending to be on the telephone with a friend and having Robert think he was in an instant messaging session with Max. She was able to manipulate Robert into thinking the Max character knew what the telephone call was about between Connie and her friend and that he was somehow able to disconnect that call. Robert fell into this trap, and when Robert called Connie, she feigned sounding amazed that her call had been cut off. This served to add credibility to Connie's scheme.

---

[101] Robert was not aware of his constitutional rights nor did he investigate this matter.

Robert felt he might be killed. "I sometimes think I'm gonna be killed" (Robert's monologue, 1997, p. 34). Robert spoke of how his relationship with Connie was manipulated and that he did have feelings for her. He felt sorry for her:

> She needs somebody to latch on to, somebody in her life. She lost so much and she lost so much more that I've not said yet. She lost something that she never knew she had.[102] And then when she found out she had it; it was wonderful. And then it was taken away. She has suffered more than a human being should ever suffer and used more than anybody should ever be used. (p. 35)

Robert's attempt to place stringent control over his money did not achieve the desired result. He held out some hope that the people who were taking his money would give it back to him.[103] "They've taken quite a bit. They do other things. They run up my credit card. They put charges on it. I currently live barely from paycheck to paycheck. They've even come into my apartment and taken money out of my wallet" (Robert's monologue, 1997, p. 37).[104]

Robert went through a long process of belief and disbelief:

> And I've learned that seeing things with your own eyes isn't really enough proof of anything. Because [Connie] saw a dead Max with her own eyes except for three or four weeks later, he's back in everyone's life, happy-go-lucky. He was never dead. They just wanted us to think he was. (Robert's monologue, 1997, p. 55)

This shows that Robert considered Connie's eyewitness report because it was the only information he had. Robert admitted he had been duped:

> As I said, when I started this in the first place, I can't tell what is real and what is not real. I'm telling you that I have been duped. I have been bamboozled and fooled by the best and they did a very complete job. And they got me believing things or thinking that I believe things that are probably so far from the truth. So, these tapes are ramblings of my experience of being fooled, but I am being fooled by people that are taking a lot of time out of their day to make sure that I am seeing things a certain way, and perhaps not seeing other things. So, I am being fooled by the best.[105] And I think whatever factual information that I have is being diluted by a lot of misinformation that they throw my way. How can I know which is fact and which is fiction? It may be proven to me one day that, yeah, these things you thought are a total fabrication, not based in any fact, but this other thing you thought is real. (Robert's monologue, 1997, p. 55)

---

[102] This loss refers to her alleged miscarriage of a pregnancy where the biological father was a doctor to whom she was engaged and was subsequently killed in an automobile crash. She told Robert she only learned she was pregnant when she was in a mental hospital from a nervous breakdown following the news of the death of the doctor.

[103] He asked them to give Connie the cash back, but they never did.

[104] At this point, Robert estimates that $50,000 has been taken directly from him. He also gave her or paid bills for her totaling another $30,000. The current total is well over $100,000.

[105] An interesting point is that Robert stated in an interview that he was shocked that Connie was able to pull off this scheme against him. Speculatively, perhaps if victims feel they have been fooled by experts, they do not feel as bad. Thus, an aspect of vulnerability is the victim's self-concept of being guarded against being victimized. Once they are harmed, their sense of ability to self-protect is compromised. By looking at the predator as highly skilled, the victim accepts the situation more readily.

Robert continued to question the identities:

> These feds, I don't see them, physically. I see them invisibly.[106] I get what they do to me, the way they've taken my money. The way they display and express to me that they have information about personal matters I discuss on the telephone. I have not, frankly, not directly, not discussed at work names, dates, places, times, indirectly because I can't keep this to myself. (A dilemma for Robert was his need to blend in with his peers; otherwise he might have brought attention onto himself. It is too much. I'm being too hurt by this. (Robert's monologue, 1997, p. 56)[107]

Robert and his parents were upset by the events:

> Even my parents have no idea what I'm saying into this tape recorder and do know I'm stressed and do understand parts of this. But, I tried to spare them, elements of this. They are very distressed and very sad, that my life has been taken over. And I am too. And why is that? I think the only thing I did was step in and try to protect [Connie]. I feel I paid a very high price in wear and tear on my body, mind, and stress, anxiety of not understanding why these people have taken over my present and made my future questionable. Why I feel I am being treated like a criminal, worse than a criminal because a criminal is charged, has his day in court, and is either found innocent and given his freedom back or found guilty and pays his penance to society.[108] And then goes back into society. This is different. This is more like an occupation. I am being occupied. [Connie] and I are under this sort of protection, but it is more of a house arrest type of existence. Anytime I've ever been any place with [Connie], they always showed up. We went to San Diego. At the drop of a hat, Jerry showed up. I didn't see him, but [Connie] said she saw him, when she went to get Demerol for her headache. She needed to do that a lot. (Robert's monologue, 1997, p. 56)

Robert lamented over feeling he was in physical jeopardy:

> I never, in 40-something years of my life, did anything that would require or result in people wanting to harm me physically. And this is no exception. I got involved with [Connie], it's true and she was being harassed, it seems by Gregg and I made a decision to try to protect her from that, but they drew me in. They brought me in deeper. They had an opportunity to divert me. All I was allowed to see was a woman in crisis. I was motivated by my own motivations, which were mostly to do the right thing. This is a girl who was desperate, falling apart and needed something. And to that I responded. (Robert's monologue, 1997, p. 57)

Robert lamented over his devastated financial situation. He discussed his large telephone and Internet usage charges:

> So my combined phone and America Online for, I don't know, a year or better was \$12/\$13/\$1,400 a month. It still pretty much lingers up there. And this isn't the way I live.

---

[106] He considered electronic messages as a type of sight, albeit invisible, but very potent.

[107] A considerable problem in this case is that Robert chose not to explain much of what he was experiencing to his coworkers.

[108] This statement is a forecast of how Robert was treated by the FBI. When he walked in and wrote out his complaint, the federal agents treated him worse than a criminal because had he been charged with a crime, he would have been read his rights (Miranda law), but in this case, he was not so advised. In retrospect, he placed himself unwittingly in harms' way.

> This isn't how I am. Before this started, I was frugal. I drive an old car; I put money into my 401(k); I don't have fancy clothes. In less than a year, I am wiped out. All my savings are gone. I can't even pay my bills without wondering if there will be enough money in my account to cover the checks that I write. Because I never know how much is in my account. It's usually less than a paycheck's worth. And sometimes it's a lot less because I never know when they are going to hit the account and take money out of it. I don't get my mail. I haven't seen bank statements in months. The only way I've been able to find out if the account [has been] hit, I have to call the bank and with prompting menus, I can find out when the most recent ATM transactions take place. And that's how I found out what my balance is, because my mail is being tampered with. (Robert's monologue, 1997, p. 59)

Thus, the feeling of a void experienced by Robert equaled losing his money. Robert's charge accounts were also very much used by Connie:

> I haven't gotten my MasterCard bill in months. I pay it because I always call MasterCard and ask them if they sent out a bill. Sometimes they say, yeah, about two weeks ago, you didn't get it? They said, yeah, it's going to be overdue in another four days, $6,000. And so I make a minimum payment of $200. When I ask them at MasterCard if there had been any charges since the last billing period, we review them. I did that just the other day; there were something like 24 charges, which I only made about 10. The rest must have been done by the feds. They've charged many things to my MasterCard account. Not just last month, every month, for months and months and months. Just most recently, they ordered magazine subscriptions for [Connie], $100 box of chocolate from Godiva; they ordered jewelry from QVC, Internet X-rated areas that are charged to my credit card, just various things out of catalogs, video tapes. (Robert's monologue, 1997, p. 59)

When the items arrived, Connie would explain to Robert that she did not know where they came from. Robert also stated that his identity was used to post messages on chat room bulletin boards. "They have me posting on the baseball chat boards saying intimidating things about Gregg Maddux, but I didn't say them" (Robert's monologue, 1997, p. 60).

Robert was reluctant to betray Connie:

> There are certain things I don't want to say, even now because I think it would be a betrayal of confidence to [Connie]. Physically and mentally she is going through a lot. She has some stomach problems and they are not just small problems, they are rather major. She has also had reason to believe that she has a tumor in her head (It was later learned that this was a lie). We don't know. I can say that I don't know what I believe. I know they are capable of making people feel sick. I know they are capable of changing medical records. (Robert's monologue, 1997, p. 63)

This was particularly clever of Connie, as now Robert was placing blame on what he occasionally referred to as the feds for making it seem that she was ill.

Robert had a personal policy of not dating crewmembers and wanted to concentrate on building his career and to become relatively affluent before looking seriously for a potential marriage partner.

Robert does not wish to utilize the services of any psychotherapist to uncover aspects of his personality, such as his vulnerability. He has become very stern in his quest to seek vindication for the actions that have resulted in his loss of career and credibility. Although

Robert is currently showing signs of improvement, he lives in an embittered state with minimal parameters of creative aspiration aside from his present quest. While it is understandable that he wishes to have his FBI record expunged of negative references to his mental state, as evidencing psychosis or delusion, this is somewhat due to his embarrassment over these labels and the obvious destruction to his career and its impact on other potential career paths he might take. Amongst pilots, the airline, and the FAA, any allusion to such difficulties, even those unproved, cause skepticism and loss of license through the prejudicial eyes of his fellow pilots and crew. Until he achieves a point of acceptable closure to his severe problems, he is living in a state of stagnation.

Robert explained why he made the taped monologue:

> I want to say something about why I decided to make these tapes. I have to hope that they are not aware of this. That's stupid, they are aware. And I think they're going to make life more difficult than ever before. Because they're going to want these tapes and I don't think I want to give them to them. I think these tapes are something that may be used one day to help me remember things or as a final goodbye or legacy if anything should happen to me. I never thought I'd be in this deep, and I never thought that the people I was supposed to trust turned out to be the ones that are destroying me.[109] They've threatened my family, not directly, but [Connie] has told me they told her if Bob gets out of character, if he wants to start blabbing his mouth and start talking to people about this, we can make life hell for his parents. We control the IRS. We can screw them [his parents] over or make them afraid of what they can do to ______ or _______.[110] They do know how to control people by threatening people who you care about. That's how they got me in the first place because I wanted to protect [Connie]. And the threat was, unless you move her to Philly with you, she'll be harmed (A person, when being threatened, should take such threats seriously if they deem them credible). So, of course, I'm gonna do what I have to do because it's the right thing to protect her. I have no doubt they can push me over the edge. I have no doubt they can drive me crazy. My mental processes are not what they used to be. I can't think of anything else other than what they've done or what they are doing and what I fear they will do. I have dreams of Max harming me, harming [Connie]; going after my family. I resent them because before I was ever aware of them, I had an orderly life. I had my finances where I could understand them. I did my job flying a jet as best I could; never doubted my abilities. Part of me does think I should take a leave of absence from my work. I know I am acting strange. People know it. People see it. I can't tell them why. I can't explain what I can't prove. (Robert's monologue, 1997, pp. 64-65)

Robert continued to consider Connie harmless:

> [Connie] is a good girl, she wouldn't hurt me, but she doesn't know what I'm feeling or what I'm seeing that's being done to her. [Connie] made me important, well, she didn't make me important; the feds took away everything and just left me standing. I think I've said a lot, but I don't think I've said anything. As I said, this is a stream of consciousness. I'm just rambling. There is not enough structure here. I think I talked about the beginning and the middle. I don't know where the end is. I am not happy with what I've said or the way I've said it. I don't even know who I'm talking to.[111] I only know that I am being taken apart slowly by people trying to

---

[109] He is referring to the identities that he was led to believe were federal agents.

[110] These people refer to Robert's brother and young nephew.

[111] The reader is reminded that these tapes were made in 1997, 5 years before Robert and the principal investigator met and 1 year since Robert gave them to this researcher. After completion, the tapes were hidden in a rafter in

> get me to believe they are with the government. They are doing it to [Connie] as well. I don't know what purpose is served in destroying her and me.[112] Sometimes she [Connie] says I remind her of her mother. I wouldn't hurt her either.[113] She knows I'm not a bad person. I always want her to believe that and always know it. I don't know why that is so important, but it is. I don't want to turn my back on her. (Robert's monologue, 1997, p. 65)

In this research, there are two dark forces at work: the one on the outside, the psychopath, involving fate or some mysterious force; and the one on the inside, Robert's unconscious yet very real and human need to stand out, which is part of the criteria: being in the face of non-being.

A complex source for drama in the relationship between Robert and Connie reside in Robert's response to the discovery of what she is. Her legerdemain is fascinating and vital to the conflict between her as an evil force and Robert as an innocent victim. Robert's response to Connie and her imaginary entities lay the groundwork for the height of the conflict: a man, reduced to a shadow of his former self, fighting against a long departed phantom (Connie) and a bureaucratic monolith (the FBI), which refuses to accept responsibility for its actions. He becomes obsessed in this fight against her as well as against the hypocrisy and self-preserving instincts of a government agency that itself operates in the context of a larger cultural hero-system and so refuses to acknowledge its own role in the harm done to one of its citizens. In the opinion of the principal investigator, the tragedy is not just in the loss of money or career—these are replaceable—but in a driven-ness to do the right thing. It is this blinding driven-ness that destroys Robert's objectivity, a hallmark of all tragic figures.

Robert's resistance to the idea that Connie might be manipulating him, despite his suspicions, and his fear of misjudging her conspire to leave him and his good intentions vulnerable to her corrupt and sadistic force. He rushes headlong into action, never allowing himself the chance to heal, to regain his objectivity and facility to explain events in a way that does not magnify his injury. He is trapped, perhaps irretrievably, in a maze of fates and his own making. In the opinion of the principal investigator, what he is left with is an image of a forlorn victim.

However, Robert's errors in judgment should not threaten the degree to which the reader or evaluator will empathize with him. In fact, such empathy may be heightened. There need not be an option of blaming the victim. In reviewing Robert's monologue and the chronology of events, it is possible to share the experience from Robert's point oß2view, thus it is possible for others to recognize their own potential for victimization. They will identify with his need to do the right thing, and his willingness to give the benefit of the doubt to Connie. They will feel their own degree of vengeance toward her, their own need for vindication. If Robert is judged, they will be condemning themselves as well.

Ernest Becker (1924-1974), a social theorist and teacher of anthropology and sociology, suggested an inherent contradiction between the inside of a person's body—his thoughts and

---

the ceiling of the closet of Robert's relatives who, to this day, have been unaware that the tapes were made in their house and hidden there.

112 Paradoxically, Robert felt it was Connie who needed to determine who is real and who is fake. It was this subterfuge that derailed Robert's own insight that this is what he, in fact, needed to be doing for himself. This became a survival tactic to force Connie to help him figure out what was going on.

113 This reveals the suggestibility component of how Connie fooled Robert into caring about her to the extent that he did.

feelings—and the outside (Becker, 1971). Although we experience only the outside, all objects in nature have some interiority.

Our contact with people is only with our physical exteriors. But we also have a private self or interior life. Taken to the extreme, such interiority can lead to a sense of isolation from others. This difficulty in projecting who we really are because of the inherent limitation of our exterior image is exacerbated when the intention is fraudulent. In this regard, a false pretense overlaps the already less important exterior self.

Based on the above illusions, it is clear that Robert was unwittingly preyed upon by a psychopathic criminal who effectively used deception and fear to have Robert override his judgment, thus highlighting Robert's vulnerability. Connie's creation of an elaborate story of intrigue using the identities (both real and fictionalized) serve to illustrate the unusual lengths she undertook to harm Robert and keep him from seeking help through law enforcement.

Robert clearly cared about Connie's well-being, as evidenced by his vigilance and noble efforts to help her both understand what was happening, but also to try to get the cyber identities, which at the time seemed like real personas, to cease their abusive conduct toward them.

Robert was interested in meeting new people and was lonely because of being in a new town. Seeking out new people to meet was his first inclination when he started using the Internet. Robert's personality includes looking forward to be a helper and rescuer, even placing himself in danger in order to protect others, including strangers. He willingly sacrificed his time and money, and took risks to try to help Connie. His risks were not considered at the time he extended his help, but the negative impact became a lasting imprint. He has a sense of duty to people. This is partly the result of flying commercial jets for many years, where he was not only doing his job, but was responsible for the well-being of hundreds of people during each flight.

Robert presents in his monologue a man who is shattered by the many bizarre and significant events that took place and which he could not prove to be untrue. He does appear to have had minimal sexual contact with Connie, and the many trips they took together and the live-in situation do resemble a non-platonic friendship, albeit one with severe relational problems because, unbeknownst to Robert, Connie was perpetrating a scam regardless of the appearance of the relationship. Because Connie had an ulterior motive, there could never have formed a close relationship. He mentioned in quite a number of places in his monologue that he cares for her (as in co-victims), and she also referred to the two of them in the ways a normal couple would refer to each other.

Perhaps the most glaring indication on the level of belief Robert placed on the situation is the fact that he questioned what he was told or what he read on the computer to be true; or at least true until he could prove otherwise. He clearly was thrown off guard. Part of the reason for the success of this technique by Connie was her development of different personality features in each of the false identities. She lured Robert into creating an alliance with one against the other, a sort of triangulation of relationships. This served to distract Robert and gave him a false notion of purpose and effectiveness to be aligned with someone he thought was a government agent out to investigate a professional baseball player who allegedly played the double position of having an association with members of organized crime.

The Construct of the Hero-Rescuer

William James (1892/1961) wrote about mankind's common instinct for reality, having always held the world to be essentially a theatre for heroism. In our culture, especially in modern times, we disguise our struggle by building wealth to reflect privately our sense of heroic worth, or by having only a little better home in the neighborhood, a bigger car, or having brighter children. By stepping out of our intense struggle, we can more easily come to the rescue of others. But underneath we strive for uniqueness, no matter how we mask it in concerns of smaller scope.

Becker (1971) wrote extensively on the cultural hero. People serve the cultural hero-system in order to earn a feeling of primary value, of cosmic specialness, of ultimate usefulness to creation, of unshakable meaning (p. 112). Man's tragic destiny: He must desperately justify himself as an object of primary value in the universe; he must stand out, act as a hero, make the biggest possible contribution to world life, and show that he counts more than anything or anyone else. This justifies his existence. By doing what is right, the hero becomes right with the universe.

In humans, a working level of narcissism is inseparable from self-esteem and a basic sense of self-worth. What people need is to feel secure in their self-esteem. Individuals have always been concerned with the hierarchy of power in nature and society and where they fit into that equation. Becker (1971) wrote of the instinct of power:

> The problem of power is the basic, natural animal question. It is also the primary question of an animal destined to strive for heroism: power must be his principal preoccupation both as a vehicle for himself, and as a hindrance to success. (p. 118)

Reality can be distorted by the phenomenon of narcissism, which is a form of the will to power (Becker, 1971). "In its benign form it is a healthy self-confidence and urge to heroism, but in its destructive and exaggerated forms, it becomes an invertedness upon oneself, an unresponsiveness to the world" (p. 162).

Jung (1969) wrote of the medieval legend wherein the saints behold the powers of the sun with the soul, itself, the custodian of such power. He thought of the notion that such power is conserved through primordial images, or archetypes. The myth of the sun-hero forms the sun archetype. "The sun in its course must represent the fate of a god or hero who, in the last analysis, dwells nowhere except in the soul of man" (p. 6). When an archetype appears in life, it can result in action. This action is seen as an explanation for the way Robert sprung to action and attempted rescues, regardless of the impact on his personal safety.

Jung (1969) articulated the contrast between the outer attitude, the persona, and the inner attitude, the animus and the anima. The inner personality is the way one behaves in relation to one's inner psychic processes; it is the inner attitude, the characteristic face that is turned towards the unconscious. "The archetypes are the unconscious images of the instincts themselves, in other words, that they are patterns of instinctual behavior" (p. 44). When the attitude is habitual, the ego can identify itself easily. When the person's behavior is out of the ordinary, it can be said that the person appears like a different entity. Certainly, Robert's conduct changed when he saw the victims of other crimes. He got involved and took on the responsibility of rescuer, despite the fact that he did not even know the victims.[114]

Robert had two experiences in his adult life that can illuminate his inner personality. In one instance, he was on a day trip to Philadelphia and, while walking down the street, he noticed a woman being mugged. He immediately confronted the mugger, who took off on foot. Robert ran after the man, who hopped on a commuter bus. Undaunted, Robert ran ahead of the bus and jumped in front of it, forcing the driver to stop abruptly. Robert boarded the bus, appealed to the driver, and tried to shock the passengers into holding the mugger while he tried desperately to explain the criminal event. The mugger was able to get off the bus, but Robert was persistent and chased him again and was able to stop him until the police were summoned. The mugger was arrested.

While living in Florida, Robert was later notified of a police department award for citizen involvement in stopping the Philadelphia mugger during his visit there. Robert chose not to attend the award ceremony, feeling he did what he was supposed to do. Robert feels a deep sense of right and wrong and continues to act as a good citizen in times of need. He does not understand the need some people have to demand public credit for acts of heroism, which he considers part of living in a civilized society. Further, Robert is quite dismayed that some persons responsible for public safety do not seem to care to become involved in resolving public problems or criminal acts. Deeper analysis also reveals that Robert does not enjoy notoriety. He prefers to stay in the background and live his life as happily as he can.

In another incident, Robert was driving and noticed a woman being assaulted by a male on the side of the road. Robert was stopped at a light and left his car to help the woman. The large man was being rough with the woman. Robert stopped his car and ran over to the scene, yelling for the man to stop. The man ceased and backed away, leaving the woman screaming. Interestingly, the woman was upset with Robert for getting involved, leaving open the interpretation as to the nature of the relationship between the two people. However, Robert's intentions were noble, though clearly risky.

In the case of his reaction to Connie's actions (later found out to be criminal), Robert verbally admitted to the principal investigator his attempt to "rescue a damsel in distress." As he thought she was in danger by others, his main objective was to help her any way he could, even to the point that he tolerated personal abuse, threatening his personal environment.

He unwittingly went along with the scheme created by Connie, partly because he did not realize at the time that the cyber identities were, in fact, false personas and partly because he could not prove that the information being told to him was untrue. In this critical junction, he expressed his vulnerability subconsciously by exposing his rescuer nature to help others, though his approach resulted in inordinate risk to himself. It is suspected that Connie, as a clever person, selected him due to his nature, and that she concocted the elaborate scheme after seeing how he reacted to the beginnings of her manipulation. Thus, his vulnerability and her antisocial behavior were a perfect blend for an interesting crime to take place.

Both hero-rescuer situations left Robert quite exposed to self-harm. This heroism can be considered a trait of Robert's. Even his choice of career as a commercial airline pilot, responsible for public safety, can be considered, in the extreme sense, to fulfill, at least potentially, the role of the hero. As a pilot, Robert managed several in-flight emergencies. His

[114] This is similar to the action-hero Superman, who changed his clothes secretly from the outfit worn by Clark Kent to take on the action identity and then he jumped into the air to fly to the crime scene and save the day.

career and the two heroic events reflect back to his interest in superheroes, where good triumphs over evil. According to the principal investigator, in some respects, Robert took on the persona of a superhero in the sense that he helped the targeted disadvantaged and also used flight to accomplish his noble objectives.

Robert's nature of hero-rescuer, coupled with the happenstance of being in the wrong place, especially early on in the Internet era, led to his downfall. This led to the conclusion that he made himself unduly exposed to an invasion by a disordered woman.

Robert liked nurses because they help people, metaphorically like angels. Once, at age 20, Robert had surgery on his nose. A nurse helped him, causing him to develop a sense of trust and respect for the profession. Robert explained these feelings to Connie early on in their interactions. She took advantage of this knowledge. Connie explained to Robert that she was traveling through an area of Pennsylvania at the exact moment of a US Airways plane crash. She told Robert that she stopped her car by the woods and tried to reach the crash site so she could help by offering her skills as a nurse. This crash was particularly traumatic for Robert because he had flown the exact aircraft several times and he also knew the pilot.

Because Connie described how she allegedly tramped through the woods to try to rescue any survivors, she potentially fit what he believed was the perfect image of how he wanted her to be. He thought maybe this could be a woman he was destined to know and be with. It was much later on that Robert realized she fabricated the story of being at the crash site and trying to help.

In a recent incident (August 2005), Robert was walking down the street in New York City and observed a woman violently screaming at her young child. Robert saw the frightened look on the child and became concerned for the child's safety. Robert noticed that other passersby were ignoring the situation. He thought about a direct confrontation with the mother, but considered against it out of concern that his intervention would exacerbate the problem for the child.

Robert noticed a police officer nearby. He quickly approached the officer and explained what he saw. The officer received an emergency radio call that someone was threatening to jump off a building, so the officer hurried away. Robert located another officer, but after explaining the situation was told bluntly that the officer only handled traffic infractions. Undaunted, Robert found a third policeman, and this person listened to his report. That officer pursued the woman and, after 10 minutes, returned to Robert and told him that they are aware of the identity of the woman, that she is a known crack addict, and that Child Protective Services is currently investigating the case. Robert offered his name and contact information in the event they need his testimony. Robert felt dismayed that the other 2 police officers he encountered did nothing to come to the aid of the child.

This event and Robert's response demonstrates his general heroic disposition. It also shows growth in his handling of a potentially serious event in that he considered the various ramifications of each possible course of action. Often, crowds displace responsibility during emergencies, but in more quiet settings, bystanders are often more likely to come to the aid of a distressed person. For the hero-rescuer, perhaps such displacement is perceived, causing the hero to act absent support from the crowd.

Significantly, because the first officer told him that unless Robert actually saw the woman strike the child, there was nothing the officer could do. Robert told the principal investigator that if he is ever called to testify in the case, he might consider lying.[115]

[115] In this regard, only on an emotional level, Robert said he would say that he saw the woman strike the child. After discussion with the principal investigator, Robert agreed that this would be inappropriate.

Chapter 7

CONCLUSIONS

INTERPRETATIONS

This research offers an idiosyncratic view of a single subject from the existential perspective. This is counter to mainstream thought that case studies should be replicable in order for them to add to extant knowledge. The subject has been shown to be vulnerable due to certain identified aspects of his personality, most notably that he is driven to rescue people, even to his own peril. Additionally, his acceptance of how the cyber identities present themselves, at least at the time of the events presented, clearly led him to be victimized. Because his personality suggests vulnerability, his presented life history is an ideal analytical tool for responding to the research questions. Robert portrayed a sense of innocence in his behavior with Connie. "Psychopaths feed on what they see as naiveté and innocence" (Babiak and Hare, 2006, p. 271).

This project leaves a lot of questions to be addressed with further research. The principal investigator recently completed an analysis of the impact on the children of their psychopathic mother's (Connie) behavior (Kreuter, 2006c). He is also developing an analysis of the personality of the psychopath through use of a single source of data: e-mail dialogue between the psychopath (Connie) and the principal investigator. As more is known about the vulnerability of victims, perhaps vulnerable individuals can be better protected from harm caused by psychopathic predators.

Based on the principal investigator's study of Robert, and the various ways he responded to the specific events in his life and to the environment in general, he exhibits mostly an extraverted personality style. He also has a sense of true altruism. Certainly, Robert's choice of career required him to be accustomed to having his every move in the cockpit both observed and recorded.

Robert's score on his intelligence test was average. Considering the highly technical nature of his occupation as a pilot, his technical acumen, and his verbal skills, and fund of knowledge, one would predict a higher score. However, questions exist as to the manner in which the test was administered. Thus, the reported result may not be conclusive.

Robert is an affable individual. His sincerity and affect are both appealing and trustworthy. The principal investigator has endeavored to verify all of Robert's self-reports with archival evidence as well as corroborating reports of those interviewed (Kreuter, 2002; 2006b). There have been no indications of falsification or embellishment of data. Robert's reports tend to be very detailed and reflect a superior memory as well as a rational thought process.

Initially, Robert seemed to be malingering, and maintaining his sense of distrust for law enforcement and psychologists. As facts of his case became known and by his candidness, the principal investigator saw in Robert a vulnerable individual, not helpless, but somehow comprised of elements that must have made him easy prey to the cunning predator as well as the unethical psychologists. Extensive research into psychopathic predator behavior and vulnerability led to the principal investigator's ultimate conclusion that Robert was victimized multiple times, and therefore his victim vulnerability deserved analysis. Hence, the essence of the principal investigators doctoral dissertation and this book was borne through this case study of Robert's life history.

Robert's relationship with his parents is very warm and affectionate. They are very supportive of his interests, though ultimately feared somewhat that he chose to become an airline pilot because of their perception of inherent danger. He learned that it was easier to keep things from his parents than to deal with their concerns. Robert was sensitive to their apprehension, which contributed to his reluctance to explain any of the problems he encountered.[116]

Von Hentig (1948) found certain distinct mechanisms that are not mutually exclusive and may exist simultaneously: the neurotic, the psychobiological, and the genetic-biological relationships. The principal investigator did not find any evidence of a hated authoritarian father or an incestuous fixation upon the mother or the inverse constellation.

There is ample evidence of a psychobiological connection between Robert and Connie. This association is the reciprocal attraction of two complementary constitutional types where one is the negative of the other. In this research, Robert needed someone to rescue, and Connie, as a psychopath, needed to find someone to infiltrate their life and steal from. Thus, she created a charade, which made it seem as if she fit the inverse of Robert. Her scheme was successful until Robert became so severely impacted that he took steps to end the situation, which ended the relationship. Ellenberger (1955) provided an example of this biological phenomenon, that of the pimp-prostitute alliance.

Importance of the Existential Perspective

Existentialism, as a recent phenomenon, has lineage traceable to the history of philosophy back as far as humanity's attempts to attain self-understanding. Early thinking included a mythological perspective, which has evolved in "attempts to treat myth allegorically, as the bearer of metaphysical truths for which no precise literal language would be adequate" (Macquarrie, 1972, p. 19). Recent theories about mythology see it as expressing in a symbolic manner truths about a person's own life and thoughts. While parallels between myths and dreams can be seen as projections of a person's inner desires, the existentialist sees in mythology the first attempts to describe identity.

Existentialism, as a construct, has been going through an evolution, in what William James (1886) called "the classic stages of a theory's career" (p. 198). As James found, new

[116] When the harm exacted on Robert became severe and he could no longer hide it, he finally did inform his parents.

theories are first attacked as absurd, then are often admitted as true. This is similar to the historical trend of organized religions, leading to the formation of cults or sects, split off from the mainstream, which then, over time, become new accepted religions in their own right. "The major themes of existentialism are vividly portrayed in nineteenth-century literature" (Brennan, 1994, p. 290). These writers included Fyoder Dostoyevsky (1821-1881) and Friedrich Nietzsche (1844-1900).

"The end of the 18th century had already brought the conflict between the rationalism of the Enlightenment and the rising spirit of Romanticism" (Macquarrie, 1972, p. 34). The existentialists have been opposed to rationalism as well as estheticism (sensibility and sensitivity) and sentimentalism (emotions).

A strong reaction to Georg Hegel's (1770-1831) metaphysical system of rationalism was expressed by Soren Kierkegaard (1813-1855), the father of modern existentialism. "The formal statement of modern existential principles resulted from a theological controversy surrounding the manner of knowing and experiencing God" (Brennan, 1994, p. 290). Kierkegaard was one of many who were critical of metaphysical systems. Years later, however, the construct of a system became less rigid. Martin Heidegger (1927/1962) thought that the existential analysis carried out in *Being and Time* were scientific (*wissenshaftlich*) in character (p. 49). This is particularly relevant to victims, who can find meaning in their suffering and move on with their lives in calculated and positive ways.

Kierkegaard had an introspective and melancholy disposition and viewed subjectivity and intensity as the criteria of truth and genuineness. In this view, reality is found in the intense moments of existence, especially moments of painful decision.

Existentialism has a metaphysical dimension, the status of which has varied throughout history. Metaphysics is defined as a theoretical philosophy of being and knowing, also called a philosophy of mind. Because human existence is the theme of existentialism, questions of a metaphysical kind arise. The existentialist denies that existence is an objectifiable empirical phenomenon. Kierkegaard's position agrees with that of St. Augustine that a person is an abyss (Macquarrie, 1972, p. 191). Today, there are various kinds of metaphysics. Speculative metaphysics may be regarded as an attempt to extend reason beyond the empirical phenomena of the world so as to grasp the supposedly supersensible reality underlying these phenomena (p. 190). Descriptive metaphysics set out to describe general categories by which we can understand our world, exploring the most general conditions of experience.

Within existence is a transcendence, thus the exploration of such is a metaphysical inquiry. Some existentialists avoid the word *metaphysics* and substitute the similar *inquiry of ontology*. Ontology is an aspect of metaphysical inquiry concerned with the question of existence apart from specific objects and events. "Allport's theories are psychological in explanation, but metaphysical in depth" i§hougassian, 1972, p. 14). Maslow (1962) reported that the expression *ontopsychology* was first suggested by Anthony Suttich in order to show how psychology nowadays is influenced by existentialism (p. 15). For Allport, "ontopsychology meant the psychology of the authentic and mature self, which in depth is a metaphysical answer to the perennial question: what is man?" (p. 14).

In the view of a popular modern existentialist, Jean-Paul Sartre (1905-1980), existence precedes essence and defines such in the individual. Sartre (1943) felt we are free to choose, but we must take responsibility for our choices. The existent has been reduced by modern thought to manifestations of appearances (p. 3). This has created a dualism between the finite and infinite. "Yet the existent in fact can not be reduced to a finite series of manifestations since each one of them is a relation to a subject constantly changing" (p. 5).

Macquarrie (1972) said, "Because man is an inexhaustible abyss and because moreover he is unintelligible apart from his environment in the widest sense, the existential analysis leads into the borders of ontological reflection" (p. 193). Therefore, an analysis of existence requires a view with a wide lens, looking at the total range of experience, especially at critical situations or the limits of a person.

The existentialist refers to ontological emotions (moods) in which the existent becomes very aware of his or her total situation. Ontological insights are possible through such awareness. These insights comprise the vision of being.

Nietzsche (1886/1966) called for a transformation in all values and created an image of a new individual who would create authentic values. Such a person lives courageously by overcoming illusions and taking responsibility for his or her life (Halling and Carroll, 1998, pp. 96-97).

"The existential style of philosophizing begins from man rather than from nature" (Macquarrie, 1972, p. 2). For the existentialist, the subject is the existent in the whole range of his existing. For Kierkegaard, existence is not to be studied, but lived. This is followed by Rogers' (1963) call for a science of the whole person. Extending Rogers' person-centered science, "Rollo May and others introduced the existential and phenomenological viewpoint into psychology and psychiatry" (Taylor and Martin, 2001, p. 22). Thus, the existential position is to focus attention on problems directly related to concrete human existence rather than abstract or speculative concepts.

Referring to the antecedents of existentialism, Jaspers (1953) expressed:

> What is new about this age . . . is that man becomes conscious of being as a whole, of himself and his limitations. He experiences the terror of the world, and his own powerlessness. He asks radical questions. Face to face with the void, he strives for liberation and redemption. By consciously recognizing his limits, he sets himself the highest goals. He experiences absoluteness in the depths of selfhood and in the lucidity of transcendence. (p. 2)

Prominent concepts in existential thinking include freedom, decision, and responsibility, finitude, guilt, alienation, despair, and death. These constitute the core of personal being through analysis and discovery of the emotional life of a person (feelings, moods, or affects). Such concepts cover the tragic elements in human existence. "It is through free and responsible decisions that man becomes authentically himself" (Macquarrie, 1972, p. 4).

Within the core of the construct of humanity is the nature or essence of individuals to make themselves become what it is in them to become, or fail to become it. Therefore, absent a blueprint to guide who they will become, individuals retain sovereignty over their decisions about their existence. Freedom, then, can be defined as individuality of the human spirit, rather than conformity.

Sartre (1943) held that values are created by our choices. Choices, themselves components of how a person responds to their environment, reflect a certain dimension of personality. When life choices return negative results, the manner of a person's adaptation and recovery from problems related to such choices is also worthy of evaluation by the existentialist.

It can be argued, then, that Maslow's theory of self-actualization might also include reaching a state of authenticity in one's life. The notable limitation of existential thinking is that it is centered on the individual, not the individual as a member of the community.

As Taylor and Martin (2001) suggested:

> The single most important contribution that humanistic psychologists have to make to modern psychology is to bring the attention of the experimenters to focus on the phenomenology of the science-making process and, once the attention of the discipline is focused on that point, to articulate a phenomenological (rather than a positivistic) epistemology as the basis for a new experimental science. (p. 26)

Existential psychology, particularly in the realm of therapy, looks more to the future than to the past, whereas Freud preferred a reconstruction of the past of the patient and to offer it back as analytical construction (Yalom, 1980, p. 347). Freud believed in the importance of the antecedent events as influential to all behavior and mental experience. "Most existential therapists tend to focus less on the past than do therapists of other persuasions, and more focus on the future tense, on the decisions beckoning one, the goals stretching out before one" (p. 349).

Jaspers (1954) viewed the human state as consisting of situations (p. 19). Situations that remain essentially the same even if their momentary aspect changes and their shattering force obscured are: I must die; I must suffer; I must struggle; I am subject to chance; and I involve myself inexorably in guilt. Jaspers called these fundamental situations of our existence *grenzsituation* (ultimate situations) (p. 20). This central concept of Jaspers is important to the understanding of existentialism. The ultimate situations are the inescapable realities in relation to which alone human life can be made genuinely meaningful. Ultimate situations cannot be changed or surmounted; they can only be acknowledged. Jaspers felt that by apprehending ultimate situations through a process of despair and rebirth, we become ourselves by a change in our consciousness of being (p. 20).

Jaspers (1954) wrote that our attitudes toward failure are crucial. "The way in which man approaches his failure determines what he will become" (p. 23). "Man seeks redemption" (p. 23). Redemption offered by religions is characterized by an objective guarantee of the truth and reality of redemption. All philosophy is a transcending of the world, analogous to redemption (p. 23).

Psychology would benefit from inclusion of the existential viewpoint, not just as a method of analysis but also for its potential impact in widening and deepening our concept of the person. As this research demonstrates features of certain aspects of the subject's personality, by evaluating his life and his environment, the principal investigator is able to understand the subject's behavior and actions in a larger, more meaningful way. This approach seems to add depth to the analysis of a person.

According to Schneider and May (1995), existential psychology is on the cusp of the change taking place in the world of psychology (p. 119). They suggested that a foundation incorporating the concepts of existential psychology "would view human being in its fullness while carefully acknowledging its tragedy and incompleteness" (p. 119).

Contemporary psycholoRß has placed a narrow range on the problems faced by patients. Adding to this limited approach, more substantive domains of psychological functioning, those of transpersonalism and postmodernism, may expand the focus.

"Transpersonal psychology encompasses those disciplines and practices that address transcendental (or nonordinary) states of consciousness" (Schneider and May, p. 121). The inclusion of existential concepts provides virtual insights into the transcendental phenomena as energy shifts, paranormal and visionary states, religious and spiritual crises, and unitive experiences (p. 122).

The postmodern approach draws upon the premise of social constructivism, which holds three basic assumptions: (1) There are no absolute truths, as all truth requires an interpretation; (2) all realities (or stories) are socially constructed; and (3) fluidity among realities is desirable (O'Hara and Anderson, 1991).

The existential approach to treatment is quite different than therapies with a cognitive-behavioral emphasis. According to Lazarus, Beutler, and Norcross (1992), the growing movement called technical eclecticism holds that the diversity of therapies can be unified by empirical means. Gendlin (1978) and Mahrer (1986) found that the problem with the postmodern approach is that the therapeutic-outcome literature is dominated by the quantitative-experimental tradition and neglects or ignores the emerging phenomenological analysis of outcome. "As a result, technical eclecticism tends to have a cognitive-behavioral bias, and existential approaches receive short shrift" (Schneider and May, 1995, p. 123). As an extension of using the existential perspective to interpret a single case of a victim, perhaps a therapy for victims based on existential principles would benefit them.

Spiegelberg (1972) wrote about the close identification of phenomenology with existentialism in psychology and psychiatry. "The new phenomenological existentialism differs from the original one by maintaining that existence can be approached phenomenologically among others in its essential structures" (p. xxix). As an offshoot of the early work of William James and Gordon Allport, the development of American phenomenological and existential psychology and psychiatry reached an important point with the publication in 1958 of *Existence: A New Dimension in Psychiatry and Psychology*, edited by Rollo May, Ernest Angel, and Henri F. Ellenberger. Ellenberger (1955) also found that the offender and his or her victim share many characteristics.

Rogers (1959) also claimed to appreciate the phenomenal field, though incidental in his writings. He wrote, "The essential point about the therapeutic process is that the way the client perceives the objects in his phenomenal field—his experiences, his feelings, his self, other persons, his environment—undergoes change in the direction of increased differentiation" (p. 142).

Rogers (1959) felt that counseling should be based on a structured, permissive relationship that allows the client to gain an understanding of the self in order to take positive steps. The emphasis is on acceptance of self. By centering on the client, the counselor has a more accurate role and the client becomes the focus of the counselor's attention (p. 27).

May's existential psychology included phenomenological themes. May felt that existence is experienced most explicitly in the I-am experience, the act of contact with and acceptance of the fact that I am (1961, p. 43). May's approach is characteristic of the Kierkegaardian emphasis on the existential connection between selfhood and anxiety as the sense of the possibility of non-being and even self-destruction (Spiegelberg, 1972, p. 162). May's main concern was to create a new existential view of individual capability of supporting a therapy that can strengthen the self in facing the anxieties of modern life.

Spiegelberg (1972) felt that "it will probably take more time and effort before the new European ingredients have been critically absorbed and integrated into the mainstream of the

American tradition" (p. 168). He felt that "the present role of phenomenology in the total picture of psychology and psychiatry, particularly in the Anglo-American world, is a minor one and has not shown significant growth in recent years except at the 'fringes'" (p. 364). Spiegelberg felt that new concrete and limited projects in depth are needed as well as the development and application of more critical standards. Further, a return to the naiveté of pre-scientific life-world was suggested by Husserl (1959), who stated, "We shall not enter the kingdom of a true psychology unless we become like children. We must look for the A B C of consciousness and thus become really A B C beginners" (p. 65). In terms of the future, Spiegelberg suggested that continued development in phenomenology focus on concreteness, limited scope of projects so as to add greater penetration, and relevance. Teamwork is also recommended with open-minded specialists in the field.

Ludwig Binswanger and Medard Boss, both psychiatrists, were among the founders of existential analysis in the field of psychotherapy and were the main existential critics of Freud. They saw their work as a metapsychological correction of the positivistic theoretical foundations of psychoanalysis, which left Freud's empirical and clinical insights largely intact (Izenberg, 1976, p. 109). Existentialism and psychoanalysis have very different concepts of the roots of selfhood. Selfhood was not disembodied consciousness but body-soul unity that showed up the emptiness and helplessness of mere will when it was arrayed against the deepest desires of the self.

The principal investigator believes that victims are better off focusing on their future rather then on their past. While the history of vulnerability of many victims is clearly notable and the harm done to their lives certainly great, many remain sentient and ambulatory. As such, they have potential to embark on a path to new destinies in their lives.

Existentialism, applied to the lives of victims, yields compassion and understanding to their individual plight. It also retains the capacity to guide them towards greater self-awareness, which, in turn, could lead to an improved sense of proportion in their life activities. With greater proportionality, victims may make better choices in terms of their future, such as commencing new education and job training.

The overriding principles of existential thought seem fully appropriate in the complete evaluation of victims. In the principal investigator's experience, the stories of many victims yield varying reactions. To those who are quick to judge, they may be viewed simply as naïve. To those with compassion, they are viewed as tragic and deserving of sympathy and help. Perhaps the existential therapeutic approach is to first understand the victim, then to coach the person towards a deeper internal understanding of the self. Through this process, the victim may be able to gain meaning from suffering and self-actualization by triumphing over despair.

The research questions have been answered by evaluating the subject from the existential perspective. Through this approach, the subject, a repeat victim, is found vulnerable due to his approach to life and how he responds to others. This book explores the subject from an atypical viewpoint. The common perspective would look to assign a certain pathological diagnosis confined to the available labels as found in the DSM. Characteristics as well as traits would be the aspects of the subject used in making such a determination. Treatment would fall into a cognitive-behavioral or psychodynamic paradigm.

By exploring the subject as a whole person, using criteria from the existential-humanistic perspective, the subject is not deemed to have pathology, but vulnerability due to his approach to life. His suffering can be seen as one aspect of his journey through life. The existential criteria open up a broader range of consideration in the interpretation of the victim. Instead of viewing his repeat victimization in the context of a defined personality disorder, the subject's actions, attitudes, and even his dreams reflect an individual who is struggling through life in order to find truer meaning of his existence.

This research provides examples of how the subject, as a victim, responded to the actions of the predator, a criminal. What was found is that the interior life-world of the subject very much revolves around heroic acts and prolonged seemingly selfless and driven efforts to rescue the oppressed, even to his own peril. Perhaps the hero-rescuer nature of the subject's interiority provide meaning to him, therefore demonstrating the need for relationships between the hero and the oppressed or even the victim and the criminal. Not only did the predator serve Robert's needs as someone to share with, but she presented as a distressed individual for him to rescue.

A paradoxical and unresolvable question is: To what extent has the principal investigator been an enabler in the subject's misfortunes without knowing it? To address this question, the principal investigator asked the subject, checked with the subject's therapist, and underwent a brief therapy himself with a focus on this issue. The answer in every case was that the subject's situation was not made worse, and in several instances may have actually been helped. The various roles of the principal investigator included tax advisor, quasi lay therapist, and objective researcher. The principal investigator does not always have control over the overlap or the outcome. The real extent of the boundary conflict, which could be created as a result of this multivaried relationship between the principal investigator and the subject, might possibly have come to light later once the principal investigator's dissertation was complete. After its completion and acceptance, the subject reviewed the document and a lively discussion followed. Certain facts regarding events in the subject's life have been clarified and the subject has been enlightened as to the findings contained in this case study. The reader is referred to the discussion in Chapter 4 (Methodology) under the subchapter heading Limitations and Delimitations.

What requires further exploration is how the subject in this research can move forward with his life and fully depart from his present quest for vindication. While the principal investigator concludes that the subject is justified in his quest due to the severity of the harm he has suffered, perhaps his vulnerability will perpetuate until the subject gives his life a more positive direction, not one solely based in retrospect.

EPILOGUE

Perhaps irony or even poetic justice struck the principal investigator recently when he was victimized by a potentially psychopathic predator. Having devoted the better part of 5 years studying the fascinating case of Robert, both in his doctoral research and now in the form of this book, encountering first-hand a person, who will be referred to as a psychopath, brought new light into the eyes of this researcher. With the rays of this new vision came deeper understanding of Robert and greater appreciation for how the heart and mind can lead to vulnerability.

In the case of the victimization of the principal investigator, like Robert, the culprit was female. And, like Robert's case, the woman used knowledge combined with the wicked use of intellect to create an elaborate scam, believable yes, but admittedly close to the edge of absurdity. The similarities between the two situations include:

- Both Robert and the principal investigator were in their 40's at the time of victimization.
- The psychopaths were about the same age (42 and 41).
- Both psychopaths used the Internet to perpetrate fraudulent illusions.
- Both psychopaths claimed to "know" high profile people.
- Both psychopaths assumed fraudulent identities in cyberspace, assuming personas of well-known people.
- Both psychopaths were not particularly attractive.
- Both psychopaths manipulated their victims by relating stories of their own traumatic lives at the hands of others as a way of garnering sympathy.
- Both psychopaths tried to convince their victims that they had been physically abused by their tormentors in the past.
- Both psychopaths attempted convince their victims that they are currently in the midst of being physically abused.
- Both psychopaths were adept at up-close psychological sleight-of-hand tricks, i.e., the subterfuge of allowing the victim to hear only one side of a phone conversation that was, in effect, an act for one person having a sole dialogue.
- Both psychopaths forged official instruments to further enhance the degree of the scam.
- Both psychopaths had a previous criminal history.
- Both psychopaths had the ability to blend into society to the extent of employment in professional capacities (however, both lost their jobs and harmed their employers).
- Both psychopaths were disenfranchised from their families.
- Both psychopaths initiated the scam and took extreme measures to keep the scam going, taking much time, energy and planning to execute the various illusions.
- Both victims were appealed to by their psychopaths to get involved with them at a personal level, i.e., to help them in some way.
- Both psychopaths insisted on long hours of telephone, e-mail, and Instant Messaging dialogue with the victims.

Most fortunately, the principal investigator used his developed awareness of these types of scams and created effective walls of protection and quickly blew the cover off the charade. However, damage was done in the form of embarrassment, loss of time, and immense disappointment. Emotions such as sadness, anger, and elation mixed badly and led to moments of despair, panic, and irrationality. Yet, through the process, the principal investigator, like Robert, asked very pertinent questions of the psychopath in order to uncover the truth or to disprove what was being told. However, many of these questions did not lead to a conclusion, but were responded to with spontaneously created lies that, for the moment, satisfied the curiosity of the victim or provided a distraction that served to take away focus on uncovering the truth. Thankfully, two weeks of confusion ended without much ado. Still, it is worthy to note that what occurred in the case of Robert, as well as this recent event, can happen to anyone. A common reaction of people who are told of this type of victimization is to be sympathetic, but there is also the appearance of distance between their compassion for the victim and any real notion that they, too, are concerned that something similar could happen to them. So, be cautious out there in the world. The problem in dealing with a psychopath is that you don't know you're dealing with a psychopath. It is like looking out for the invisible man. There are dangerous wolves appearing as sheep. If you are not careful you will surely be sheared. A small token of advice: if you sense a scam, go to the police. Many victims refuse to report scams because of potential embarrassment. Psychopaths are aware of this trepidation so they feel quite immune from prosecution. Perhaps this book will help bring out courage in future victims to help society by reporting scams. We might not be able to get them before they strike, but we can at least try to get them after they cause harm.

Just as the study of victimization, at least from the existential perspective, is new, the phenomenon of law enforcement's inability to recognize the effect on victims of assaults by psychopathic predators and deal with victims in an effective and appropriate manner also requires further study. The victim, like the eye witness, is in the best position to help understand the psychopathic perpetrator. Unfortunately, law enforcement appreciates witnesses when they can cite physical crimes, but the psychological crime is much more difficult to garner respect, although such harm is often just as serious.

Original oil painting done by: Robert's mother

References

Abrams K and Robinson G (1998a) Stalking Part I: an overview of the problem. Canadian *Journal of Psychiatry* 43.

Abramson, P. (1992). *A case for case studies*. Newbury Park, CA: Sage.

Abramson, L.Y., Seligman, M. E. P., and Teasdale, J. D. (1978). Learned helplessness in humans: Critique and reformulation. *Journal of Abnormal Psychology, 87*, 49-74.

Adler, A. (1924). *The practice and theory in individual psychology* (P. Radin, Trans.). New York: Harcourt Brace Jovanovich.

Adler, A. (1998). *Understanding human nature*. Center City, MN: Hazledden. (Original work published 1927)

Allport, G. (1933). The study of personality by the experimental method. *Character and Personality, 1, 259-264.*

Allport, G. (1937). *Personality: A psychological interpretation*. New York: Henry Holt.

Allport, G. (1965). *Letters from Jenny*. New York: Harcourt, Brace and World.

Allport, G. W. (1927). Concepts of trait and personality. *Psychological Bulletin, 24*, 284-293.

Allport, G. W. (1960). *Personality and social encounter*. Boston: Beacon Press.

Allport, G. W. (1961). *Pattern and growth in personality*. New York: Holt, Rinehart and Winston.

Allport, G. W., and Vernon, P. E. (1930). The field of personality. *Psychological Bulletin, 27*, 677-730.

American Psychiatric Association. (1980). *Diagnostic and statistical manual of mental disorders* (3rd ed.). Washington, DC: Author.

American Psychiatric Association. (1987). *Diagnostic and statistical manual of mental disorders* (3rd ed., rev.). Washington, DC: Author.

American Psychiatric Association (2000). *Diagnostic and statistical manual of mental disorders* (4th ed., text revision). Washington, DC: Author.

American Society of Victimology. (2005, January 24). *The third American symposium on victimology.* Retrieved January 24, 2005, from http://www .American-Society-Victimology.us/Jan.24.

Arons, M., and Richards, R. (2001). Two noble insurgencies: Creativity and humanistic psychology. In K. J. Schneider, J. F. T. Bugental, and J. F. Pierson (Eds.), *The handbook of humanistic psychology: Leading edges in theory, research, and practice* (pp. 127-142). Thousand Oaks, CA: Sage.

Babiak, P, and Hare, R.D. (2006). *Snakes in suits: When psychopaths go to work.* New York: HarperCollins.

Bandura, A. (1986). *Social foundations of thought and action.* Englewood Cliffs, NJ: Prentice-Hall.

Becker, E. (1971). *The birth and death of meaning: An interdisciplinary perspective on the problem of man* (2nd ed.). New York: The Free Press.

Black, W. J. (1972). *The works of William Shakespeare.* Roslyn, NY: Black's Readers Service.

Blackburn, R. (1998). Psychopathy and the contribution of personality to violence. In R. D. Davis, T. Millon, E. Simonsen, and M. Birket-Smith (Eds.), *Psychopathy: Antisocial, criminal, and violent behavior* (pp. 50-68). New York: Guilford Press.

Blair, J, Mitchell, D. and Blair, K. (2005). *The psychopath: Emotion and the brain.* Malden, MA: Blackwell Publishing.

Bocij, P. (2004). Cyberstalking: *Harassment in the Internet age and how to protect your family.* Westport, CT: Greenwood Publishing Group.

Bocij, P., Bocij, H., and McFarlane, L. (2003) Cyberstalking: A case study concerning serial harassment in the UK. *British Journal of Forensic Practice, 5*(2) 25-32.

Bojij, P. (2005). Reactive stalking: a new perspective on victimisation, *The British Journal of Forensic Practice,* 2.

Bodner, E., and Mikulciner, M. (1998). Learned helplessness and the occurrence of depressive-like and paranoid-like responses: The role of attentional focus. *Journal of Personality and Social Psychology, 74*(4), 1010-1023.

Bolgar, H. (1965). The case study method. In B. Wolman (Ed.), *Handbook of clinical psychology* (pp. 28-38). New York: McGraw-Hill.

Brennan, J. F. (1994). *History and systems of psychology* (5th ed.). Upper Saddle River, NJ: Prentice-Hall.

Breslau, N., Davis, G. C., and Andreski, P. (1995). Risk factors for PTSD related traumatic events: A prospective analysis. *American Journal of Psychiatry, 152*, 529-535.

Briere, J. (2002). *Psychological assessment of adult posttraumatic states.* Washington, DC: American Psychological Association.

Bromley, D. B. (1977). *Personality description in ordinary language.* New York: Wiley.

Brown, I., and Inouye, D. K. (1978). Learned helplessness through modeling: The role of perceived similarity in competence. *Journal of Personality and Social Psychology, 36,* 900-908.

Brune, M. (2003). Erotomania (De Clerambault's Syndrome) revisited – Clues to its origin from evolutionary theory. In S. P. Shohov (Ed.), *Advances in psychology research, 21*, (pp. 185-212). New York: Nova Science Publishers.

Bugental, J. F. T. (1978). *Psychotherapy and process: The fundamentals of an existential-humanistic approach.* Boston: McGraw-Hill.

Burgess, A., and Hazelwood, R. (Eds.). (1995). *Practical aspects of rape investigation: A multidisciplinary approach* (2nd ed.). New York: CRC Press.

Byrne, M. (2003). Trauma reactions in the offender. *International Journal of Forensic Psychology 1*(1) 59-70.

Campbell, D. T., and Stanley, J. C. (1966). *Experimental and quasi-experimental designs for research.* Chicago: Rand McNally.

Carlen, P. (1986). Psychiatry in prisons: Promises, premises, practices and politics. In P. Miller and N. Rose (Eds.), *The power of psychiatry* (pp. 241-66). London: Polity.

Carozza, D. (2005). Battling elusive identity theft. *Fraud Magazine, 19*(4), 36-40.

Chisum, W. J. (1999). An introduction to crime reconstruction. In B. Turvey (Ed.), *Criminal profiling: An introduction to behavioral evidence analysis* (pp. 73-85). San Diego, CA: Academic Press.

Cleckley, H. (1976). *Mask of insanity*. St. Louis, MO: C.V. Mosby. (Original work published 1941)

Cole, C. S., and Coyne, J. C. (1977). Situational-specificity of laboratory-induced learned helplessness. *Journal of Abnormal Psychology, 86*, 615-623.

Collins, M. J., and Wilkas, M. B. (2001). Stalking trauma syndrome and the traumatized victim. In J. A. Davis (Ed.), *Stalking crimes and victim protection: Prevention, intervention, threat assessment, and case management* (pp. 317-334). Boca Raton, FL: CRC Press.

Cooper, M. (2003). *Existential therapies*. London: Sage.

Davis, J. (1999, June). *Personality psychology, trait theory, behavioral contiguity and reciprocal determinism: The key to the assessment of potential threat.* Inservice presentation, Association for Threat Assessment Professionals (ATAP), San Diego, CA.

Davis, J., and Chipman, M. A. (1997). Stalkers and other obsessional types: A forensic psychological typology of those who stalk. *Journal of Clinical Forensic Medicine, U.K., 4*, 166-172.

Davis, R. D., and Millon, T. (1998). Ten subtypes of psychopathy. In. R. D. Davis, T. Millon, E. Simonsen, and M. Birket-Smith (Eds.), *Psychopathy: Antisocial, criminal, and violent behavior* (pp. 161-170). New York: Guilford Press.

De Clerambault, G. G. (1942). *Les psychoses passionelles.* In J. Fretet (Ed.), *Oeuvres psychiatriques*. Paris: Presses Universitaires de France.

Dersch, J., Palatin, P. B., and Gotchel, R. J. (2002). Chronic pain and psychopathology: Research findings and theoretical considerations. *Psychosomatic Medicine, 64*, 773-786.

Douglas, D., and Anisman, H. (1975). Helplessness or expectation incongruence: Effects of aversive stimulation of subsequent performance. *Journal of Experimental Psychology: Human Perception and Performance, 1*, 411-417.

Douglas, J. (2003). *Anyone you want me to be: A true story of sex and death on the Internet.* New York: Scribner.

Drapkin, I., and Viano, E. (Eds.) (1975). *Victimology: A new focus* (vol. I). Lexington, MA: Lexington Books.

Dvoskin, J. A., and Patterson, R. F. (1998). Administration of treatment programs for offenders with mental disorders. In R. M. Wettstein (Ed.), *Treatment of offenders with mental disorders* (pp. 1-43). New York: Guilford Press.

Eisner, E.W. (1991). *The enlightened eye: Qualitative inquiry and the enhancement of educational practice*. New York: Macmillan.

El-Assra, A. (1989). Erotomania in a Saudi woman. *British Journal of Psychiatry, 155*, 553-555.

Ellenberger, H. F. (1955). Psychological relationships between criminal and victim. *Archives of Criminal Psychodynamics, 1*(2), 257-290.

Ellenberger, H. F. (1958). A clinical introduction to psychiatric phenomenology and existential analysis. In R. May, E. Angel, and H. F. Ellenberger (Eds.), *Existence: A new dimension in psychiatry and psychology* (pp. 92-127). New York: Basic Books.

European Forum for Victim Services. (2005, January 24). *Repeat victimization*. Retrieved January 24, 2005, from *http://www.victimology.nl/on/pub/eurforsocrtsvic98a.html.*

Feifel, H. (1959). Attitudes toward death in some normal and mentally ill populations. In H. Feifel (Ed.), *The meaning of death* (pp. 114-132). New York: McGraw-Hill.

Ferris, J. R. (2002). *Internet addiction disorders: Causes, symptoms, and consequences.* Retrieved February 20, 2005, from: *http://www.chem.vt.edu/chem.dept/dessy/honors/papers/ferris.html*

Frankl, V. (1984). *Man's search for meaning: An introduction to logotherapy.* New York: Pocket Books. (Original work published 1959)

Frankl, V. E. (1963). Existential dynamics and neurotic escapism (paper read before the Conference on Existential Psychiatry, Toronto, May 6, 1962). *Journal of Existential Psychiatry, IV*, 27-42.

Frankl, V. E. (1986). *The doctor and the soul: From psychotherapy to logotherapy* (3rd ed.). (Trans. R. Winston and C. Winston). New York: Vintage.

Frankl, V. E. (1988). *The will to meaning: Foundations and applications of logotherapy.* London: Meridian.

Frankl, V. E. (2000). *Recollections: An autobiography.* (J. Fabry and J. Fabry, Trans.). Cambridge, MA: Perseus.

Freud, S. (1923). *The ego and the* id: *The standard edition of the complete psychological works, Vol. 19.* London: Hogarth.

Freud, S. (1952). *On dreams* (J. Strachey, Trans. and Ed.). New York: W. W. Norton.

Freud, S. (1961). *Introductory lectures of psycho-analysis: The standard edition of the complete psychological works, Vol. 16 (Part 3),* (J. Strachey, Trans. and Ed.). London: Hogarth.

Fuller, R. (1988). Psychological religiousness: Resisting the tide of disenchantment. *Pastoral Psychology, 36*(3), 146-163.

Geiger, T. C., and Crick, N. R. (2001). A developmental psychopathology perspective on vulnerability to personality disorders. In R. E. Ingram and J. M. Price (Eds.), *Vulnerability to psychopathology* (pp. 57-102). New York: Guilford Press.

Gendlin, E. (1978). *Focusing.* New York: Bantam.

Ghougassian, J. P. (1972). *Gordon W. Allport's ontopsychology of the person.* New York: Philosophical Library.

Giorgi, A. (1970). *Psychology as a human science.* New York: Harper and Row.

Green, B., Grace, M. C., and Glaser, C. G. (1985). Identifying survivors at risk: Long-term impairment following the Beverly Hills Supper Club fire. *Journal of Consulting and Clinical Psychology, 53*, 672-678.

Greening, T. (2003). Four existential challenges: Three responses to each, adapted from: Greening, T. Existential challenges and responses. *The Humanistic Psychologist, 20*(1), Spring, 1992.

Gross, H. (1901). Zur frage des reflectoiden handelns. *Archiv fur Kriminal- Anthropologie und Kriminalistik, 7*, 154-158.

Gross, L. (2000). *Surviving a stalker: Everything you need to know to keep yourself safe.* New York: Marlowe.

Guggenbuhl-Craig, A. (1999). *The emptied soul: On the nature of the psychopath* (G. V. Hartman, Trans.). Woodstock, CT: Spring. (Original work published 1980)

Guignon, C. B. (2002). Existentialism. *Routledge encyclopedia of philosophy.* Retrieved July 25, 2005, from *http://www.rep.routledge.com*

Hall, C. S., and Lindzey, G. (1978). *Theories of personality.* New York: John Wiley.

Hall, D. M. (1998). The victims of stalking. In J. R. Meloy (Ed.), *The psychology of stalking: Clinical and forensic perspectives,* (pp. 115-136). San Diego, CA: Academic Press.

Halling, S., and Carroll, A. (1998). Existential-phenomenological psychology. In D. Moss (Ed.), *Humanistic and transpersonal psychology* (pp. 95-124). Westport, CT: Greenwood.

Hare, R. (1970). *Psychopathy: Theory and research.* New York: Wiley.

Hare, R. (1986). Twenty years of experience with the Cleckley psychopath. In W. Reid, D. Dorr, J. Walker, and J. Bonner (Eds.), *Unmasking the psychopath* (pp. 3-27). New York: Norton.

Hare, R. D. (1991). *The Hare Psychopathy Checklist – Revised.* Toronto, Ontario: Canada Systems.

Hare, R. D. (1993). *Without conscience: The disturbing world of the psychopaths among us.* New York: Guilford Press.

Hare, R. D. (1996). Psychopathy and antisocial personality disorder: A case of diagnostic confusion. *Psychiatric Times, 13*(2), 32-39.

Hare, R. D. (1998). Psychopaths and their nature: Implications for the mental health and criminal justice systems. In R. D. Davis, T. Millon, E. Simonson, and M. Birket-Smith, (Eds.), *Psychopathy: Antisocial, criminal, and violent behavior* (pp. 95-109). New York: Guilford Press.

Harmon, R., Rosner, R., and Owens, H. (1995). Obesssional harassment and erotomania in a criminal court population. *Journal of Forensic Sciences, 40*(2), 188-196.

Harris, G. T., Rice, M. E., and Cormier, C. A. (1991). Psychopathy and violent recidivism. *Law and Human Behavior, 15*, 625-37.

Harvard Medical School. (2006, January). *Client-centered therapy, 22*(7), 1-3. Author.

Healy, W., and Healy, M. T. (1969). *Pathological lying, accusation, and swindling: A study in forensic psychology.* Montclair, NJ: Patterson Smith.

Heidegger, M. (1962). *Being and time* (J. Macquarrie and E. Robinson, Trans.). San Francisco: Harper Collins. (Original work published 1927)

Hiroto, D. S., and Seligman, M. E. P. (1975). Generality of learned helplessness in man. *Journal of Personality and Social Psychology, 31,* 311-327.

Hollon, S. D. (1999). Psychotherapy and pharmacotherapy: Efficacy, generalizability, and cost-effectiveness. In N. E. Miller and K. M. Magruder (Eds.), *Cost-effectiveness of psychotherapy: A guide for practitioners, researchers, and policymakers* (pp. 14-26). New York: Oxford University Press.

Hollon, S. D., and Cobb, R. (1993). Relapse and recurrence in psychopathological disorders. In C. G. Costello (Ed.), *Basic issues in psychopathology* (pp. 377-402). New York: Oxford University Press.

Hollon, S. D., Evans, M. D., and DeRubeis, R. J. (1990). Cognitive mediation of relapse prevention following treatment for depression: Implications of differential risk. In R. E. Ingram (Ed.), *Contemporary psychological approaches to depression: Theory, research, and treatment* (pp. 117-136). New York: Plenum.

Holloway, H. C., and Fullerton, C. S. (1994). The psychology of terror and its aftermath. In R. J. Ursano, C. S. Fullerton, and B. G. McCaughey (Eds.), *Individual and community response to trauma and disaster: The structure of human chaos* (pp. 31-45). Cambridge, England: Cambridge University Press.

Hughes, R. (1993). *Culture of complaint: The fraying of America.* New York: Oxford University Press.

Husserl, E. (1959). Dank an Husserl. In H. L. Van Breda (Ed.), *Edmund Husserl, 1859-1938* (pp. 1-41). The Hague: Nijhoff.

Husserl, E. (1960). *Cartesian meditations: An introduction to phenomenology.* The Hague, Netherlands: Nilhoff. (Original work published 1931)

Identity Fraud, Inc. (2005, January 21). Protect your identity: Engaging solutions for identity protection. Retrieved January 21, 2005, from: http://www.identityfraud.com/main/index.aspx

Ingram, R. E., and Fortier, M. (2001). The nature of adult vulnerability. In R. E. Ingram and J. M. Price, (Eds.), *Vulnerability to psychopathology* (pp. 39-54). New York: Guilford Press.

Ingram, R. E., and Price, J. M. (2001). The role of vulnerability in understanding psychopathology. In R. E. Ingram and J. M. Price, (Eds.). *Vulnerability to psychopathology* (pp. 3-19). New York: Guilford Press.

Izenberg, G. N. (1976). *The existentialist critique of Freud.* Princeton, NJ: Princeton University Press.

James, H. (Ed.). (1920). *The letters of William James* (Vol. II, pp. 253-254). Boston: Atlantic Monthly Press.

James, W. (1886). Notes on echolalia in Mrs. Piper. In F. H. Burkhardt, F. Bowers, and I. Skrupskelis, (Eds.), *The collected works of William James: Essays in psychical research.* Cambridge, MA: Harvard University Press.

James, W. (1961). *Psychology: The briefer course.* New York: Harper. (Original work published 1892)

Jaspers, K. (1953). *The origin and goal of history* (M. Bullock, Trans.). New Haven, CT: Greenwood Press.

Jaspers, K. (1954). *Way to wisdom: An introduction to philosophy.* (R. Manheim, Trans.). New Haven, CT: Yale University Press.

Jaspers, K. (1986). *Karl Jaspers: Basic philosophical writings.* (E. Ehrlich, L. H. Ehrlich, and G. B. Pepper, Trans.). New Brunswick, NJ: Humanities Press.

Jung, C. G. (1960). *On the nature of the psyche.* (R. F. C. Hull, Trans.). Princeton, NJ: Princeton University Press.

Jung, C. G. (1969). *The archetypes and the collective unconscious: Collected works.* (R. F. C. Hull, Trans.). Princeton, NJ: Princeton University Press.

Jung, C. G. (1976). *Psychological types: Collected works.* (R. F. C. Hull, Trans.). Princeton, NJ: Princeton University Press.

Kessler, R. C., Sonnega, A., Bromet, E., Hughes, M., and Nelson, C. B. (1995). Posttraumatic stress disorder in the national comorbidity survey. *Archives of General Psychiatry, 52*, 1048-1060.

Kiesler, C. A., and Sibulkin, A. E. (1987). *Mental hospitalization: Myths and facts about a national crisis.* Newbury Park, CA: Sage.

Klingberg, H., Jr. (1995). Tracing logotherapy to its roots. *Journal des Viktor-Frankl-Instituts, I,* 9-20.

Koch, S. (1993). 'Psychology' or 'the psychological studies.' *American Psychologist, 48*, 902-904.

Kraepelin, E. (1883). Compendium der psychiatrie. *Zum Gebrauche fur Studirende und Arzte. 1. Aufl. Leipzig: Ambrosius Abel*, 305-308.

Kratochwill, T. R. (1978). *Single subject research*. New York: Academic Press.

Kreuter, E. A. (2002). *Case study of a pilot's loss of license due to faulty psychological evaluations*. Unpublished manuscript, Saybrook Graduate School and Research Center, San Francisco.

Kreuter, E. A. (2003a). *Theories of psychopathy: History, types, diagnosis, and treatment.* Unpublished manuscript, Saybrook Graduate School and Research Center, San Francisco.

Kreuter, E. A. (2003b). *Theories of victim vulnerability and non-random selection by psychopathic predators*. Unpublished manuscript, Saybrook Graduate School and Research Center, San Francisco.

Kreuter, E. A. (2003c). The impact of identity theft through cyberspace. *The Forensic Examiner, 12*(5), 30-35.

Kreuter, E. A. (2004). Investigation of a psychopathic criminal's behavior as the wheels of justice slowly turn. *The Forensic Examiner, 13*(4), 28-35.

Kreuter, E. A. (2005). Transformation through poetic awareness of the inner pain of the prisoner. *Journal of Poetry Therapy, 18*(2), 97-101.

Kreuter, E. A. (2006a). Prose and cons: Use of poetry in existential-humanistic therapy for prisoners. *Journal of Poetry Therapy, 19*(1), 1-6.

Kreuter, E.A. (2006b). *Victim vulnerability: An existential-humanistic interpretation of a single case study.* Unpublished doctoral dissertation, Saybrook graduate School and Research Center, San Francisco.

Kreuter, E. A. (2006c). The psychopathic criminal mother: A case study of her two daughters' expression of basic mistrust. In F. Columbus (Ed.), *Archives in psychology research, Vol. 41.* (pp. 75-90) Hauppauge, NY: Nova Science.

Kubler-Ross, E. (1997). *On death and dying: What the dying have to teach doctors, nurses, clergy, and their own families*. New York: Touchstone.

Kvale, S. (1996). *InterViews: An introduction to qualitative research interviewing*. Thousand Oaks, CA: Sage.

Lagache, D. (1950). *Psycho-criminogenese*. Paris: Congres International de Criminologie.

Laing, R. D. (1965). *The divided self: An existential study in sanity and madness.* Harmondsworth, England: Penguin.

Laing, R. D. (1967). *The politics of experience*. New York: Random House.

Lazarus, A., Beutler, L., and Norcross, J. (1992). The future of technical eclecticism. *Psychotherapy,* 29(1), 11-20.

Leitz Spitz, M. A. (2003). Stalking: Terrorism at our doors—how social workers can help victims fight back. *Social Work, 48*(4), 504-512.

Levy, L. (1970). *Conceptions of personality*. New York: Random House.

Leys, R. (1991). Types of one: Adolf Meyer's life chart and the representation of Individuality. *Representations*, *34,* 1-28.

Locke, L. F., Spirduso, W. W., and Silverman, S. J. (2000). *Proposals that work: A guide for planning dissertations and grant proposals* (4th ed.). Thousand Oaks, CA: Sage.

Lucks, B. O. (2001). Electronic crime, stalkers, and stalking: Relentless pursuit, harassment, and terror online in cyberspace. In J. A. Davis (Ed.), *Stalking crimes and victim protection: Prevention, intervention, threat assessment, and case management* (pp. 161-204). Boca Raton, FL: CRC Press.

Lundberg, G. A. (1926). Case work and the statistical method. *Social Forces, 5*, 61-65.

Luthar, S. S., and Zigler, E. (1991). Vulnerability and competence: A review of research on resilience in childhood. *American Journal of Orthopsychiatry, 61,* 6-22.

Macquarrie, J. (1972). *Existentialism.* Harmondsworth, England: Penguin.

Mahrer, A. (1986). *Therapeutic experiencing: The process of change*. New York: Norton.

Maier, S. F., Seligman, M. E. P., and Solomon, R. L. (1969). Pavlovian fear conditioning and learned helplessness: Effects on escape and avoidance behavior of (a) the CS-US contingency, and (b) the independence of the US and voluntary responding. In B. A. Campbell and R. M. Church (Eds.), *Punishment* (pp. 42-57). New York: Appleton-Century-Crofts.

Maslow, A. H. (1954). *Motivation and personality*. New York: Harper.

Maslow, A. H. (1962). *Toward a psychology of being*. Princeton, NJ: D. Van Nostrand.

May, R. (1961). The emergence of existential psychology. In R. May (Ed.), *Existential psychology* (pp. 11-51). New York: Random House.

McCallum, D. (2001). *Personality and dangerousness: Genealogies of antisocial personality disorder*. Cambridge, MA: University Press.

McClurkin, D. (2001). *Eternal victim, eternal victor*. Lanham, MD: Pneuma Life.

McHugh, P. R. (2001, August). *Psychiatric research report.* Retrieved August 16, 2001, from *http://www. Hopkinsmedicine.org/press/2001/august/McHugh.htm*

McNally, R. J. (2001). Vulnerability to anxiety disorders in adulthood. In R. E. Ingram and J. M. Price (Eds.), *Vulnerability to psychopathology* (pp. 304-321). New York: Guilford Press.

Meloy, J. R. (1989). Unrequited love and the wish to kill: Diagnosis and treatment of Borderline erotomania. *Bulletin of the Meninger Clinic*, *53*, 477-92.

Meloy, J. R. (1998). *The psychology of stalking: Clinical and forensic perspectives.* San Diego, CA: Academic Press.

Meloy, J. R. (2002). *The psychopathic mind: Origins, dynamics, and treatment*. Northvale, NJ: Jason Aronson.

Mendelson, B. (1974). The origin of the doctrine of victimology. In L. Drapkin and E. Viano (Eds.), *Victimology* (pp. 50-74). Lexington, KY: Lexington Books.

Merleau-Ponty, M. (1962). *Phenomenology of perception*. London: Routledge and Kegan Paul.

Meyer, A. (1948). *The commonsense psychiatry of Dr. Adolf Meyer*. New York: McGraw-Hill.

Mikulciner, M., and Solomon, Z. (1988). Attributional style and combat-related posttraumatic stress disorder. *Journal of Abnormal Psychology, 97*, 308-313.

Millon, T., and Davis, R. (2000). *Personality disorders in modern life*, New York: Wiley.

Mills, J. (1997). The false *Dasein*: From Heidegger to Sartre and psychoanalysis. *Journal of Phenomenological Psychology, 28*(1), 42-65.

Moran, F. H. (1940). The *sex criminal on parole, tenth report of the Division of Parole.* Albany, NY: Author.

Murphy, G., and Kovach, J. K. (1972). *An historical introduction to modern psychology,* New York: Harcourt Brace. (Original work published 1949)

Murray, H. A., Barrett, W. G., Langer, W. C., Morgan, C. D., Homburger, E., Mekeel, H. S. et al. (1938). Explorations in personality: *A clinical and experimental study of fifty men of college age.* New York: Oxford University Press.

Murray, H. A. (1955). Introduction. In A. Burton and R. Harris (Eds.), *Clinical studies of personality* (Vol. I, pp. 7-9). New York: Harper and Row.

Nemours Foundation. (2005, March 25). *Dealing with bullying*. Retrieved March 25, 2005, from http://kidshealth.org/teen/your_mind/problems/bullies.html

Nicholson, I. A. M. (2003). *Inventing personality: Gordon Allport and the science of selfhood.* Washington, DC: American Psychological Association.

Nietzsche, F. (1966). *Beyond good and evil* (W. Kaufmann, Trans.). New York: Vintage Books. (Original work published 1886)

Ogloff, J. R., Wong, S., and Greenwood, A. (1990). Treating criminal psychopaths in a therapeutic community program. *Behavioral Science and the Law, 8,* 81-90.

O'Hara, M., and Anderson, W. (1991, September). Welcome to the postmodern world. *Networker,* 19-25.

Orion, D. (1997). *I know you really love me: A psychiatrist's journal of erotomania, stalking, and obsessive love.* New York: Macmillan.

Overmier, J. B., and Leaf, R. C. (1965). Effects of discriminate Pavlovian fear conditioning upon previously or subsequently acquired avoidance responding. *Journal of Comparative and Physiological Psychology, 60*, 213-218.

Overmier, J. B. and Seligman, M. E. P. (1967). Effects of inescapable shock upon subsequent escape and avoidance learning. *Journal of Comparative and Physiological Psychology, 63,* 23-33.

Pathé, M. and Mullen, P. (1997) The impact of stalkers on their victims. *British Journal of Psychiatry*,170, 12-7.

Patrick, C. J. (2006). Preface. In C. J. Patrick (Ed.), *Handbook of psychopathy* (pp. xiii-xvi). New York: Guilford Press.

Patterson, G. R. (1993). Orderly change in a stable world: The antisocial trait as a chimera. *Journal of Consulting and Clinical Psychology, 61*, 911-919.

Peak.Org. (2005, February 17). Retrieved February 17, 2005, from: http://www.peak.org/dadaists/English/graphics

Peterson, C., Maier, S. F., and Seligman, M. E. P. (1993). *Learned helplessness: A theory for the age of personal control.* New York: Oxford University Press.

Piantanida, M., and Garman, N. B. (1999). *The qualitative dissertation: A guide for students and faculty*. Thousand Oaks, CA: Corwin Press.

Pinsent, J. (1969). *Greek mythology*. London: Paul Hamlyn.

Price, J. M., and Lento, J. (2001). The nature of child and adolescent vulnerability: History and definitions. In R. E. Ingram and J. M. Price (Eds.), *Vulnerability to psychopathology* (pp. 20-38). New York: Guilford Press.

Raschka, L. B. (1979). The incubus syndrome: A variant of erotomania. *Canadian Journal of Psychiatry, 24*, 549-553.

Robert's taped telephone calls. Unpublished raw data.

Robert's e-mail. Unpublished raw data.

Robert's monologue. (1997). Transcribed from audiotapes. [Unpublished raw data].

Rogers, C. R. (1959). A theory of therapy, personality and interpersonal relationships as developed in the client-centered framework. In S. Koch (Ed.), *Psychology: A study of science* (Vol. 3, pp. 184-256). New York: McGraw-Hill.

Rogers, C. R. (1963). Toward a science of the person. *Journal of Humanistic Psychology, 3*(2), 72-92.

Rorty, R. (1979). *Philosophy and the mirror of nature*. Princeton, NJ: Princeton University Press.

Rowley, J. (1997, November 14). 1 in 12 women pursued by stalkers, survey shows. *Times Picayune*, p. A18.

Runyan, W. M. (1982). *Life histories and psychobiography: Explorations in theory and method.* New York: Oxford University Press.

Rutter, M. (1987). Psychosocial resilienM^ and protective mechanisms. *American Journal of Orthopsychiatry*, *57,* 316-331.

Sartre, J. P.(1943). *Being and nothingness: The principal text of modern existentialism*. New York: Washington Square Press.

Scarce, M. (1997). Same-sex rape of male college students. *Journal of American College Health, 45,* 171-173.

Schneider, H. J. (2002). Victimological developments in the world during the past three decades: A study of comparative victimology, part 2 [Abstract]. *Violence and Abuse Abstracts, 8,3*.

Schneider, K. J. (1999). *The paradoxical self: Towards an understanding of our contradictory nature.* New York: Plenum.

Schneider, K. J. (2004). *Rediscovery of awe: Splendor, mystery, and the fluid center of life.* St. Paul, MN: Paragon House.

Schneider, K. J., and May, R. (1995). *The psychology of existence: An integrative, clinical perspective.* New York: McGraw-Hill.

Schneidman, E. S. (Ed.). (1981). *Endeavors in psychology: Selections from the personology of Henry A. Murray.* New York: Harper and Row.

Seeman, M. V. (1978). Delusional loving. *Archives of General Psychiatry, 35*, 1265-1267.

Segal, J. H. (1989). Erotomania revisited: From Kraepelin to DSM-III-R. *American Journal of Psychiatry, 146,* 1261-1266.

Seligman, M. E. P. (1998). *Learned optimism: How to change your mind and your life* New York: Simon and Schuster.

Seligman, M. E. P., Maier, S. F., and Solomon, R. L. (1971). Unpredictable and uncontrollable aversive events. In F. R. Brush (Ed.), *Aversive conditioning and learning* (pp. 18-25). New York: Academic Press.

Simkin, D. K., Lederer, J. P., and Seligman, M. E. P. (1983). Learned helplessness in groups. *Behaviour Research and Therapy*, *21,* 613-622.

Spence-Diehl, E. (1999). *Stalking: A handbook for victims*. Holmes Beach, FL: Learning.

Spiegelberg, H. (1972). *Phenomenology in psychology and psychiatry: A historical introduction.* Evanston, IL: Northwestern University Press.

Spinelli, E. (1989). *The interpreted world: An introduction to phenomenological psychology.* London: Sage.

Statutes and Constitution. (2005). Retrieved May 27, 2005, from http://www.flSenate.gov/statutes/index.cfm:App_made=Display_StatuteandURL=Cho784/cho784.htm

Struckman-Johnson, C. (1988). Forced sex on dates: It happens to men, too. *Journal of Sex Research, 24,* 234-241.

Suler, J. (1999, March). *The psychology of cyberspace: Computer and cyberspace addiction.* Retrieved March 15, 1999, from: *http://www.rider.edu/users/suler/psycyber/cybaddict.html*

Sullivan, H. S. (1970). *The interpersonal theory of psychiatry*. New York: W. W. Norton.

Sykes, C. J. (1992). *A nation of victims: The decay of the American character*. New York: St. Martin's.

Taylor, E. I. (1992). The case for a uniquely American Jamesian tradition in psychology. In M. Donnelly (Ed.), *Reinterpreting the legacy of William James* (pp. 3-28). Washington, DC: American Psychological Association.

Taylor, E. I. (2000). "What is man psychologist that thou art so unmindful of him?": Henry A. Murray on the historical relation between classical personality theory and humanistic psychology. *Journal of Humanistic Psychology, 40*(3), 29-42.

Taylor, E. I. (2004). *Personality theory and the case teaching method.* Unpublished position paper, Saybrook Graduate School and Research Center, San Francisco.

Taylor, E. I., and Martin, F. (2001). Humanistic psychology at the crossroads. In K. J. Schneider, J. F. T. Bugental, and J. F. Pierson (Eds.), *The handbook of humanistic psychology: Leading edges in theory, research, and practice* (pp. 21-27). Thousand Oaks, CA: Sage.

Taylor, S. J., and Bogdan, R. (1984). *Introduction to qualitative research: The search for meanings.* New York: John Wiley.

Tillich, P. (1952). *The courage to be* (2nd ed.). New Haven, CT: Yale University Press.

Turvey, B. E. (1999a). Victimology: Profiling the victim. In B. E. Turvey (Ed.), *Criminal profiling: An introduction to behavioral evidence analysis* (pp. 106-110). San Diego, CA: Academic Press.

Turvey, B. E. (1999b). Offender characteristics. In B. E. Turvey (Ed.), *Criminal profiling: An introduction to behavioral evidence analysis* (pp. 183-191). San Diego, CA: Academic Press.

Turvey, B. E. (2001a). Victimology: Risk assessment. In B. E. Turvey (Ed.), *Criminal profiling: An introduction to behavioral evidence analysis* (pp. 114-120). San Diego, CA: Academic Press.

Turvey, B. E. (2001b). Victimology: Profiling the victim. In B. E. Turvey (Ed.), *Criminal profiling: An introduction to behavioral evidence analysis* (pp. 105-112). San Diego, CA: Academic Press.

Ugolini, J. A., and Kelly, K. (2001). Case management strategies regarding stalkers and their victims: A practical approach from a private industry perspective. In J. A. Davis (Ed.), *Stalking crimes and victim protection: Prevention, intervention, threat assessment, and case management* (pp. 301-315). Boca Raton, FL: CRC Press.

Vaknin, S. (2006). Narcissistic personality disorder – Narcissist vs. psychopath. Retrieved August 4, 2006, from *http://www.buzzle.com/editorials/7-10-2006-101743.asp*

Van Deurzen, E. (2002). *Existential counseling and psychotherapy in practice* (2nd ed.). London: Sage.

Van Dusen, W. (1958). Wu Wei, No mind, and the fertile void in psychotherapy. *Psychologia, 1*, 253-6.

Van Dusen, W. (2001). *The design of existence: Emanation from source to creation.* Westchester, PA: Swedenborg Foundation.

Vernon, P., and Allport, G. (1931). A test for personal values. *Journal of Abnormal and Social Psychology*, *26*, 231-248.

Viano, E. C. (2000). Victimology today: Major issues in research and public policy [Abstract]. *Violence and Abuse Abstracts, 6*,3.

Von Hentig, H. (1948). *The criminal and his victim.* New Haven, CT: Yale University Press.

Watson, J. B. (1925). *Behaviorism*. New York: Norton.

Wells, S. J. (2002). Stolen identity. *HR Magazine, 47*(12), 30-38.

Wertz, F. J. (1985). Method and findings in a phenomenological psychological study of a complex life-event: Being criminally victimized. In A. Giorgi (Ed.), *Phenomenology and psychological research* (pp. 155-218). Pittsburgh, PA: Duquesne University Press.

White, B. H., and Robinson Kurpius, S. E. (2002). Effects of victim sex and sexual orientation on perceptions of rape. *Sex Roles: A Journal of Research, 1,* 191-202.

White, R. W. (1966). *Lives in progress: A study of the natural growth of personality.* New York: Holt, Rinehart and Winston.

White, R. W. (1987). *Seeking the shape of personality: A memoir.* Marlborough, NH: The Homestead Press.

Whiteley, D. (1998). The victim and the justification of punishment. *Criminal Justice Ethics, 17*(2), 42-54.

Williams, W. L., Lane, J. C., and Zona, M. (1996). Stalking and successful intervention strategies. *The Police Chief Magazine, 1,* 104-116.

Wikipedia. (2005, February 17). *Dadaism*. Retrieved February 17, 2005, from *http://en.wikipedia.org/wiki/dadaism*

Winkel, F. W., Blaauw, E., Sheridan, L., and Baldry, A. C. (2003). Repeat criminal victimization and vulnerability for coping failure: A prospective examination of a potential risk factor. *Psychology, Crime and Law, 9*, 87-95.

Winkel, F. W., and Vrij, A. (1998). Who is in need of victim support?: The issue of accountable and empirically validated selection and victim referral. *Expert Evidence, 6,* 23-41.

Winter, D. G., and Barenbaum, N. B. (1999). History of modern personality theory and research. In L. A. Pervin and O. P. John (Eds.), *Handbook of personality theory and research* (2nd ed., pp 3-27). New York: Guilford Press.

Worchel, S. (1984). The darker side of helping. In E. Staub et al., (Eds.), *The development and maintenance of prosocial behavior* (pp. 75-93). New York: Plenum.

Yalom, I. D. (1980). *Existential psychotherapy.* New York: Basic Books.

Yin, R. K. (1994). *Case study research: Design and methods.* Applied Social Research Methods Series (Vol. 5). Thousand Oaks, CA: Sage.

Zona, M. A., Palarea, R. E., and Lank¢ J. C., Jr. (1998). *Psychiatric diagnosis and the offender-victim typology of stalking: Clinical and Forensic Perspectives*, San Diego: Academic Press.

Zona, M. A., Sharma, K. K., and Lane, J. (1993). A comparative study of erotomanic and obsessional subjects in a forensic sample. *Journal of Forensic Sciences, 38*(4), 894-903.

Zubin, J., and Spring, B. (1977). Vulnerability: A new view of schizophrenia. *Journal of Abnormal Psychology, 86,* 103-126.

Zur, O. (2005). The psychology of victimhood. In R. H. Wright and N. A. Cummings (Eds.), *Destructive trends in mental health: The well-intentioned path to harm.* (pp. 45-65). New York: Routledge.

About the Author

Eric Anton Kreuter recently completed a doctorate (Ph.D.) in clinical psychology at Saybrook Graduate School and Research Center in San Francisco, California. He is a Certified Public Accountant, a Certified Management Accountant, a Certified Fraud Examiner, a Fellow and Diplomat with the American College of Forensic Examiners, International, and a Senior Professional in Human Resource Management. He is a Shareholder of a regional accounting firm – Marden, Harrison and Kreuter, CPAs, P.C. Dr. Kreuter is also an adjunct professor of Human Resource Management at Mercy College in Dobbs Ferry, NY, teaching in the graduate program in human resource management. He is a volunteer at a prison for women in New York and president of Hermandad, Inc. - a non-governmental community development organization serving the poor farming communities of southwestern Dominican Republic. Dr. Kreuter has published numerous articles, several book chapters and has three published books and has presented seminars on a number of occasions. He has also run 52 marathons in 26 states and 5 countries.

INDEX

A

B

C

Q

R

W

Y